Upgrading to PHP 5

Other resources from O'Reilly

Upgrading to PHP 5

Adam Trachtenberg

O'REILLY®

Beijing · Cambridge · Farnham · Köln · Paris · Sebastopol · Taipei · Tokyo

Upgrading to PHP 5
by Adam Trachtenberg

Published by O'Reilly Media, Inc., 1005 Gravenstein Highway North, Sebastopol, CA 95472.

O'Reilly books may be purchased for educational, business, or sales promotional use. Online editions are also available for most titles (*safari.oreilly.com*). For more information, contact our corporate/institutional sales department: (800) 998-9938 or *corporate@oreilly.com*.

Editors:	Nathan Torkington and Tatiana Apandi Diaz
Production Editor:	Genevieve d'Entremont
Cover Designer:	Ellie Volckhausen
Interior Designer:	Melanie Wang

Printing History:

July 2004:	First Edition.

 This book uses RepKover™, a durable and flexible lay-flat binding.

ISBN: 0-596-00636-5

[C]

To my grandparents:

Bruce & Selma Zorn

and

Oscar & Shoshana Trachtenberg

Table of Contents

Preface

PHP is a powerful yet easy-to-use tool for creating dynamic web content. The perfect language for projects great and small, PHP is used by Yahoo!, millions of personal home pages, and everything in-between. Best of all, PHP is open source and runs on Unix, Windows, and Mac OS X.

The latest version, PHP 5, contains robust support for object-oriented programming, an integrated suite of XML tools, an all-new MySQL extension, web services with SOAP and REST, and hundreds of other improvements.

There are so many updates and new features, it's difficult to get a handle on all the changes. Documentation is scarce, scattered, and rarely in-depth. This book steadily guides you from the world of PHP 4 to PHP 5, covering what's completely new, what's received an overhaul, and what's just slightly different enough to slip you up.

Who This Book Is For

This is the PHP 5 book for PHP 4 programmers. If you're currently using PHP and want to learn what's new in PHP 5, you should buy this book. Unlike other PHP 5 books, *Upgrading to PHP 5* assumes you're familiar with PHP, so it doesn't waste your time discussing how to process forms and query databases.

Instead, *Upgrading to PHP 5* shows you a complete collection of detailed examples covering all the latest and greatest features of PHP 5. Object-oriented programming? Check. MySQL? Check. XML? Check. If it's part of PHP 5, it's part of this book.

Besides showing off PHP 5, this book also eases your migration from PHP 4 to PHP 5. As a veteran PHP programmer, you have pages and pages of existing

PHP code. Not all of it will work perfectly under PHP 5. That's why *Upgrading to PHP 5* provides you with detailed side-by-side comparisons of PHP 4 *and* PHP 5 solutions. This lets you clearly see the exact changes you need to make to your current code.

In addition to covering what's new and how it's new, this book tells you *why* it's new. PHP 5 isn't change for the sake of change. *Upgrading to PHP 5* explains the logic behind the changes and shows how you can take advantage of them to the benefit of your code.

Finally, it provides an address book program. This concrete example combines the new features of PHP 5, demonstrating their usefulness in the context of a complete application. The address book shows you exactly how PHP 5 makes it faster and easier to develop more powerful and flexible web applications.

Who This Book Is Not For

This book is not for people new to PHP. If you're looking to learn the language, check out these three excellent alternatives:

Learning PHP 5, by David Sklar. This book provides a gentle introduction to PHP for web designers and other nontechnical people familiar with HTML and the Web, but not with programming and databases.

Programming PHP, by Rasmus Lerdorf and Kevin Tatroe. Co-authored by the creator of PHP, *Programming PHP* is aimed at anyone looking to learn PHP. An exhaustive reference, this book covers all aspects of PHP, from basic concepts to advanced techniques.

Web Database Applications with PHP and MySQL, by Hugh E.Williams and David Lane. If you're comfortable programming but have only just started using SQL, this book teaches you how to create an entire database-backed web site. *Web Database Applications with PHP and MySQL* works you through the entire process, including design, coding, and implementation.

These books are all published by O'Reilly Media, Inc.

What's in This Book

This book is divided into 10 chapters and 3 appendixes. The material in the first half of this book covers vital components of everyday web programming: object-oriented programming, MySQL, SQLite, and XML. It's hard to use PHP 5 without them. Specifically:

- Chapter 1, *Introduction*, explains the background of PHP 5 and its new extensions.
- Chapter 2, *Object-Oriented Programming*, covers object-oriented programming under PHP 5.
- Chapter 3, *MySQL*, examines MySQLi, a new MySQL database extension. It also details SQL features of MySQL 4.0 and 4.1.
- Chapter 4, *SQLite*, talks about SQLite, an embedded database library.
- Chapter 5, *XML*, teaches everything XML: DOM, XSLT, SimpleXML, SAX, and XPath.

The second half of the book discusses more specialized PHP 5 features. Iterators, exceptions, streams, SOAP, and other extensions are all extremely useful for solving specific tasks. The more you program in PHP 5, the more you'll find yourself integrating these features into your code.

- Chapter 6, *Iterators and SPL*, shows how iterators and SPL let you loop through directories, database queries, and XML documents.
- Chapter 7, *Error Handling and Debugging*, helps you handle errors with exception handling.
- Chapter 8, *Streams, Wrappers, and Filters*, introduces streams, wrappers, and filters.
- Chapter 9, *Other Extensions*, discusses the SOAP and Tidy extensions and the Reflection classes.
- Chapter 10, *PHP 5 in Action*, puts the whole book together with a sample PHP 5 application.

The three appendixes complement the rest of the book:

- Appendix A, *Introduction to XML*, provides an introduction to XML and Namespaces.
- Appendix B, *Additional New Features and Minor Changes*, documents the changes in PHP 5 not covered elsewhere in the book.
- Appendix C, *Installing PHP 5 Alongside PHP 4*, details how to integrate PHP 5 into your existing web server and PHP 4 setup.

Other Resources

These web sites and books are excellent companions to *Upgrading to PHP 5*.

Web Sites

There is a tremendous amount of PHP reference material online. With everything from the annotated PHP manual to sites with periodic articles and tutorials, a fast Internet connection rivals a large bookshelf in PHP documentary usefulness.

The Annotated PHP Manual (http://www.php.net/manual/)
  The official PHP Manual contains thousands of pages covering all aspects of PHP. It's an invaluable resource for looking up functions.

PHP mailing lists (http://www.php.net/mailing-lists.php)
  Discuss PHP on the PHP mailing lists. Don't be shy, there's a list for every topic: programming, databases, and even Windows. A mailing list archive lives at *http://news.php.net/*.

PHP Presentation archive (http://talks.php.net/)
  A great way to keep up-to-date on all the latest PHP developments, this archive contains conference presentation slides.

PEAR (http://pear.php.net/)
  Don't reimplement the wheel, download it from PEAR. PEAR—the PHP Extension and Application Repository—contains PHP classes that simplify forms processing, provide a database abstraction layer, generate class documentation, and solve hundreds of other tasks.

PECL (http://pecl.php.net/)
  PECL is PEAR's sister. PECL—the PHP Extension Community Library—is a collection of PHP extensions written in C. They're just like the bundled PHP extensions, except they're targeted at a specialized audience. PECL contains may useful extensions, including a PHP cache and optimizer, extensions to let you talk to Perl and Python from PHP, and an XML pull parser.

PHP DevCenter (http://www.onlamp.com/php/)
  A large collection of PHP articles and tutorials freely available on the web.

PHPCommunity.org (http://www.phpcommunity.org/)
  A gathering place where members of the PHP community can hang out and meet other PHP programmers.

Books

These books are all helpful problem-solving guides and references. Most of the books in the list are web-specific, and the top six books are my favorite PHP and MySQL texts.

PHP Cookbook,[*] by David Sklar and Adam Trachtenberg (O'Reilly, 2003).

Essential PHP Tools: Modules, Extensions, and Accelerators, by David Sklar (Apress, 2004).

Advanced PHP Programming, by George Schlossnagle (SAMS, 2004).

MySQL Reference Manual, by Michael "Monty" Widenius, David Axmark, and MySQL AB (O'Reilly, 2002); also available at *http://dev.mysql.com/doc/.*

MySQL Cookbook, by Paul DuBois (O'Reilly, 2003).

High Performance MySQL, by Jeremy D. Zawodny and Derek J. Balling (O'Reilly, 2004).

XML in a Nutshell, Second Edition, by Elliotte Rusty Harold and W. Scott Means (O'Reilly, 2002).

HTTP Developer's Handbook, by Chris Shiflett (SAMS, 2003).

Web Security, Privacy & Commerce, Second Edition, by Simson Garfinkel and Gene Spafford (O'Reilly, 2001).

Mastering Regular Expressions, Second Edition, by Jeffrey E. F. Friedl (O'Reilly, 2002).

Conventions Used in This Book

The following programming and typesetting conventions are used in this book.

Programming Conventions

The <?php and ?> opening and closing markers that begin and end a PHP program are generally omitted from examples in this book, except in examples where the body of the code includes an opening or closing marker.

The examples in this book were written to run under PHP 5 on both Unix and Windows, except where noted in the text.

At the time this book went to press, the latest available version of PHP 5 was Release Candidate 3 (RC3). Also, MySQL 4.1 was in beta. It is possible that some changes may occur between RC3 and the final release. Please check the online errata at *http://www.oreilly.com/catalog/upgradephp5/errata/* for any last-minute updates.

---

[*] While I admit to some bias in favor of *PHP Cookbook,* I frequently find myself looking up recipes when I need to refresh my memory on a particular topic or technique.

Typesetting Conventions

The following typographical conventions are used in this book:

Italic

> Indicates new terms, URLs, email addresses, filenames, file extensions, pathnames, and directories.

`Constant width`

> Indicates commands, options, switches, variables, attributes, keys, functions, types, classes, namespaces, methods, modules, properties, parameters, values, objects, events, event handlers, XML tags, HTML tags, macros, the contents of files, or the output from commands.

`Constant Width Bold`

> Indicates the output from code examples.

`Constant width italic`

> Shows text that should be replaced with user-supplied values.

> This icon signifies a tip, suggestion, or general note.

> This icon indicates a warning or caution.

Using Code Examples

This book is here to help you get your job done. In general, you may use the code in this book in your programs and documentation. You do not need to contact us for permission unless you're reproducing a significant portion of the code. For example, writing a program that uses several chunks of code from this book does not require permission. Selling or distributing a CD-ROM of examples from O'Reilly books *does* require permission. Answering a question by citing this book and quoting example code does not require permission. Incorporating a significant amount of example code from this book into your product's documentation *does* require permission.

We appreciate, but do not require, attribution. An attribution usually includes the title, author, publisher, and ISBN. For example: "*Upgrading to PHP 5*, by Adam Trachtenberg. Copyright 2004 O'Reilly Media, Inc., 0-596-00636-5."

If you feel your use of code examples falls outside fair use or the permission given here, feel free to contact us at *permissions@oreilly.com*.

We'd Like to Hear from You

Please address comments and questions concerning this book to the publisher:

O'Reilly Media, Inc.
1005 Gravenstein Highway North
Sebastopol, CA 95472
(800) 998-9938 (in the United States or Canada)
(707) 829-0515 (international or local)
(707) 829-0104 (fax)

We have a web page for this book, where we list errata, examples, and any additional information. You can access this page at:

http://www.oreilly.com/catalog/upgradephp5/

To comment or ask technical questions about this book, send email to:

bookquestions@oreilly.com

For more information about our books, conferences, Resource Centers, and the O'Reilly Network, see our web site at:

http://www.oreilly.com/

Acknowledgements

This book would not exist without the assistance of many, many, many people. They have my sincere gratitude and thanks.

My largest debt belongs to the entire PHP community. *Upgrading to PHP 5* could not exist without your efforts. I want to specifically thank these people for their special assistance, whether they knew they were giving it or not: Marcus Boerger, Zak Greant, Andi Gutmans, Sterling Hughes, Derick Rethans, Rob Richards, Georg Richter, George Schlossnagle, Christian Stocker, and Hans Zaunere.

Thanks also to the members of NYPHP (*http://nyphp.org/*) for sharing problems, ideas, and solutions. I'm lucky to have the world's best PHP user group in my hometown.

Portions of Chapter 7 were inspired in part by Gunjan Doshi's *Best Practices for Exception Handling* article on ONJava.com (*http://www.onjava.com/pub/a/onjava/2003/11/19/exceptions.html*). I offer him my thanks.

Bret Martin and Rik Faith provided hosting. Because of them, the technical review process was smooth and easy.

Two people diligently reviewed *Upgrading to PHP 5*. Their comments and suggestions immensely improved all aspects of the book. Chris Shiflett and David Sklar are the two best technical reviewers an author could have. I am proud to call them my friends.

I want to thank all the associates of O'Reilly Media, Inc. for their help. I've met many O'Reilly employees over the years, and there's not a bozo in the bunch.

These people, both directly and indirectly, contributed to the words, images, and pages you hold in your hands:

- Genevieve d'Entremont prepared this book for production and repaired my prose.
- chromatic published my PHP articles on ONLamp.com.
- A cornered Andy Oram and Bruce Epstein graciously provided editorial guidance and support one late night at FOO Camp.
- Rob Romano transformed my crayon sketches into works of art.
- Betsy Waliszewski got the word out early and often.

However, two people contributed more messages to my inbox than the others combined: Tatiana Diaz and Nat Torkington.

I have no idea how Tatiana Diaz put up with my all-too-often claims of "Oh sure, I can make that deadline," without reaching through the Internet and strangling me. Without her gentle prodding, *Upgrading to PHP 5* wouldn't be available until PHP 6.

Nat Torkington is a great editor. He gave me a push when I got stuck and helped me reframe chapters when they became misaligned. He even lets me make Perl 6 jokes at his expense. I pay him the greatest compliment I can: this book would be far less helpful without him.

Thanks to my family and friends for their support and encouragement.

Extra special thanks go to Elizabeth Hondl, my beautiful princess and talking frog.

CHAPTER 1

Introduction

PHP 4 is a wildly popular web programming language. Web servers on over 15,000,000 domains support PHP. PHP is the most popular Apache module by almost a 2-to-1 margin. But if PHP's so great, why do we need PHP 5?

Well, PHP 4 isn't perfect. While it makes developing web applications quick and easy, it's occasionally weighted down by its legacy baggage. This makes tackling some problems unnecessarily difficult.

In particular, PHP's version of object-oriented programming (OOP) lacks many features, the MySQL extension doesn't support the new MySQL 4.1 client protocol, and XML support is a hodgepodge.

Fortunately, PHP 5 improves on PHP 4 in three major areas:

- Object-oriented programming
- MySQL
- XML

These items have all been completely rewritten, turning them from limitations into star attractions. While these changes alone warrant a new version of PHP, PHP 5 also provides:

- SQLite for an embedded database
- Iterators
- Error handling using exceptions
- Streams
- SOAP

Some of these features, such as iterators and exceptions, are available only due to fundamental changes in PHP's core. Others, such as streams and SQLite, are PHP 4.3 features that have matured into prime-time use in PHP 5.

This book shows you how to take advantage of these new features in your applications. Additionally, it places a special emphasis on not just telling you what's new, but showing you how and why it's new.

Whenever possible, there's a direct comparison between the PHP 4 method of solving a task and the PHP 5 solution. The PHP 5 way is frequently shorter, more elegant, and provides you with greater flexibility. The before-and-after examples demonstrate in clear code what's better about PHP 5 and provide you with concrete examples to ease the transition from PHP 4 to PHP 5.

This chapter serves as a dual introduction to both PHP 5 and *Upgrading to PHP 5*. It begins with a brief history of PHP that provides the motivation behind PHP 5. The next section provides a short description of all the major new features of PHP 5 and, at the same time, explains how the book is organized. This chapter ends with a discussion of how to install and configure PHP 5.

Why PHP 5?

To understand why PHP 5 came to exist, it's necessary to quickly review the evolution of PHP as a language.

When Rasmus Lerdorf created PHP back in 1995, it wasn't even called PHP—his Personal Home Page/Forms Interpreter language was known as PHP/FI. At the time, PHP/FI's main focus was solving small-time web tasks: guest books, hit counters, and basic forms processing. Its major benefit was its simplicity; PHP/FI made it easy to handle all the messy tasks thrown at a web developer. Additionally, it's C-like syntax was already understood by many programmers.

Over the next two years, PHP/FI gradually grew in popularity. However, by 1997, PHP/FI was already showing its age. As the Internet gathered steam, programmers began to create more complex applications, such as e-commerce shopping carts. PHP/FI's quirks and limitations hindered development. It was too slow and was missing some basic features, such as for and foreach loops.

These problems caused Zeev Suraski and Andi Gutmans, of Zend fame, to begin work on a new version of PHP/FI. This version, which became PHP 3, solved many difficulties faced by PHP/FI developers while remaining true to the essential nature of PHP/FI.

In particular, PHP 3 was faster and more efficient than PHP/FI. The new parser also provided the opportunity to iron out some language oddities, making PHP more consistent. PHP 3's other major advance was an easy-to-use extension API. Developers from all over contributed extensions to PHP, effectively turning PHP from a programming language into an entire web development environment.

PHP 3 retained PHP/FI's procedural syntax, but it also introduced a very simplistic object-oriented syntax. Originally the result of a weekend hack, developers flocked to objects, much to the surprise of Zeev and Andi. Unfortunately, PHP 3 was ill-equipped to provide all the object-oriented features developers demanded.

A few months after PHP 3 went final in June of 1998, work started on PHP 4. Again, the problem was speed. The new extension infrastructure provided the opportunity to create larger and more complex web sites than ever imagined. In the words of Alan Greenspan, "irrational exuberance" was at hand.

While PHP 4 provided yet another burst of power, its secondary objective was backward compatibility. There was a strong emphasis on not breaking PHP 3 scripts under PHP 4. As a result, beefing up the core language was not a main focus of PHP 4. PHP 4 was released in May 2000, almost two years after PHP 3.

A lot has happened over the last four years. Perl may be the "duct tape of the Internet," but PHP is the real glue that holds the Web together. However, PHP still faces challenges. The problems of performance and flexibility have long been conquered, but now PHP is under attack from the twin foes of Java and C#.

Over the past 10 years, Java and C# have introduced advanced object-oriented programming concepts to web development. Yet in many ways, despite all the improvements, PHP 4.3 is still the same procedural language that Rasmus wrote a decade ago. PHP 5 finally grants developers their wish, providing a full set of object-oriented features.

These features, which are discussed in Chapter 2, allow developers to more easily develop large-scale applications without resorting to the cumbersome workarounds necessary in PHP 4. They also let you write cleaner code that's less error-prone and more maintainable.

What's New in PHP 5?

Better object-oriented features aren't the only new features of PHP 5. Many extensions have been rewritten to take advantage of PHP 5's new capabilities, and many new extensions have been added to the distribution.

MySQL

The MySQL database is PHP's partner in crime. Many developers power their web sites with MySQL, yet PHP's original MySQL extension dates back to the days of PHP/FI. It's showing its age.

In retrospect, some design decisions for the MySQL extension weren't the best solution after all. Also, the latest versions of MySQL, 4.1 and 5.0, introduce many new features, some of which require significant changes to the extension.

As a result, PHP 5 comes with a completely new and improved MySQL extension. Dubbed MySQLi, for the MySQL Improved extension, MySQLi offers prepared statements, bound parameters, and SSL connections. It even takes advantage of PHP 5's new object-oriented support to provide an OO interface to MySQL. This extension is covered in Chapter 3.

SQLite

While MySQL is greater than ever, it's actually "too much database" for some jobs. SQLite is an embedded database library that lets you store and query data using an SQL interface without the overhead of installing and running a separate database application. It's the topic of Chapter 4.

PHP 5 bundles SQLite, providing developers with a database that's guaranteed to work on all PHP 5 installations. Despite the name, SQLite is a nowhere close to a "lite" database. It supports transactions, subqueries, triggers, and many other advanced database features.

Like MySQLi, SQLite also comes with dual procedural and OO interfaces.

XML

XML is a key part of web development, so PHP 5 offers a full selection of new XML tools. A major goal of XML in PHP 5 is interoperability among each of the different XML extensions, making them a unified unit instead of individual agents.

The new Document Object Model (DOM) extension is leaps and bounds better than PHP 4's experimental version. It also uses new PHP 5 features to comply with the DOM specification, fulfilling the goal of DOM as a language-neutral API for XML.

There's also a new Extensible Stylesheet Language Transformations (XSLT) extension that operates on XML documents and DOM objects. You can transform DOM objects using XSLT and receive translated documents from

XSLT. You can even pass XML nodes back and forth between XSLT and PHP from within a stylesheet.

Perhaps the most innovative part of PHP 5 is the SimpleXML extension. This lightweight interface to XML lets you easily iterate through XML documents without the overhead of DOM or the oddness of XSLT. It's perfect for documents where you know the specification and want to quickly extract data.

Chapter 5 covers all these topics, plus the original Simple API for XML (SAX) extension and an XPath extension, used for querying XML documents. If you're new to XML or want a refresher on some of its more difficult parts, such as namespaces, be sure to read Appendix A.

Iterators and SPL

Iterators are a completely new PHP 5 feature and the topic of Chapter 6. They allow you to use a foreach loop to cycle through different types of data: directory listings, database results, and even XML documents.

SPL—the Standard PHP Library—is a collection of iterators that provide this functionality and also filter, limit, cache, and otherwise modify iterator results. Iterators are an incredibly handy way to abstract away messy details from your code.

Error Handling and Debugging

PHP 5 offers a completely different model of error checking than what's available in PHP 4. It's called *exception handling*. With exceptions, you're freed from the necessity of checking the return value of every function. Instead, you can separate programming logic from error handling and place them in adjoining blocks of code.

Exceptions are commonly found in object-oriented languages such as Java and C++. When used judiciously, they streamline code, but when used willy-nilly, they create spaghetti code.

Chapter 7 covers exceptions.

Streams, Filters, and Wrappers

Streams allow you to place a file interface on reading and writing data using protocol-specific objects known as wrappers. Streams also let you modify the data flowing through them by attaching filters.

First introduced in PHP 4.3, streams are an underutilized part of PHP. PHP 5 expands upon the existing streams infrastructure to allow more extensive wrappers, and to let you create filters directly in PHP instead of in C.

Chapter 8 demonstrates how to create a shared memory wrapper and two streams, one for encoding HTML entities and another for decoding them.

Other Extensions

Chapter 9 covers three new pieces of PHP 5: SOAP, Tidy, and the Reflection classes.

SOAP is a key component of the fast-growing web services field. This extension lets developers create SOAP clients with or without a Web Services Description Language (WSDL) file, and also implement SOAP servers in PHP.

The Tidy extension makes it easy to ensure that your output is valid HTML and XHTML. Its smart parser brings even the most unruly of files into compliance with the latest W3C specifications.

Nothing less than complete code introspection is the goal of the Reflection classes. This set of classes lets you examine classes, methods, parameters, and more, to discover object attributes.

It is now simple and easy to create PHP class browsers, debuggers, and other tools that rely on gathering details about objects and functions.

PHP 5 in Action

It's one thing to see each of the individual parts of PHP 5 in isolation; it's another to see them in harmony. Chapter 10 provides you with a small address book application that combines the new PHP 5 features into a complete unit.

This chapter pulls together the concepts introduced in the rest of the book and provides you with an example that shows exactly why application development in PHP 5 is so great. Even in a short program, you can take advantage of SQLite, DOM, SimpleXML, iterators, abstract classes, exceptions, and property overloading to create an application that's flexible in many dimensions, yet easy to write and understand.

This address book lets you add contact information and search stored records using both a web and command-line interface. The output is completely separated from application logic, and the program uses a simple series of template classes to control its formatting.

Everything Else

PHP 5 is such a major update that it's impossible to cover it completely in only 10 chapters. Additionally, some features are so minor, they're only worth mentioning briefly.

Appendix B contains all the small changes and fixes that aren't mentioned in the chapters. It's definitely worth a read because, in many ways, it's easiest to be tripped up by minor changes. You know you're on new ground with the mysqli extension, but, unless you read Appendix B, you probably would not know that you can now pass optional parameters by reference, or that strrpos( ) behaves slightly differently than before, or even that the command-line version of PHP has the ability to execute code on every line of input.

Installing and Configuring PHP 5

You can download PHP 5 from *http://www.php.net/downloads.php*. The installation process is identical to PHP 4; however, PHP 5 does have some new configuration options. See Table C-1 in Appendix C for a complete list.

During the transition from PHP 4 to PHP 5, it's common to want to run both versions of PHP simultaneously. This lets you easily test code under PHP 5 without switching completely away from PHP 4. It also allows you to slowly migrate scripts from PHP 4 to PHP 5, as you can control which version of PHP parses specific sets of pages.

One option is to run two separate web servers, either on different machines or on different ports on the same machine. The primary advantage of using two web servers is that you can run both PHP 4 and PHP 5 as a module. The disadvantages are that you either need multiple computers at your disposal or need to be familiar with installing Apache (or your particular web server of choice). It's also a lot of work for a temporary situation.

Another solution is to continue using your existing web server and install one version of PHP as a module and another as a CGI. This gets you up and running with both versions with minimal fuss; however, the CGI version of PHP lacks certain features included in the Apache module.

Appendix C provides detailed instructions for setting up PHP 4 and PHP 5 under Apache on both Unix and Windows. It shows how to configure Apache to switch between the versions both on a directory-by-directory basis and by setting up a virtual server on another port.

CHAPTER 2
Object-Oriented Programming

This chapter introduces object-oriented programming (OOP) and explains all the object-oriented (OO) features in PHP 5. The chapter assumes no prior knowledge of OOP, so if this is your first time learning it, that's okay.

However, there's lots here for PHP 4 OO programmers, too. PHP 5, besides adding many OO bells and whistles, modifies fundamental parts of PHP 4's OO behavior. Running PHP 4 programs under PHP 5 will result in unexpected results and errors if you're not up-to-date on all the changes.

Additionally, the new features allow you to implement many OOP best practices that just aren't possible in PHP 4. This chapter shows you how and why you should modify your existing code to take full advantage of PHP 5.

Early versions of PHP were strictly procedural: you could define functions, but not objects. PHP 3 introduced an extremely rudimentary form of objects, written as a late-night hack. Back in 1997, nobody expected the explosion in the number of PHP programmers, nor that people would write large-scale programs in PHP. Therefore, these limitations weren't considered a problem.

Over the years, PHP gained additional object-oriented features; however, the development team never redesigned the core OO code to gracefully handle objects and classes. As a result, although PHP 4 improved overall performance, writing complex OO programs with it is still difficult, if not nearly impossible.

PHP 5 fixes these problems by using Zend Engine 2. The first version of the Zend Engine was written for PHP 4 to handle PHP's core functionality, such as what type of objects you can use, and to define the language's syntax.

Zend Engine 2, which powers PHP 5, enables PHP to include more advanced object-oriented features, while still providing a high degree of backward compatibility to the millions of PHP scripts already written.

If you don't have experience with object-oriented programming outside of PHP, then you're in for a bit of a surprise. While some of the new features allow you to do things more easily, many features don't let you do anything new at all. In many ways, they *restrict* what you can do.

Even though it seems counterintuitive, these limitations actually help you quickly write safe code because they promote code reuse and data encapsulation. These key OO programming concepts are explained throughout the chapter.

What Is Object-Oriented Programming?

Object-oriented programming is a way to group functions and data together into a prepackaged unit. This unit is known as an *object*.

Many people prefer OOP because it encourages a behavior known as *encapsulation*. Inevitably, whenever you write code, there's some part—the way you store the data, what parameters the functions take, how the database is organized—that doesn't work as well as it should. It's too slow, too awkward, or doesn't allow you to add new features, so you clean it up.

Fixing code is a good thing, unless you accidently break other parts of your system in the process. When a program is designed with a high degree of encapsulation, the underlying data structures and database tables are not accessed directly. Instead, you define a set of functions and route all your requests through these functions.

For example, you have a database table that stores names and email addresses. A program with poor encapsulation directly accesses the table whenever it needs to fetch a person's email address:

```
$name   = 'Rasmus Lerdorf';
$db     = mysql_connect();
$result = mysql_query("SELECT email FROM users
                              WHERE name  LIKE '$name'", $db);
$row    = mysql_fetch_assoc($r);
$email  = $row['email'];
```

A better-encapsulated program uses a function instead:

```
function getEmail($name) {
    $db = mysql_connect();
    $result = mysql_query("SELECT email FROM users
                              WHERE name  LIKE '$name'", $db);
    $row    = mysql_fetch_assoc($r);
    $email  = $row['email'];
    return $email
}

$email = getEmail('Rasmus Lerdorf');
```

Using getEmail( ) has many benefits, including reducing the amount of code you need to write to fetch an email address. However, it also lets you safely alter your database schema because you only need to change the single query in getEmail( ) instead of searching through every line of every file, looking for places where you SELECT data from the users table.

It's hard to write a well-encapsulated program using functions, because the only way to signal to people "Don't touch this!" is through comments and programming conventions.

Objects allow you to wall off implementation internals from outside access. This prevents people from relying on code that may change and forces them to use your functions to reach the data. Functions of this type are known as *accessors*, because they allow access to otherwise protected information. When redesigning code, if you update the accessors to work as before, none of the code will break.

More information on encapsulation appears later, but first, here's an introduction to using objects in PHP 5.

Using Objects

Typically, objects represent "real-world" or tangible entities, such as a person. Here is one version of a Person object in PHP:

```
$rasmus = new Person;
$rasmus->setName('Rasmus Lerdorf');
print $rasmus->getName( );
Rasmus Lerdorf
```

The first line assigns a value to a $rasmus variable. This value is an object of type Person. Person is a previously specified structure containing code that describes how a "Person object" should operate. This structure is called a *class*.

The difference between an object and a class is that an object is an actual variable that you can manipulate. You can pass it to functions, delete it, copy it, and so forth. It holds a specific set of data.

A class is the template that defines how the object can be used and what data it can hold.

Convert a class into an object by using the new keyword:

```
$rasmus = new Person;
```

This command causes PHP to look for a class labeled as Person, create a new copy, and assign it to $rasmus. This process is known as *instantiating* an object or creating a new instance of a class.

For now, don't worry about the actual syntax for defining Person. Also, it's not necessary to know how Person stores data. This information is encapsulated away, and you're forced to work without it. (And this is a good thing!)

What you do need to know is that Person allows you to call something that looks like a function called setName( ):

```
$rasmus->setName('Rasmus Lerdorf');
```

When you define a class, you can specify functions that belong to the class. To call an object's function, place an arrow (->) after the object and then add the function name. This tells PHP to invoke the setName( ) function on that specific instance of the class.

The proper term for setName( ) isn't "function"; it's a *method* or an *object method*. Here's how you use the term in a full sentence: "I called the setName( ) method on the object," or "You must call the object's setName( ) method."

The setName( ) method sets the "name" attribute of $rasmus. In this case, it's set to Rasmus Lerdorf.

You can retrieve this value by calling getName( ):

```
print $rasmus->getName( );
Rasmus Lerdorf
```

The getName( ) method looks up the value stored by an earlier call to setName( ) and returns it. Because of encapsulation, you don't know how Person stores this data—the specific details are irrelevant.

In object-oriented programming, there is an implicit contract between the class's author and the users of the class. The users agree not to worry about the implementation details. The author agrees that as long as a person uses accessor methods, such as setName( ) and getName( ), they'll always work, even if the author redesigns the class.

The full details on class creation come later, but here's a first look at the elements of a simple class. For example, the Person class can look like this:

```
class Person {
    setName($name) {
        $this->name = $name;
    }

    getName( ) {
        return $this->name;
    }
}
```

You define and name a class like you define and name a function, except that you use the word class instead of function, and parentheses (( )) don't follow the class name.

Inside the class, declare class methods like you declare regular functions:

```
function setName($name) {
    $this->name = $name;
}

function getName( ) {
    return $this->name;
}
```

These two methods store and return a name using a special class variable called $this. That's why $rasmus->getName( ) is able to remember and return the value passed in by $rasmus->setName('Rasmus Lerdorf').

That's all for now on writing classes. It's time to go back to using classes and objects.

In PHP 5, you can call a method on an object returned by a function:

```
function getRasmus( ) {
    $rasmus = new Person;
    $rasmus->setName('Rasmus Lerdorf');
    return $rasmus;
}

print getRasmus( )->getName( );
Rasmus Lerdorf
```

This isn't possible in PHP 4. Instead, you store the object in a temporary variable as an intermediate step:

```
function getRasmus( ) {
    $rasmus = new Person;
    $rasmus->setName('Rasmus Lerdorf');
    return $rasmus;
}

$rasmus = getRasmus( )
print $rasmus->getName( );
```

Calling setName( ) on different objects causes that method to operate on a different set of data. Each instance operates independently of every other instance, even if they're of the same class.

```
$rasmus = new Person;
$zeev   = new Person;

$rasmus->setName('Rasmus Lerdorf');
$zeev->setName('Zeev Suraski');
```

```
print $rasmus->getName( );
print $zeev->getName( );
```
Rasmus Lerdorf
Zeev Suraski

This example creates two instances of the Person class, $rasmus and $zeev. These objects are separate, so the call $zeev->setName('Zeev Suraski'); doesn't undo the earlier call of $rasmus->setName('Rasmus Lerdorf');.

Besides methods, objects also have properties. A property is to an object as an element is to an array. You refer to it by a name and can store in it every type of data: strings, arrays, and even other objects.

The syntax for property access is like method access, except that there are no parentheses following the property name:

```
$rasmus = new Person;
$rasmus->name = 'Rasmus Lerdorf';
print $rasmus->name;
```
Rasmus Lerdorf

This assigns the string Rasmus Lerdorf to the name property of $rasmus. Then, it retrieves the string and prints it out. An object with only properties and no methods is more or less a fancy array.

Autoload

When you attempt to instantiate a class that's not defined, PHP 4 dies with a fatal error because it can't locate what you're looking for. PHP 5 solves this problem by loading the missing code on the fly with its new autoload feature.

Extensive use of classes requires you to either define all your classes in a single file or else place an include statement for each class you use at the top of every script. Since PHP 5 calls __autoload( ) when you instantiate undefined classes, you can make it include all the classes used by your script with only a little work:

```
function __autoload($class_name) {
    include "$class_name.php";
}

$person = new Person;
```

The __autoload( ) function receives the class name as its single parameter. This example appends a *.php* extension to that name and tries to include a file based on $class_name. So, when you instantiate a new Person, it looks for *Person.php* in your include_path.

If you adopt the PEAR-style naming convention of placing an underscore between words to reflect the file hierarchy, use the code in Example 2-1.

Example 2-1. Autoloading classes using PEAR naming conventions

```
function __autoload($package_name) {
    // split on underscore
    $folders = split('_', $package_name);
    // rejoin based on directory structure
    // use DIRECTORY_SEPARATOR constant to work on all platforms
    $path    = join(DIRECTORY_SEPARATOR, $folders);
    // append extension
    $path    .= '.php';

    include $path;
}
```

With the code in Example 2-1, you can do the following:

```
$person = new Animals_Person;
```

If the class isn't defined, `Animals_Person` gets passed to `__autoload()`. The function splits the class name on underscore (`_`) and joins it on `DIRECTORY_SEPARATOR`. This turns the string into `Animals/Person` on Unix machines (and `Animals\Person` on Windows).

Next, a *.php* extension is appended, and then the file *Animals/Person.php* is included for use.

While using `__autoload()` slightly increases processing time during the addition of a class, it is called only once per class. Multiple instances of the same class does not result in multiple calls to `__autoload()`.

Data Encapsulation

Although using properties instead of accessor methods is less work up front, it's not a good idea, because it reduces encapsulation. Reading and writing to name directly instead of calling setName() and getName() undermines the layer of abstraction that prevents code from breaking after redesigns. Since this is a big benefit of object-oriented programming, you should avoid using properties instead of accessor methods.

PHP 5 allows you to enforce the distinction between what should and shouldn't be accessed directly. All of the methods and properties shown so far have been *public* methods and properties. This means anyone can call or edit them.

In PHP 4, all properties and methods are public. In PHP 5, however, you can use the private label to restrict access to only those methods defined inside the class. When this label is applied to a method or property, it is known as *private*. Marking something as private signals that it may change in the future, so people shouldn't access it or they'll violate encapsulation.

This is more than a social convention. PHP 5 actually prevents people from calling a private method or reading a private property outside of the class. Therefore, from an external perspective, these methods and properties might as well not exist because there's no way to access them. More information on access control appears in "Access Restrictions," later in this chapter.

Constructors and Destructors

Objects in PHP 5 also have the ability to call constructors and destructors. A *constructor* is a method that is called automatically when an object is instantiated. Depending upon how the constructor is implemented, you may be able to pass it arguments.

For example, a constructor for a class that represents a database may take the address of the database you wish to connect to, as well as the username and password necessary for authentication:

```
$db = new Database('db.example.com', 'web', 'jsd6w@2d');
```

This creates an new instance of a Database class and passes three pieces of information to the constructor. The class's constructor will use that data to create a connection to the database and then store the result handle in a private property.

PHP 4 has object constructors, but object *destructors* are new to PHP 5. Destructors are like constructors, except that they're called when the object is deleted. Even if you don't delete the object yourself using unset( ), PHP 5 still calls the destructor when it determines that the object is no longer used. This may be when the script ends, but it can be much earlier.

You use a destructor to clean up after an object. For instance, the Database destructor would disconnect from the database and free up the connection. Unlike constructors, you cannot pass information to a destructor, because you're never sure when it's going to be run.

Memory Management

In PHP 4, when you copy a variable or pass it to a function, you don't transfer the original variable. Instead, you pass a copy of the data stored in the variable. This is known as *pass-by-value* because you're copying the variable's values and creating a duplicate.

As a result, the new variable is completely disassociated from the original. Modifying one doesn't affect the other, similar to how calling $zeev-> setName( ) didn't affect $rasmus in the earlier example.

Object References

Objects in PHP 5 behave differently from other variables. You don't pass them by value, like you do with scalars and arrays. Instead, you pass them by reference. A *reference*, or *object reference*, is a pointer to the variable. Therefore, any alterations made to the passed object are actually made to the original.

Here's an example:

```
$rasmus = new Person;
$rasmus->setName('Rasmus Lerdorf');

$zeev = $rasmus;
$zeev->setName('Zeev Suraski');

print $rasmus->getName();
Zeev Suraski
```

In this case, modifying $zeev does change $rasmus!

This is not what occurs in PHP 4. PHP 4 prints Rasmus Lerdorf because $zeev = $rasmus causes PHP to make a copy of the original object and assign it to $zeev.

However, in PHP 5, this command assigns $zeev a reference to $rasmus. Any changes made to $zeev are actually made to $rasmus.

A similar behavior occurs when you pass objects into functions:

```
function editName($person, $name) {
    $person->setName($name);
}

$rasmus = new Person;
$rasmus->setName('Rasmus Lerdorf');

setName($rasmus, 'Zeev Suraski');
print $rasmus->getName();
Zeev Suraski
```

Normally, changes made inside of editName() don't alter variables outside of the function, and to update the original object you need to return the modified variable. That's what you need to do in PHP 4.

Since PHP 5 passes objects by reference, changing them inside a function or a method alters the original object. There's no need for you to pass them explicitly by reference or return the modified copy. This action is also referred to as *passing an object handle*, since "handle" is a synonym of reference or pointer.

Other variable types, including strings and arrays, are still passed by value by default, unless declared otherwise in the function prototype by placing an ampersand (&) before the variable name.

This change in PHP 5 makes it much easier to use objects because it's far more common to need to pass objects by reference than by value. When your data is encapsulated inside of objects, you frequently pass an instance or two to a method and alter the objects inside of the method.

Without this switch, to cleanly propagate these changes back to the original instances you must place ampersands everywhere you need PHP to pass the objects by reference. However, if you omit even a single ampersand, you end up with a bug that's difficult to isolate and broken code.

To copy the data inside an object and not just the reference to it, instead of a direct assignment using an equals sign (=), use the clone operator:

```
$rasmus = new Person;
$rasmus->setName('Rasmus Lerdorf');

$zeev = clone $rasmus;
$zeev->setName('Zeev Suraski');

print $rasmus->getName( );
print $zeev->getName( );
Rasmus Lerdorf
Zeev Suraski
```

This tells PHP not to assign a reference, but to duplicate the values stored in $rasmus and store them in a new object that gets assigned to $zeev. This also means $ramsus and $zeev are independent entities, so calling $zeev->setName( ) doesn't update $rasmus.

PHP 4 programs that rely heavily on PHP 4's pass- and copy-by-value behaviors can enable the zend.ze1_compatibility_mode configuration directive. This causes PHP 5 to clone objects instead of using a reference.

This directive also re-enables a few quirks of PHP 4 that have been ironed out in PHP 5. For instance, you can no longer cast an object to an integer or floating-point number. In PHP 4, objects with properties become 1 and objects without properties become 0.

Turning on the compatibility mode may ease your transition to PHP 5, but it should not be a long-term solution. It reduces application portability, and you cannot share code between applications that enable the compatibility mode and those that assume it's disabled. New sites should be developed with this directive set to its default (Off).

Garbage Collection

Some languages, most notably C, require you to explicitly request memory from the computer whenever you create strings or data structures. Once you've allocated the memory, you can then store information in the variable.

You're also responsible for releasing, or freeing, the memory when you're finished using the variable. This allows the machine to provide the memory to other variables in your program and prevents your computer from running out of RAM. This is also a big pain.

PHP handles memory allocation for you. When you instantiate an object, it automatically doles out memory. When it's deleted, it frees the memory.

The process of cleaning up unused objects is known as *garbage collection*. The type of garbage collection used by PHP is called *reference counting*.

When you create a value—such as a string, number, or object—PHP records its existence and sets a counter to one, indicating that there's one copy of the value. From then on, PHP tracks the value, incrementing and decrementing its counter accordingly.

The counter goes up by one when you create a reference to the value, either by passing it into a function by reference or by assigning it by reference to another variable. (Objects are always assigned by reference, unless you use clone; non-objects are assigned by reference using the =& operator.) The counter goes down by one when you remove a reference to a value, which happens when you exit a function or delete the variable. For example:

```
$rasmus1 = new Person( );  // New object:          Reference count = 1
$rasmus2 = $rasmus1;       // Copy-by-reference:   Reference count = 2
unset($rasmus1);           // Delete a reference:  Reference count = 1
sendEmailTo($rasmus);      // Pass-by-reference:
                           // During function execution:
                           //                      Reference count = 2
                           // After function completes:
                           //                      Reference count = 1
unset($rasmus2);           // Delete a reference:  Reference count = 0
```

When the counter hits zero, PHP knows the object is no longer used anywhere in your program, so deletes it and releases its memory. Before it does that, however, PHP calls your object's destructor to let you clean up any higher-level resources you've opened in the object.

At the end of a script, PHP cleans up all the remaining values that still have a nonzero reference count.

Basic Classes

To define a class, use the class keyword followed by the class name:

```
class Person {

}
```

This code creates a `Person` class. This is not a very exciting class, because it lacks methods or properties. Class names in PHP are case-insensitive, so you cannot define both a `Person` and a `PERSON` class.

Use this class name to instantiate a new instance of your object:

```
$rasmus = new Person;
```

Alternatively, to determine a class from an object instance, use get_class( ):

```
$person = new Person;
print get_class($person)
Person
```

Even though class names are case-insensitive, PHP 5 preserves their capitalization. This is different from PHP 4, where PHP converts the name to lowercase. In PHP 4, calling get_class( ) on an instance of the `Person` class produced person. PHP 5 returns the correct class name.

Properties

List class properties at the top of the class:

```
class Person {
    public $name;
}
```

This creates a `public` property named name. When a property is public, it can be read from and written to anywhere in the program:

```
$rasmus = new Person;
$rasmus->name = 'Rasmus Lerdorf';
```

Properties in PHP 4 are declared using a different syntax: var. This syntax is deprecated in favor of `public`, but for backward compatibility, var is still legal. The behavior of a property declared using `public` and var is identical.

Never use `public` properties. Doing so makes it easy to violate encapsulation. Always use accessor methods instead.

You don't need to predeclare a property inside the class to use it. For instance:

```
$rasmus = new Person;
$rasmus->email = 'rasmus@php.net';
```

This assigns rasmus@php.net to the email property of $rasmus. This is valid, even though email was not mentioned in the class definition.

Even though you don't have to, always predeclare your properties. First, these properties are implicitly public, so they're already bad. Second, predeclaring properties forces you to think about the best way to handle data. It also makes it easier for anyone reading the class (including yourself two months later) to see all of the class's properties without wading through the entire code of the class.

Methods

Define methods underneath properties. They're declared using the standard function syntax:

```
class Person {
    public $name;

    public function setName($name) {
        $this->name = $name;
    }
}
```

The public keyword indicates that anyone can call the setName( ) method. In PHP 4, methods are not preceded by a visibility identifier such as public. For backward compatibility, these methods are assumed to be public.

Unlike properties, public methods are okay to use. Accessor methods, for instance, are frequently declared as public.

To refer to an object instance inside of a class, use the special variable $this. For example:

```
public function setName($name) {
    $this->name = $name;
}
```

In this code, the setName( ) method sets the name property of the current object to the value of the $name variable passed into the method.

Be careful not to place a dollar sign before the property name, such as $this->$name. This causes PHP to access the property with the value stored in the $name variable. This is occasionally the desired result, but often is not.

PHP 4 doesn't prevent you from assigning a new object to $this:

```
public function load($object) {
    $this = $object;
}
```

but this is illegal in PHP 5. You can only alter object properties. Trying to set $this to a new value produces an error:

```
PHP Fatal error:  Cannot re-assign $this
```

Access Restrictions

To prevent a property or method from being accessed from outside a class, use the private keyword:

```
class Person {
    private $name;

    public function setName($name) {
        $this->name = $name;
    }
}

$rasmus = new Person;
$rasmus->setName('Rasmus Lerdorf');
print $rasmus->name;
PHP Fatal error:  Cannot access private property Person::$name... on line 12
```

When name is declared as private, it cannot be accessed outside of the class. It's still safe to manipulate it inside of setName( ) because that's an internal method. What you cannot do is something like:

```
print $rasmus->name;
```

This causes a fatal error, which is why you need to implement a getName( ) method:

```
class Person {
    private $name;

    public function setName($name) {
        $this->name = $name;
    }

    public function getName() {
        return $this->name;
    }
}

$rasmus = new Person;
$rasmus->setName('Rasmus Lerdorf');
print $rasmus->getName();
Rasmus Lerdorf
```

This code works as expected and prints Rasmus Lerdorf.

Declare private methods by placing the word private in front of function:

```
class Person {
    private $email;

    public function setEmail($email) {
        if ($this->validateEmail($email)) {
            $this->email = $email;
        }
    }

    private function validateEmail($email) {
        // email address validation
```

```
        // regular expression
        // omitted for clarity
    }
}

$rasmus = new Person;
$rasmus->setEmail('rasmus@php.net');
```

This code declares two methods, one public and one private. The public method, setEmail( ), lets you set a person's email address. The private method, validateEmail( ), is used internally by the class to check whether the address is valid. Since that method is not relevant to a user, it is declared as private.

This example also shows how to access a method from within a class. The syntax is akin to accessing a class's property. Use $this to represent the object, as is done inside setEmail( ):

```
public function setEmail($email) {
    if ($this->validateEmail($email)) {
        $this->email = $email;
    }
}
```

This code calls the validateEmail( ) method of the Person class and passes it the $email variable. Since this call occurs in a method defined in the same class, it works even though validateEmail( ) is declared as private.

Constructors and Destructors

Object constructors act the same in PHP 4 and PHP 5, but PHP 5 introduces a new naming convention. In PHP 4, an object's constructor has the same name as its class:

```
class Database {
    function Database($host, $user, $password) {
        $this->handle = db_connect($host, $user, $password);
    }
}

$db = new Database('db.example.com', 'web', 'jsd6w@2d');
```

Creating a new instance of the Database class causes PHP to call the Database( ) method.

To designate an object constructor in PHP 5, name the method __construct( ):

```
class Database {
    function __construct($host, $user, $password) {
        $this->handle = db_connect($host, $user, $password);
    }
}

$db = new Database('db.example.com', 'web', 'jsd6w@2d');
```

To ease the transition from PHP 4, if PHP 5 cannot find a method named __construct( ) within your object hierarchy, it reverts to the PHP 4 constructor naming scheme and searches accordingly. Since a PHP 4 constructor has the same name as its class, unless you have class methods called __construct( ) that are serving another purpose, your existing code should not break under PHP 5. (The reason for this name change is discussed in "Constructors," later in this chapter.)

There are no backward compatibility issues with destructors, because they aren't available in PHP 4. However, that doesn't mean people didn't try to recreate them using other language features. If you emulated destructors, you will want to port your code, because PHP 5's destructors are more efficient and easier to use.

In PHP 4, you can mimic destructors by defining a method that you want to act as a destructor and then using register_shutdown_function( ) to make PHP invoke it at the end of the script, as in Example 2-2.

Example 2-2. Mimicking destructors in PHP 4

```
register_shutdown_function('destruct');
$GLOBALS['objects_to_destroy'] = array( );

function destruct( ) {
    foreach($GLOBALS['objects_to_destroy'] as $obj) {
        $obj->destruct( );
    }
}

class Database {
    function database($host, $user, $password) {
        $this->handle = db_connect($host, $user, $password);
        $GLOBALS['objects_to_destroy'][ ] = &$this;
    }

    function destruct( ) {
        db_close($this->handle); // close the database connection
    }
}
```

PHP has a special function, register_shutdown_function( ), that's called by PHP right before the script ends. You can use register_shutdown_function( ) to ensure PHP runs whatever clean-up code you want before it does its own housekeeping.

Example 2-2 sets things up so that PHP calls the destruct( ) function. This function iterates through a list of destroyable objects stored in the global variable $objects_to_destroy and calls each object's destruct( ) method.

When an object needs a destructor, it must add itself to the $objects_to_ destroy array and also implement a destruct( ) method. The destruct( ) method should contain any code needed to clean up the resources that were consumed when the object was created and used.

In this example, the Database class adds itself in the constructor by doing $GLOBALS['objects_to_destroy'][ ] = &$this;. This ensures all objects are properly accounted for. Its destruct( ) method calls db_close( ) to shut the database connection.

In many cases, such as closing connections to databases and unlocking files, PHP will do this for you automatically. However, this clean up occurs only when the script is complete. Therefore, it's a good idea to release them yourself in the destructor. It's best to clean up as soon as possible because other programs may want to use your database connection or access the locked file.

When the majority of PHP scripts were short and fast, letting PHP tidy up your mess wasn't a large concern, because the time between the moment you finished using the resource and the end of the script was very short. Now that PHP is used on the command line and for more complex tasks, long-running scripts are commonplace, so it's a practical concern.

You may notice that since this implementation of destructors uses register_ shutdown_function( ), there's no time benefit, because the destructor isn't called until the end of the script. This is one of the big differences between destructors in PHP 5 and this PHP 4 emulation.

In PHP 5, objects are destroyed when they're no longer used, so connections are freed earlier. Also, this implementation is far from clean and object-oriented. You need to use global variables and global functions to track your objects, and it's easy to break the scheme by overwriting the array.

Thankfully, PHP 5 implements object destructors in the language itself, so PHP automatically tracks which objects have destructors and calls them as soon as you're finished using the object. This can be much earlier than when your program ends, so resources such as database connections and file locks won't be held open for the entire script; instead, they are released as soon as possible.

Like constructors, destructors in PHP 5 have a fixed name: __destruct( ). Since you don't call the destructor manually, you're not allowed to pass it any parameters. If your destructor needs any object-specific information, store it as a property:

```php
// PHP 5 Destructor
class database {
    function __destruct() {
        db_close($this->handle); // close the database connection
    }
}
```

Since destructors are now a language-level feature, there's no need for use register_shutdown_function( ). Everything is done for you.

You cannot assume that PHP will destroy objects in any particular order. Therefore, you should not reference another object in your destructor, as PHP may have already destroyed it. Doing so will not cause a crash, but it will cause your code to behave in an unpredictable (and buggy) manner.

Class Intermediates

The topics in the previous section covered the limit of PHP 4's object-oriented abilities. This section introduces a few concepts new to PHP 5: interfaces, type hinting, and static methods and properties.

Interfaces

In object-oriented programming, objects must work together. Therefore, you should be able to require a class (or more than one class) to implement methods that are necessary for the class to interact properly in your system.

For instance, an e-commerce application needs to know a certain set of information about every item up for sale. These items may be represented as different classes: Book, CD, DVD, etc. However, you need to know that your application can find the name, price, and inventory number of each object, regardless of its type.

The mechanism for forcing classes to support the same set of methods is called an *interface*. Defining an interface is similar to defining a class:

```
interface Sellable {
    public function getName( );
    public function getPrice( );
    public function getID( );
}
```

Instead of using the keyword class, an interface uses the keyword interface. Inside the interface, define your method prototypes, but don't provide an implementation.

This creates an interface named Sellable. Any class that's Sellable must implement the three methods listed in the interface: getName( ), getPrice( ), and getID( ).

When a class supports all the methods in the interface, it's called *implementing the interface*. You agree to implement an interface in your class definition:

```
class Book implements Sellable {

    public function getName( ) { ... }
```

```
        public function getPrice( ) { ... }
        public function getID( ) { ... }
    }
```

Failing to implement all the methods listed in an interface, or implementing them with a different prototype, causes PHP to emit a fatal error.

A class can agree to implement as many interfaces as you want. For instance, you may want to have a Listenable interface that specifies how you can retrieve an audio clip for an item. In this case, the CD and DVD classes would also implement Listenable, whereas the Book class wouldn't.

When you use interfaces, it's important to declare your classes before you instantiate objects. In PHP 4, you can arrange your code in any order and PHP will still find a the class definition.

In PHP 5, that's still mostly true; however, when a class implements interfaces, PHP 5 can sometimes become confused. To avoid breaking existing applications, this requirement is not enforced, but it's best not to rely upon this behavior.

Type Hinting

Another way of enforcing controls on your objects is by using *type hints*. A type hint is a way to tell PHP that an object passed to a method must be of a certain class.

In PHP 4, you must check that an argument is of the correct type by yourself. This results in many calls to get_class( ) and is_array( ) inside your code.

To ease this burden, PHP 5 allows you to transfer the job of type checking to PHP. You can optionally specify a class name in function and method prototypes. This only works for classes, though, not for any other variable types. You cannot, for example, require that an argument be an array.

For example, to require the first argument to your AddressBook class's add( ) method to be of type Person:

```
class AddressBook {

    public function add(Person $person) {
        // add $person to address book
    }
}
```

Then, if you call add( ) but pass a string, you get a fatal error:

```
$book = new AddressBook;

$person = 'Rasmus Lerdorf';
```

```
$book->add($person);
PHP Fatal error:  Argument 1 must be an object of class Person in...
```

Placing a type hint of Person in the first argument of your function declaration is equivalent to adding the following PHP code to the function:

```
public function add($person) {
        if (!($person instanceof Person)) {
                die("Argument 1 must be an instance of Person");
        }
}
```

The instanceof operator checks whether an object is an instance of a particular class. This code makes sure $person is a Person.

PHP 4 does not have an instanceof operator. You need to use the is_a( ) function, which is deprecated in PHP 5.

Type hinting has the side benefit of integrating API documentation directly into the class itself. If you see that a class constructor takes an Event type, you know exactly what to provide the method. Additionally, you know that the code and the "documentation" must always be in sync, because it's baked directly into the class definition.

However, type hinting does come at the cost of less flexibility. There's no way to allow a parameter to accept more than one type of object, so this places some restrictions upon how you design your object hierarchy.

Also, the penalty for violating a type hint is quite drastic—the script aborts with a fatal error. In a web context, you may want to have more control over how errors are handled and recover more gracefully from this kind of mistake. Implementing your own form of type checking inside of methods lets you print out an error page if you choose.

Last, unlike some languages, you cannot use type hinting for return values, so there's no way to mandate that a particular function always returns an object of a particular type.

Static Methods and Properties

Occasionally, you want to define a collection of methods in an object, but you want to be able to invoke those methods without the hassle of instantiating a object. In PHP 5, declaring a method static lets you call it directly:

```
class Format {
    public static function number($number, $decimals = 2,
                                  $decimal = ',', $thousands = '.') {
        return number_format($number, $decimals, $decimal, $thousands);
    }
}
```

```
print Format::number(1234.567);
1,234.57
```

Since static methods don't require an object instance, use the class name instead of the object. Don't place a dollar sign ($) before the class name.

Static methods aren't referenced with an arrow (->), but with double colons (::)—this signals to PHP that the method is static. So, in the example, the number( ) method of the Format class is accessed using Format::number( ).

Number formatting doesn't depend upon any other object properties or methods. Therefore, it makes sense to declare this method static. This way, for example, inside your shopping cart application, you can format the price of items in a pretty manner with just one line of code and still use an object instead of a global function.

Static methods do not operate on a specific instance of the class where they're defined. PHP does not "construct" a temporary object for you to use while you're inside the method. Therefore, you cannot refer to $this inside a static method, because there's no $this on which to operate. Calling a static method is just like calling a regular function.

PHP 5 also has a feature known as *static properties*. Every instance of a class shares these properties in common. Thus, static properties act as class-namespaced global variables.

One reason for using a static property is to share a database connection among multiple Database objects. For efficiency, you shouldn't create a new connection to your database every time you instantiate Database. Instead, negotiate a connection the first time and reuse that connection in each additional instance:

```
class Database {
    private static $dbh = NULL;

    public function __construct($server, $username, $password) {
        if (self::$dbh == NULL) {
            self::$dbh = db_connect($server, $username, $password);
        } else {
            // reuse existing connection
        }
    }
}

$db  = new Database('db.example.com', 'web', 'jsd6w@2d');
// Do a bunch of queries

$db2 = new Database('db.example.com', 'web', 'jsd6w@2d');
// Do some additional queries
```

Static properties, like static methods, use the double colon notation. To refer to a static property inside of a class, use the special prefix of self. self is to static properties and methods as $this is to instantiated properties and methods.

The constructor uses self::$dbh to access the static connection property. When $db is instantiated, dbh is still set to NULL, so the constructor calls db_connect() to negotiate a new connection with the database.

This does not occur when you create $db2, since dbh has been set to the database handle.

Inheritance

Besides encapsulation, another major advantage of object-oriented code is reuse. Reusing code reduces development time and the number of bugs. Object-oriented programming promotes reuse through a process known an inheritance.

Extending Classes

With inheritance, you can modify a class by adding or rewriting its methods. This allows your new class to be more specific than the original one, while still allowing you access to all the methods of the first class. The original class is known as the parent, and the new class is called the child.

Creating a child class is also called *extending a class* or *subclassing an object*. The original class that's extended can also be called a *super class* or a *base class*.

For instance, you can extend Person to create an Employee class, where an Employee is a Person with a salary.

When extending a class, abide by the "is a" rule. You should always be able to say, "Child class is a Parent class." Following this rule leads to clean relationships between your classes. This example is okay because an Employee is a Person:

```
class Person {
    private $name;

    public function setName($name) {
        $this->name = $name;
    }

    public function getName() {
        return $this->name;
    }
}
```

```
class Employee extends Person {
    private $salary;

    public function setSalary($salary) {
        $this->salary = $salary;
    }

    public function getSalary() {
        return $this->salary;
    }

}

$billg = new Employee;
$billg->setName('Bill Gates');
$billg->setSalary(865114); // Actual 2003 salary (excluding stock)
```

This code creates a new Employee class; instantiates a new instance of Employee, $billg; and sets his name and salary.

The extends keyword at the top of the class definition indicates to PHP that this class should inherit all the properties and methods of the parent class. This allows you to interact with a child object in the same way as its parent because when PHP cannot find a property or method in the child class, it searches the parent class.

Therefore, you can call setName( ) on an Employee, even though this method isn't defined in the class, because it's defined in Person and Employee extends Person.

Inheritance also lets you modify the parent class. This allows you to create two new methods, setSalary( ) and getSalary( ), and a property, $salary, to store the salary information.

When using inheritance, a third visibility level, protected, is useful. A public method is callable by anyone; a private method is callable by any method in the same class, but not by any methods in a subclass; a protected method, like a private method, restricts access to only the methods within the class, but it *also* allows access from children classes.

You should use protected instead of private in your classes, unless you have a particularly strong reason to deliberately prevent a subclass from accessing a method or property.

In the previous example, it did not matter that the name property was declared private, because it's altered only by setName( ) and getName( ), and these methods are in the same class as name. However, you could not add a new method to Employee that references name. This would not be the case if name were declared as protected.

Class Hierarchies

Inheritance isn't limited to one level. You can further extend `Employee`:

```
class Executive extends Employee {

    public function swindleShareholders() {

    }
}
```

Since an instance of the `Executive` class inherits everything from `Employee`, it also inherits everything from `Person`. This simple concept allows you to build up a tree of classes that start with an extremely basic class and become further specialized as they continue to extend each other. This is known as a *class hierarchy*.

You can branch classes in your class hierarchy. For instance, in addition to an `Employee` line, you can have a `Student` class that also extends `Person`. This results in the hierarchy shown in Figure 2-1.

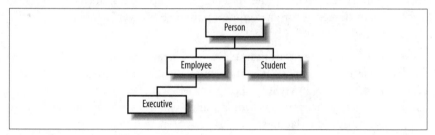

Figure 2-1. Class hierarchy

Some languages, most notably C++, allow a class to extend multiple parents. This is known as *multiple inheritance*. Multiple inheritance is handy when your child needs to take on characteristics of two different sets of parents.

For instance, consider an object that is an `Employee` and a `Parent`. Many people fit both criteria, but it doesn't make sense for `Parent` to subclass `Employee` or vice versa, because it's possible to be one and not the other.

This is easy to check because it violates the "is a" rule. An `Employee` is *not* a `Parent` any more than a `Parent` is an `Employee`.

The "is a" relationship also applies to the `instanceof` operator. For example, an instance of `Employee` is also a `Person`:

```
$billg = new Employee;
if ($billg instanceof Person) {
    print "Employees are people too!";
}
Employees are people too!
```

Since Employee subclasses Person, it's also considered an instance of Person.

Type hinting does an instanceof check, so a type hint for a Person can be either an instance of the Person class or any class that extends Person, such as Employee.

PHP does not support multiple inheritance, because multiple inheritance introduces many complexities. For instance, what happens when a class inherits different methods with the same name? It's not clear which method is the "correct" one. Instead, PHP handles these situations like Java does: by using interfaces.

As you may remember, an interface is a way to require a class to support a specific set of methods. When a class is required to implement an interface, you know that you can use the class as you need without corrupting the object hierarchy. Additionally, PHP 5 allows a class to implement multiple interfaces, so you're not constrained to a single class and a single interface.

Sometimes you have a slightly different problem. You have a series of objects that are related using the "is a" relationship, so it makes logical sense to have them descend from a common parent. However, while the children are tangible, the parent is abstract.

Take, for example, the Database class used previously in this chapter. A database is a real object, so it makes sense to have a Database class. However, although Oracle, MySQL, Postgres, MSSQL, and hundreds of other databases exist, you cannot download and install a generic database. You must choose a specific database.

Abstract Classes

PHP 5 provides a way for you to create a class that cannot be instantiated. This class is known as an *abstract class*. Here's an updated version of the Database class:

```
abstract class Database {
    abstract public function connect();
    abstract public function query();
    abstract public function fetch();
    abstract public function close();
}
```

Mark a class as abstract by placing the abstract keyword before class.

Abstract classes must contain at least one method that is also marked abstract. These methods are called *abstract methods*. Database contains four abstract methods: connect( ), query( ), fetch( ), and close( ). These four methods are the basic set of functionality necessary to use a database.

If a class contains an abstract method, the class must also be declared abstract. However, abstract classes can contain nonabstract methods (even though there are no regular methods in Database).

Abstract methods, like methods listed in an interface, are not implemented inside the abstract class. Instead, abstract methods are implemented in a child class that extends the abstract parent. For instance, you could use a MySQL class:

```
class MySQL extends Database {
    protected $dbh;
    protected $query;

    public function connect($server, $username, $password) {
        $this->dbh = mysql_connect($server, $username, $password);
    }

    public function query($sql) {
        $this->query = mysql_query($sql, $this->dbh);
    }

    public function fetch() {
        return mysql_fetch_row($this->query, $this->dbh);
    }

    public function close() {
        mysql_close($this->dbh);
    }
}
```

If a subclass fails to implement all the abstract methods in the parent class, then it itself is abstract and another class must come along and further subclass the child. You might do this if you wanted to create two MySQL classes: one that fetched information as objects and another that returned arrays.

There are two requirements for abstract methods:

- Abstract methods cannot be defined private, because they need to be inherited.
- Abstract methods cannot be defined final, because they need to be overridden.

PHP 5 offers the ability to restrict child classes from overriding a method in their parent. A final method is one that cannot be overridden by a child class. This is discussed in more detail in "Final Classes, Methods, and Properties," later in this chapter.

Constructors

Inheritance is the reason PHP 5 changed constructor names from the class's name to __construct( ). When constructors are tied to class names, it's easy to break code without realizing it. In PHP 4, to call the parent constructor inside of your class, you must hardcode the parent class name:

```
// Hardcoded parent constructor name
class MyDatabase extends MySQL {
    function MyDatabase() {
        // automatically populate connection values
        parent::MySQL('db.example.com', 'web', 'jsd6w@2d');

    }
}
```

This class, MyDatabase, is a wrapper for the main MySQL class. The two classes act identically, except that MyDatabase hardcodes the information necessary to connect to the database.

It uses the parent prefix to explicitly reference the constructor in the parent class. Otherwise, it may accidentally reference a method named MySQL in the current class. It is unlikely that you'd create such a method, but this eliminates any potential problems and makes parental reference clear.

However, moving this class under a different parent, or even renaming the parent, forces you to edit the constructor, replacing the call to parent:: MySQL() with the new parent constructor's name.

The more flexible solution makes you jump through a few hoops to dynamically determine the name of the parent's class:

```
// Dynamic parent constructor name
class MyDatabase extends MySQL {
    function MyDatabase() {
        // automatically populate connection values
        $parent = get_parent_class($this);
        parent::$parent('db.example.com', 'web', 'jsd6w@2d');
    }
}
```

This code is inefficient because you must call get_parent_class() every time you create a new instance of the class.

Using a fixed name for constructors reduces the brittleness of OO code. Calling a parent constructor is now easy and safe:

```
// Hardcoded parent constructor name
class MyDatabase extends MySQL {
    function MyDatabase() {
        // automatically populate connection values
        parent::__construct('db.example.com', 'web', 'jsd6w@2d');

    }
}
```

With the new naming scheme, you can always use parent::__construct( ) and know that it's the right thing to do.

Final Classes, Methods, and Properties

Inheritance is normally a good thing, but it can make sense to restrict it. The most common reason to declare a method final is that the method is "perfect." When you believe there's no way to update the method to make it better, declare it using the final keyword. This prevents subclasses from ruining it by reimplementing the method in an inferior manner.

Make a method final by placing the final keyword at the beginning of the method declaration:

```
final public function connect($server, $username, $password) {
    $this->dbh = mysql_connect($server, $username, $password);
}
```

This prevents someone from subclassing MySQL or creating a different connect( ) method.

To prevent subclassing of an entire class, don't mark each method final. Instead, make a final class:

```
final class MySQL extends Database {

}
```

A final class cannot be subclassed. This differs from a class in which every method is final because that class can be extended and provided with additional methods, even if you cannot alter any of the pre-existing methods.

PHP 5 also lets you mark properties as final; however, it does not call them final properties. Instead, it reuses its concept of constants.

```
class Math {
    const pi = 3.14159; // universal
    const e  = 2.71828; // constants
}

$area = math::pi * radius * raidus;
```

Like static properties, you can access constants without first instantiating a new instance of your class, and they're accessed using the double colon (::) notation. Prefix the word self:: to the constant name to use it inside of a class.

Unlike properties, constants do not have a dollar sign ($) before them:

```
class Circle {
    const pi = 3.14159;
    protected $radius;
```

```php
    public function __construct($radius) {
        $this->radius = $radius;
    }

    public function diameter() {
        return 2 * self::pi * $this->radius;
    }
}

$c = new circle(1);
print $c->diameter();
6.28318
```

This example creates a circle with a radius of 1 and then calls the diameter method to calculate its diameter. To use the class's pi constant, refer to it as self::pi; otherwise, PHP tries to access the value of the global pi constant:

```php
define('pi', 10); // global pi constant

class Circle {
    const pi = 3.14159; // class pi constant
    protected $radius;

    public function __construct($radius) {
        $this->radius = $radius;
    }

    public function diameter() {
        return 2 * pi * $this->radius;
    }

}

$c = new circle(1);
print $c->diameter();
20
```

Oops! PHP has used the value of 10 instead of 3.14159, so the new answer is 20 instead of 6.28318.

Although it's unlikely that you will accidentally redefine π (you'll probably use the built-in M_PI constant anyway), this can still slip you up.

You cannot assign the value of an expression to a constant, nor can they use information passed into your script:

```php
// invalid
class permissions {
    const    read = 1 << 2;
    const   write = 1 << 1;
    const execute = 1 << 0;
}
```

```
// invalid and insecure
class database {
    const debug = $_REQUEST['debug'];
}
```

Neither the constants in permissions nor the debug constant in database are acceptable because they are not fixed. Even the first example, 1 << 2, where PHP does not need to read in external data, is not allowed.

Magical Methods

PHP 5 has a few methods that are implicitly invoked behind the scenes. You've already seen two, __construct( ) and __destruct( ), but these are not the only special methods in PHP 5.

There are seven special methods, and they are as follows:

__construct( )
> Called when instantiating an object

__destruct( )
> Called when deleting an object

__get( )
> Called when reading from a nonexistent property

__set( )
> Called when writing to a nonexistent property

__call( )
> Called when invoking a nonexistent method

__toString( )
> Called when printing an object

__clone( )
> Called when cloning an object

These methods are easy to spot, since they all begin with two underscores (__).

__get( ) and __set( )

You've read a lot about the benefits of encapsulation and why your classes must have accessor methods. Writing these methods, however, induces numbness as you repeatedly create methods for each property in your class. PHP 5 has two special methods, __set( ) and __get( ), to ease your pain.

In PHP 4, the only way to handle accessors is to write your own set of methods for each property. By convention, these methods often begin with the word set and end with the property name. So, to set a Person's name, you call setName( ).

Using PHP 4 and accessors, the code looks like this:

```
class Person {
    var $name;
    var $email;

    function setName($name) {
        $this->name = $name;
    }

    function getName() {
        return $this->name;
    }
}

$rasmus = new Person;
$rasmus->setName('Rasmus Lerdorf');
print $ramsus->getName()
Rasmus Lerdorf
```

This isn't a problem when there's only a single property, but when Person adds email, age, address, and other details, the class quickly spirals into a long list of almost identical accessors.

PHP 4 requires you to manually write specific accessor functions for every property.* That quickly becomes tiresome as the number of object properties increases, and it makes changing from one backend to another complicated because you need to edit every single method.

Using methods such as getName( ) and setName( ) provides a great degree of protection against broken code, but forcing people to call getName( ) instead of reading name is clunky. In PHP 4, you don't have a choice, because that's the only way to implement accessors.

However, since accessors are so important, PHP 5 has two specific methods that implement them: __get( ) and __set( ). The __get( ) method automatically intercepts access to any undefined property reads. Likewise, __set( ) does the same for property writes.

Example 2-3 reimplements the class in PHP 5 using __get( ) and __set( ).

Example 2-3. Implementing magic accessor methods

```
class Person {
    private $data;

    public function __get($property) {
        if (isset($this->data[$property])) {
```

---

* Unless you use the experimental overload extension. If you do, you should know that you can no longer pass the accessor functions a variable by reference as a final parameter to get( ) or set( ).

Example 2-3. Implementing magic accessor methods (continued)

```
            return $this->data[$property];
        } else {
            return false;
        }
    }

    public function __set($property, $value) {
        $this->data[$property] = $value;
    }
}

$rasmus = new Person;
$rasmus->name = 'Rasmus Lerdorf';
print $rasmus->name;
Rasmus Lerdorf
```

With __get( ) and __set( ), you can use what appear to be public properties, such as $rasmus->name, without violating encapsulation. This is because the programmer isn't reading from and writing to those properties directly, but is instead being routed through accessor methods.

The __get( ) method takes the property name as its single parameter. Within the method, you check to see whether that property has a value inside $data. If it does, the method returns that value; otherwise, it returns false.

This lets you continue accessing properties using the familiar property syntax, even though the actual data is someplace else.

 When you read $rasmus->name, you actually call __get('name') and it's returning $data['name'], but for all external purposes that's irrelevant.

The __set( ) method takes two arguments: the property name and the new value. Otherwise, the logic inside the method is similar to __get( ).

There are two downsides to using __get( ) and __set( ). First, these methods only catch missing properties. If you define a property for your class, __get( ) and __set( ) are not invoked by PHP.

This is the case even if the property you're trying to access isn't visible in the current scope (for instance, when you're reading a property that exists in the class but isn't accessible to you, because it's declared private). Doing this causes PHP to emit a fatal error:

PHP Fatal error: Cannot access private property...

Second, these methods completely destroy any notion of property inheritance. If a parent object has a __get( ) method and you implement your own version of __get( ) in the child, your object won't function correctly, because the parent's __get( ) method is never called.

__call( )

PHP 5 also has a __call( ) method. It captures any calls to undefined methods in a class. The __call( ) method is useful for implementing an OO concept known as *aggregation*.

With aggregation, one object acts as a container for one or more additional objects. This is another way of solving the problem of multiple inheritance because you can easily piece together an object out of smaller components.

For example, a Person object can contain an Address object. Clearly, People have addresses. However, addresses aren't unique to people; they also belong to businesses and other entities. Therefore, instead of hardcoding address information inside of Person, it makes sense to create a separate Address class that can be used by multiple classes.

Example 2-4 shows how this works in practice.

Example 2-4. Aggregating an Address object

```
class Address {
    protected $city;
    protected $country;

    public function setCity($city) {
        $this->city = $city;
    }

    public function getCity() {
        return $this->city;
    }

    public function setCountry($country) {
        $this->country = $country;
    }

    public function getCountry() {
        return $this->country;
    }
}

class Person {
    protected $name;
    protected $address;

    public function __construct() {
```

Example 2-4. Aggregating an Address object (continued)

```
        $this->address = new Address;
    }

    public function setName($name) {
        $this->name = $name;
    }

    public function getName( ) {
        return $this->name;
    }

    public function __call($method, $arguments) {
        if (method_exists($this->address, $method)) {
            return call_user_func_array(
                array($this->address, $method), $arguments);
        }
    }
}
```

The Address class is set up just like the Person class you have seen before. However, it stores a city and country instead of a name.

Person has setName( ) and getName( ), like before, but it also has two new methods: __construct( ) and __call( ).

Its constructor instantiates an Address object and stores it in a protected $address property. This allows methods inside Person to access $address, but prevents others from talking directly to the class.

Ideally, when you call a method that exists in Address, PHP would automatically execute it. This does not occur, since Person does not extend Address. You must write code to glue these calls to the appropriate methods yourself.

Wrapper methods are one option. For example:

```
    public function setCity($city) {
        $this->address->setCity($city);
    }
```

This setCity( ) method passes along its data to the setCity( ) method stored in $address. This is simple, but it is also tedious because you must write a wrapper for every method.

Using __call( ) lets you automate this process by centralizing these methods into a single place:

```
    public function __call($method, $arguments) {
        if (method_exists($this->address, $method)) {
            return call_user_func_array(
                array($this->address, $method), $arguments);
        }
    }
```

The __call( ) method is invoked with two arguments: the name of the method and an array holding the parameters passed to the method. The first argument lets you see which method was called, so you can determine whether it's appropriate to dispatch it to $address.

Here, you want to pass along the method if it's a valid method of the Address class. Check this using method_exists( ), providing the object as the first parameter and the method name as the second.

If the function returns true, you know this method is valid, so you can call it. Unfortunately, you're still left with the burden of unwrapping the arguments out of the $arguments array. That can be painful.

The seldom used and oddly named call_user_func_array( ) function solves this problem. This function lets you call a user function and pass along arguments in an array. Its first parameter is your function name, and the second is the array of arguments.

In this case, however, you want to call an object method instead of a function. There's a special syntax to cover this situation. Instead of passing the function name, you pass an array with two elements. The first element is the object, and the other is the method name.

This causes call_user_func_array( ) to invoke the method on your object. You must then return the result of call_user_func_array( ) back to the original caller, or your return values will be silently discarded.

Here's an example of Person that calls both a method defined in Person and one from Address:

```
$rasmus = new Person;
$rasmus->setName('Rasmus Lerdorf');
$rasmus->setCity('Sunnyvale');

print $rasmus->getName() . ' lives in ' . $rasmus->getCity() . '.';
Rasmus Lerdorf lives in Sunnyvale.
```

Even though setCity( ) and getCity( ) aren't methods of Person, you have aggregated them into that class.

You can aggregate additional objects into a single class, and also be more selective as to which methods you expose to the outside user. This requires some basic filtering based on the method name.

When deciding if aggregation is the right technique, ask yourself if the "has a" rule applies. Here a Person has an Address, so it makes sense to aggregate. However, keep in mind that aggregate relationships are weaker than inheritance relationships because they're not as intricately bound to the object's identity.

__toString( )

PHP 5 provides objects with a way to control how they are converted to strings. This allows you to print an object in a friendly way without resorting to lots of additional code.

PHP 4 requires you to call a method that returns a string. For example:

```php
class Person {
    var $name;
    var $email;

    function setName($name) {
        $this->name = $name;
    }

    function setEmail($email) {
        $this->email = $email;
    }

    function toString() {
        return "$this->name <$this->email>";
    }
}

$rasmus = new Person;
$rasmus->setName('Rasmus Lerdorf');
$rasmus->setEmail('rasmus@php.net');
print $rasmus->toString();
```

Rasmus Lerdorf <rasmus@php.net>

This is effective, but there's no requirement that the string conversion method is always toString( ), so you can't rely on it from class to class.

Also, it adds visual clutter to your code because you're constantly writing ->toString( ) whenever you want to print an object. PHP should know that when you try to print an object, you want a special string representation of the contents of the object.

PHP 5 introduces a special method that lets you to control how PHP displays objects. PHP calls an object's __toString( ) method when you echo or print the object by itself.

The PHP 5 Person class is identical to the PHP 4 version, except that toString( ) has been renamed __toString( ):

```php
class Person {
    protected $name;
    protected $email;
```

```
    public function setName($name) {
        $this->name = $name;
    }

    public function setEmail($email) {
        $this->email = $email;
    }

    public function __toString() {
        return "$this->name <$this->email>";
    }
}
```

Now, instead of writing:

```
$rasmus = new Person;
$rasmus->setName('Rasmus Lerdorf');
$rasmus->setEmail('rasmus@php.net');
print $rasmus->toString();
```

you can write:

```
$rasmus = new Person;
$rasmus->setName('Rasmus Lerdorf');
$rasmus->setEmail('rasmus@php.net');
print $rasmus;
Rasmus Lerdorf <rasmus@php.net>
```

This feature does not work for interpolated or concatenated strings:

```
print  "PHP was created by $rasmus";
print  'PHP was created by '. $rasmus;
printf('PHP was created by %s', $rasmus);
PHP was created by Object id #1
PHP was created by Object id #1
PHP was created by Object id #1
```

The one exception is a dusty corner of PHP that uses echo and a comma (,) instead of period (.) to combine items:

```
echo  'PHP was created by ', $rasmus;
PHP was created by Rasmus Lerdorf <rasmus@php.net>
```

PHP 5 will *not* autoconvert objects to strings when you pass them to a function that requires a string argument. You should call __toString() on them instead:

```
print htmlentities($rasmus);                // bad
print htmlentities($rasmus->__toString());  // good
```

While such limited support for __toString() reduces its usefulness, future versions of PHP should extend this behavior to also call __toString() when you:

- Place the object inside double quotes or a heredoc
- Concatenate with the object using dot (.)

- Cast the object to a string using (string) or strval( )
- Treat the object as a string in printf( ) by indicating it should be formatted with %s

Therefore, it's best to start using the __toString( ) naming convention when you transition to PHP 5 because then there will be less code to modify when you want to take advantage of the newer features.

__clone( )

Since PHP 5 copies objects by reference instead of value, you need to use clone to duplicate the contents of an object. Otherwise, the second object is simply a reference to the first.

This cloning process copies every property in the first object to the second. This includes properties holding objects, so the cloned object may end up sharing object references with the original.

This is frequently not the desired behavior. For example, consider the aggregated version of Person that holds an Address object, shown earlier in Example 2-4. The key point to remember is that the $address property holds an Address object.

With this class, here's what happens when you clone an object:

```
$rasmus = new Person;
$rasmus->setName('Rasmus Lerdorf');
$rasmus->setCity('Sunnyvale');

$zeev = clone $rasmus;
$zeev->setName('Zeev Suraski');
$zeev->setCity('Tel Aviv');

print $rasmus->getName() . ' lives in ' . $rasmus->getCity() . '.';
print $zeev->getName() . ' lives in ' . $zeev->getCity() . '.';
Rasmus Lerdorf lives in Tel Aviv.
Zeev Suraski lives in Tel Aviv.
```

Interesting. Calling setName( ) worked correctly because the $name property is a string, so it's copied by value. However, since $address is an object, it's copied by reference, so getCity( ) doesn't produce the correct results, and you end up relocating Rasmus to Tel Aviv.

This type of object cloning is known as a *shallow clone* or a *shallow copy* because PHP does not clone objects held in properties. In contrast, a *deep clone* occurs when all objects involved are cloned. This is PHP 4's cloning method.

Control how PHP 5 clones an object by implementing a __clone( ) method in your class. When this method exists, PHP allows __clone( ) to override its default behavior:

```php
class Person {

    // ... everything from before

    public function __clone() {
        $this->address = clone $this->address;
    }
}
```

Inside of __clone( ), you're automatically presented with a shallow copy of the variable, stored in $this, the object that PHP provides when __clone( ) does not exist.

Since PHP has already copied all the properties, you only need to overwrite the ones you dislike. Here, $name is okay, but $address needs to be explicitly cloned.

Now the clone behaves correctly:

```php
$rasmus = new Person;
$rasmus->setName('Rasmus Lerdorf');
$rasmus->setCity('Sunnyvale');

$zeev = clone $rasmus;
$zeev->setName('Zeev Suraski');
$zeev->setCity('Tel Aviv');

print $rasmus->getName() . ' lives in ' . $rasmus->getCity() . '.';
print $zeev->getName() . ' lives in ' . $zeev->getCity() . '.';
Rasmus Lerdorf lives in Sunnyvale.
Zeev Suraski lives in Tel Aviv.
```

Using the clone operator on objects stored in properties causes PHP to check whether any of those objects contain a __clone( ) method. If one exists, PHP calls it. This repeats for any objects that are nested even further.

This process correctly clones the entire object and demonstrates why it's called a deep copy.

CHAPTER 3

MySQL

PHP 5 sports a new MySQL extension. While this extension is similar in spirit to the original MySQL extension, it has many new features and other improvements. To differentiate it from the original version, this extension is called the "Improved MySQL extension," or `mysqli` for short.

The changes to `mysqli` come from two places. The majority are from new features available in MySQL 4.1. However, PHP 5 also allows `mysqli` to add an object-oriented interface.

Here's a list of the major advances in `mysqli`:

- Compatibility with MySQL 4.1 and above
- Prepared statements and bound parameters
- Object-oriented interface
- Secure connections using SSL

Additionally, MySQL 4.1 has new SQL-level capabilities that you can use from PHP. They include:

- Subselects
- Transactions
- Fulltext searching
- Unicode support
- Geospacial support (GIS)

On the downside, there are a few wrinkles if you want to start using `mysqli` with your existing PHP projects:

- Its client libraries are *not* bundled with PHP 5.
- It does *not* work with MySQL 4.0 and below.
- It's missing some `mysql` functions.

In a nutshell, if all your projects use MySQL 4.1 and later, and you have no legacy MySQL code, then all you need to do is download the MySQL client libraries and start using mysqli. On the other hand, you'll have some work to do if you:

- Want to use MySQL 4.1, but have existing mysql-based code
- Must write code that runs under MySQL 4.0 (and below) *and* 4.1 (and above)
- Want to have some applications use a MySQL 4.0 database and others use a MySQL 4.1 database

The section "Porting Code and Migrating Databases" at the end of this chapter discusses a few strategies for handling these types of situations. However, before discussing *how* to move from mysql to mysqli, this chapter covers *why* you'd want to make the switch.

The chapter begins by showing how to use the mysqli extension, with sections on both the procedural and object-oriented interfaces. Next comes prepared statements and bound parameters. These are database features that require a different set of functions to communicate with MySQL than before, but offer improved speed and ease-of-use.

The middle of the chapter covers subselects and transactions. These are new MySQL 4.1 features that aren't unique to mysqli and PHP, but are part of the MySQL 4.1 server. Subselects let you nest a query inside of another, and transactions allow you to group a series of SQL queries as an integrated unit. Queries wrapped inside a transaction are guaranteed to either all work or all fail.

MySQL 4.1 allows you to group multiple queries into a single request. This is useful when you're using PHP to restore a database or need to populate a database from scratch. The section "Before and After: Making Multiple Queries" covers the new interface for processing the results of a multi-query, which is more complicated than a regular query.

Another MySQL 4.1 feature is the ability to encrypt the connection between PHP and MySQL using Secure Sockets Layer (SSL). The next section shows how to configure PHP and MySQL to support SSL connections and how to use mysqli to pass authentication credentials.

At the end of the chapter, there's a discussion of various migration strategies for moving your code to both mysqli and MySQL 4.1. Due to various incompatibilities, this process requires a careful plan of attack.

While this chapter covers many MySQL topics, it omits some advanced topics, such query optimization, backups, and replication. For more information on those topics, read *High Performance MySQL*, by Jeremy D. Zawodny and Derek J. Balling (O'Reilly). That book covers those three issues and more, including a complete chapter on securing MySQL from crackers.

Installing and Configuring

You must download and install MySQL 4.1 or greater to use `mysqli`. In particular, if you use the MySQL library bundled with PHP 4, you now must download and install a new version of MySQL.

While PHP 4 bundles a copy of the MySQL client libraries, PHP 5 does not. As of MySQL 4.1, the entire MySQL application is licensed under the GNU General Public License (GPL). Since PHP uses a different type of open source license, PHP was legally unable to bundle the libraries without modifying their license.

MySQL eventually added a special license exemption for many free and open source products, including PHP. However, the PHP Group decided not to restore the libraries. Since many people already had the libraries on their systems, bundling the libraries actually caused conflicts when the bundled library differed from the preinstalled version.

As a result, if you don't already have a copy of the MySQL client libraries, you need to install one. You can download MySQL from *http://www.mysql.com/*. If you're using `mysqli`, be sure to use a copy of MySQL 4.1.2 or greater, as earlier versions won't work with PHP.

Before installing MySQL 4.1, you should read the section "Porting Code and Migrating Databases." You may have migration problems, particularly if you're upgrading directly from MySQL 3.2.x and skipping MySQL 4.0. Reading this section isn't necessary if MySQL 4.1 is your first version of MySQL.

After you've installed MySQL, you can enable the `mysqli` extension with the `--with-mysqli` flag during the PHP configure process.

Unlike for `mysql`, you don't tell PHP where MySQL is located by adding the path to the MySQL base installation. Instead, PHP uses MySQL's new *mysql_config* file.

Here's an example of the difference between the configuration options for `mysql` and `mysqli` for a MySQL installation in */usr/local/mysql*:

```
// mysql
--with-mysql=/usr/local/mysql

// mysqli
--with-mysqli=/usr/local/mysql/bin/mysql_config
```

You can enable both mysql and mysqli at the same time, which is useful when you need to support legacy applications. You should link PHP against the same set of MySQL libraries to prevent compiler errors.

Procedural Interface

The procedural interface to mysqli is largely identical to the older mysql extension. Except, of course, all the function names begin with mysqli instead of mysql:

```
$db = mysqli_connect($server, $user, $password) or
    die("Could not connect: " . mysqli_error());
mysqli_select_db($db, "users");

$result = mysqli_query($db, "SELECT username FROM users");

while ($row = mysqli_fetch_assoc($result)) {
    print $row['username'] . "\n";
}

mysqli_free_result($result);
mysqli_close($db);
```

This code connects to a MySQL database, selects the users table, makes a query, and then fetches each row as an associative array. These functions all behave the same as their mysql counterparts, except that the mysqli functions require a database handle as their first argument instead of optionally allowing one as the final argument. "Porting Code and Migrating Databases" covers all the API changes in detail.

There is also a minor change in mysqli_fetch_array(). When there are no additional rows, it returns NULL. The original extension returns false. This difference won't affect code like that shown here, where it only assigns the result to a variable, but if you use !== to do a strict check against false, you must now check against NULL.

Alternative Fetch Methods

If you prefer different MySQL fetch methods, they're also in mysqli. Given the same query of SELECT username FROM users, these example functions all print the same results:

```
// Fetch numeric arrays:
while ($row = mysqli_fetch_row($result)) {
    print $row[0] . "\n";
}
```

```
// Alternative syntax:
while ($row = mysqli_fetch_array($result, MYSQLI_NUM)) {
    print $row[0] . "\n";
}

// Alternative associative array syntax:
while ($row = mysqli_fetch_array($result, MYSQLI_ASSOC)) {
    print $row['username'] . "\n";
}

// Both numeric and associative:
while ($row = mysqli_fetch_array($result, MYSQLI_BOTH)) {
    print $row[0] . "\n";
    print $row['username'] . "\n";
}

// Fetch as "object"
while ($row = mysqli_fetch_object($result)) {
    print $row->username . "\n";
}
```

Before and After: Connecting to the Database Server

Before you can issue queries, you need to connect to the MySQL server. This sounds so basic that you'd think it would be the same in both versions of the MySQL extension, but there are quite a few changes.

Connecting isn't just specifying the location of your database and providing a username and password. You also specify a variety of configuration options, such as whether to use SSL and the number of seconds before the connection times out.

mysql: Making a Connection

The mysql connection functions take five parameters:

```
mysql_connect(server, username, password, new_link, client_flags)
```

All of these parameters are actually optional, because the extension defaults to values specified in a series of MySQL-related configuration directives, such as mysql.default_host.

The *server* parameter is usually the same as the host, but you can also append a port name or a path to a socket. For example, if your database runs on port 3307 on *db.example.org*:

```
mysql_connect('db.example.org:3307');
```

Separate the hostname and port with a colon (:) so PHP can tell them apart.

The username and password variables are not the username and password for your local account, but for MySQL's account system.

By default, if you try to reconnect to the same database with the same set of credentials, PHP will reuse the existing connection. Setting *new_link* to true forces PHP to always make another link to MySQL.

Use the final parameter, *client_flags*, to control the session. You can modify it by passing any combination of the following three constants: MYSQL_CLIENT_COMPRESS, MYSQL_CLIENT_IGNORE_SPACE, and MYSQL_CLIENT_INTERACTIVE. These tell MySQL to compress the connection, ignore spaces after functions, and modify how it determines when to close the connection, respectively.

mysqli: Making a Connection

Under mysqli there are two different ways to connect to MySQL: the familiar mysqli_connect( ) and a new method, mysqli_real_connect( ).

Don't feel that mysqli_real_connect( ) is somehow superior to mysqli_connect( ) because it contains the word real. It's not. This name comes simply from the underlying MySQL C API. Besides, mysqli_connect( ) uses the same C functions as mysqli_real_connect( ); it just wraps them in an easy-to-use form.

Unfortunately, while mysqli_connect( ) looks similar to mysql_connect( ), it is not identical. For one, it now takes six parameters, all of them still optional:

```
mysqli_connect(hostname, username, password, database, port, socket)
```

The first three options—*hostname*, *username*, and *password*—are the same as mysql_connect( ), but the remaining three are different. The *database* parameter controls which database you want to query. Using this parameter is the same as calling mysql_select_database( ). This function is still available as mysqli_select_database( ), but you should not need to use it unless you are reusing the same connection to switch from one database to another on the same server.

The *port* option controls which port to contact on the database server, and *socket* specifies which socket to use. This is identical to adding *:port* or *:/path/to/socket* after the *hostname* in mysql_connect( ). (You cannot use this syntax in mysqli.) These two parameters are mutually exclusive. If you use one, there's no purpose in using the other.

Here's an example that uses the first five options:

```
mysqli_connect('db.example.org', 'web', 'xyz@123', 'users', 3306);
```

This function tries to connect to a MySQL server running on db.example.com on port 3306. It uses a MySQL username of web with password xyz@123. If it's authorized, it then sets the database to events, just like entering USE events; in the MySQL prompt.

The mysql_pconnect( ) function has been removed. You cannot create persistent connections using MySQLi. While the goal of persistent connections—reducing the overhead time necessary to establish a connection—was a good idea, they caused problems. On high traffic sites they actually prevented PHP from accessing MySQL because they were holding onto available connections.

The mysql extension had an optional *client_flags* parameter, which let you set options such as whether the connection should compress data. These options now require a different set of connection functions:

```
$db = mysqli_init( );
mysqli_real_connect($db, 'db.example.com', 'web', 'xyz@123', 'users',
                    3306, NULL, MYSQLI_CLIENT_COMPRESS);
```

The mysqli_init( ) function returns a MySQL object that can then be used by mysqli_real_connect( ) to make the connection.

The mysqli_real_connect( ) function has the same syntax as mysqli_connect( ), except that you can add client flags as a seventh parameter. The call just shown is identical to the example using mysqli_connect( ), except that it also compresses the connection.

Table 3-1 shows the five constants you can pass to mysqli_real_connect( ). It includes the three flags available with mysql, but also adds two new ones: MYSQLI_CLIENT_FOUND_ROWS and MYSQLI_CLIENT_SSL. The pre-existing constants have also been renamed to begin with MYSQLI.

Table 3-1. mysqli_real_connect( ) options

Name	Description
MYSQLI_CLIENT_COMPRESS	Compress the connection.
MYSQLI_CLIENT_FOUND_ROWS	Return the number of found rows instead of the number of changed rows.
MYSQLI_CLIENT_IGNORE_SPACE	Allow spaces after function names.
MYSQLI_CLIENT_INTERACTIVE	Close the connection after interactive_timeout seconds instead of wait_timeout seconds. These values are usually the same unless you've modified your MySQL configuration.
MYSQLI_CLIENT_SSL	Encrypt the connection using SSL (should be automatically invoked when you add SSL information).

For more information on these options, see *http://www.mysql.com/doc/en/ mysql_options.html*.

Using mysqli_init( ) also allows you to set a variety of other configuration options before establishing the link:

```
$db = mysqli_init( );
mysqli_options($db, MYSQLI_OPT_CONNECT_TIMEOUT, 120);
mysqli_options($db, MYSQLI_OPT_LOCAL_INFILE, false);

mysqli_real_connect($db, 'db.example.com', 'web', 'xyz@123', 'users',
                    3306, NULL, MYSQLI_CLIENT_COMPRESS);
```

The mysqli_options( ) function provides you with the ability to control more esoteric details about the connection. Since these options usually allow you to specify a parameter, they can't be passed alongside the other client flags.

This example sets the connection timeout to 120 seconds and disables the ability to use LOAD LOCAL INFILE. See Table 3-2 for a list of all the connection options usable in mysqli_options( ) and mysqli_real_connect( ).

Table 3-2. mysqli_options( ) options

Name	Description
MYSQLI_READ_DEFAULT_GROUP	Read the options for this group from your MySQL configuration file.
MYSQLI_READ_DEFAULT_FILE	Use this file as your MySQL configuration file instead of *my.cnf*.
MYSQLI_OPT_CONNECT_TIMEOUT	Number of seconds before MySQL times out.
MYSQLI_OPT_LOCAL_INFILE	Enable the LOAD LOCAL INFILE command.
MYSQLI_INIT_COMMAND	Always issue this command when connecting (and reconnecting) to the server.

Additional details on these options are available at *http://www.mysql.com/doc/en/mysql_options.html*.

Object-Oriented Interface

The mysqli extension also allows you to manipulate the data using an object-oriented interface. Everything that can be done using the procedural interface is available this way. Here is the same sample transaction from the last section translated into the OO style:

```
$mysqli = new mysqli('db.example.org', 'web', 'xyz@123');
$mysqli->select_db('users');

$result = $mysqli->query("SELECT username FROM users");

while ($row = $result->fetch_assoc( )) {
    print $row['username'] . "\n";
}

$result->close( );
```

With the OO interface, there's no need to pass database handles as the first parameter to a mysqli method. Instead, the extension stores that handle as part of the mysqli object.

If you're porting code from mysql and use the default link option, you may find it easier to switch to the OO syntax because it doesn't require you to modify the argument list of every mysql function.

You can also use mysqli_init( ) and mysqli_real_connect( ):

```
$mysqli = new mysqli( );
$mysqli->init( );
$mysqli->options(MYSQLI_OPT_CONNECT_TIMEOUT, 120);
$mysqli->options(MYSQLI_OPT_LOCAL_INFILE, false);

$mysqli->real_connect('db.example.com', 'web', 'xyz@123', 'users',
                      3306, NULL, MYSQLI_CLIENT_COMPRESS);
```

A new mysqli object does not automatically call mysqli_init( ) in its constructor. This is still your responsibility.

Certain mysqli functions are object properties instead of methods, in particular, mysqli_error( ), mysqli_errno( ), and mysqli_insert_id( ). Here's an example using mysqli_insert_id( ):

```
// place new e-mail address on list:
$email = 'rasmus@php.net';
$list  = 'php-general';

// escape data
$email = $mysqli->real_escape_string($email);
$list = $mysqli->real_escape_string($list);

$mysqli = new mysqli($server, $user, $password);
$mysqli->query("INSERT INTO addresses VALUES(NULL, '$email')");
$id = $mysqli->insert_id; // no ( ) necessary!
$mysqli->query("INSERT INTO lists VALUES($id, '$list')");
```

A complete list of MySQLi classes, methods, and properties can be found at *http://www.php.net/mysqli*.

Before and After: Querying and Retrieving Data with Prepared Statements

One way to speed up MySQL is to use prepared statements. Every time you make an SQL query, MySQL parses the request, checks its validity, and executes it. While MySQL does this efficiently, prepared statements make this process even faster.

A prepared statement is a way to tell MySQL what your query will look like before you actually execute it. This description doesn't contain the exact query; it's more like a query template. Most of the query is hardcoded, but there are placeholders where you want to customize the information.

You pass this template to MySQL. It parses and validates the query, and returns a statement handle. You then use that handle to execute the request.

In contrast to a traditional query, when you execute this type of request, there's no need to parse the SQL. As a result, MySQL executes the query faster. If you make the same query more than once, it's faster to use a prepared statement than a direct query. Additionally, prepared statements automatically escape quotes, so you don't need to worry about stray characters. This is a big benefit that makes prepared statements worthwhile even for single queries.

Prepared statements also let you control data retrieval. There's no longer a need to first retrieve a row into an array and then assign each element to an individual variable. You can instruct MySQL to place each piece of data directly into a variable.

PHP 4: Traditional Input Queries

Example 3-1 demonstrates the traditional way to insert data into a table.

Example 3-1. Executing a traditional query

```
// User-entered data
$username = 'rasmus';
$password = 'z.8cMpdFbNAPw';
$zipcode  = 94088;

// Escape data
$username = mysqli_real_escape_string($db, $username);
$password = mysqli_real_escape_string($db, $password);
$zipcode  = intval($zipcode);

// Create SQL query
$sql = "INSERT INTO users VALUES ('$username', '$password', $zipcode)";

// Make SQL query
mysqli_query($db, $sql) or die('Error');
```

There are three distinct parts of the process: escaping the data, creating the query, and executing the query.

It's vital not to omit the three lines at the top. When you insert user-entered information into a database, you must prevent the possibility that the user can create an invalid query or even maliciously alter the query. The mysqli_real_ escape_string( ) function ensures strings are treated as data by escaping single quotes, and the intval( ) function converts the data to an integer, stripping away non-numbers in the process. This prevents MySQL from interpreting them as part of the query.

The mysqli_real_escape_string( ) function differs from mysql_escape_string( ) because mysqli_real_escape_string( ) respects the character encoding of your data. The older mysql_escape_string( ) is obsolete and is not available under mysqli.

After escaping the data, you take the fields and create an SQL statement. Although you can build the SQL directly inside mysqli_query( ), assigning it to a variable such as $sql makes debugging easier because you can easily do a print $sql (or another form of logging) to discover if what you're actually passing MySQL is what you think you're passing.

When the SQL's complete, it's passed to MySQL using mysqli_query( ). MySQL then receives the data, parses it, reports errors if they exist, executes the query, and returns a result.

This is standard stuff to most PHP programmers. You can continue to use this method in PHP 5 under mysqli, but as you'll see, there's a better method.

PHP 5: Binding Input Parameters

MySQL 4.1 introduces a new way to query a database. With this approach, you create a statement with input parameter placeholders. This template is then filled in with data when you execute the query.

Example 3-2 is a revised version of Example 3-1.

Example 3-2. Querying with bound input parameters

```
// User-entered data
$username = 'rasmus';
$password = 'z.8cMpdFbNAPw';
$zipcode = 94088;

// Prepare statement
$sql = 'INSERT INTO users VALUES(?, ?, ?)';
$stmt = mysqli_stmt_init($db);
if (mysqli_stmt_prepare($stmt, $sql)) {

    // Associate placeholders with data type and variable name
    // 'ssi' tells MySQL you're passing two strings and an integer
    mysqli_stmt_bind_param($stmt, 'ssi', $username, $password, $zipcode);

    // Executing statement
    mysqli_stmt_execute($stmt);
}
```

This is a big twist. There are question marks (?) in the SQL where your variables used to be, and the calls to mysql_real_escape_string( ) and intval( ) have disappeared.

The new method separates querying a database into three parts. Before, you passed MySQL the SQL with the data and told MySQL to execute it in one step. Here, you first tell MySQL the query without any data. This is known as *preparing the query*. Next, you tell MySQL what types of information are going in each spot in the query and which PHP variables hold the data. This is called *binding parameters*. Finally, you pass along the data and execute the query. This is called *executing the query*.

When you prepare the query, you create an SQL statement that looks identical to what you normally write, but you substitute a question mark for each variable. Here's a before and after example:

```
// Before
$sql = "INSERT INTO events VALUES ('$name', '$password', $zipcode)";

// After
$sql = 'INSERT INTO events VALUES(?, ?, ?)';
```

The new SQL statement is like a template that's going to be filled in later on, and the question marks tell MySQL where to place the data. Notice how there's no need to place single quotation marks around the first and second parameters. When you tell MySQL a parameter is a string, MySQL automatically quotes the variable for you. Parameter type identification is explained shortly.

The next step is to create a new MySQL statement. First, initialize a blank statement handle with mysqli_stmt_init( ). Pass this and your SQL to mysqli_stmt_prepare( ). This sends your statement to MySQL, where the server can check whether your syntax is correct. This function returns true if everything is okay and false if there's a problem.

```
if (mysqli_stmt_prepare($stmt, $sql)) {
```

All future interaction with the query goes through the statement handle, $stmt, instead of the database handle, $db.

Now that the statement is prepared, bind the parameters using mysqli_stmt_bind_param( ):

```
// Associate placeholders with data type and variable name
mysqli_stmt_bind_param($stmt, 'ssi', $username, $password, $zipcode);
```

This function takes a variable number of arguments. The first parameter is the statement handle. The second is a string that describes each SQL placeholder. If you want MySQL to treat the variable as text, use s; for integers, i;

for all other numbers, d; and for blobs, b. In this example, the first two placeholders are strings and the last one is an integer, so the argument is ssi.

The remaining arguments are the variables that you want PHP to pass to MySQL when the query is executed. This is different from passing the variables themselves, as in a traditional function call. MySQL *does not* take what's currently stored in the variables; instead, it takes what *will be* stored in the variables at the time of the query's execution. This is a big difference.

In this case, the end result would be the same either way because you don't alter the values of $username and the other two variables in between binding them and executing the query, but later on you see an example where the distinction is crucial.

You must have an equal number of question marks in your statement, characters in the placeholder types parameter, and arguments following that parameter. (Here there are three of each.) Failing to do so causes MySQL to return an error.

Finally, you instruct MySQL to execute the statement:

```
// Executing statement
mysqli_stmt_execute($stmt);
```

Since you've already prepared the SQL and bound the variables, MySQL needs no new information, so mysqli_stmt_execute( ) is the least complicated part of the process.

You can also use prepared statements with mysqli's OO interface. This example does the same thing as Example 3-2:

```
// User-entered data
$username = 'rasmus';
$password = 'z.8cMpdFbNAPw';
$zipcode  = 94088;

// Prepare statement
$sql = 'INSERT INTO users VALUES(?, ?, ?)';
$stmt = $db->stmt_init();
if ($stmt->prepare($sql)) {

    // Associate placeholders with data type and variable name
    // 'ssi' tells MySQL you're passing two strings and an integer
    $stmt->bind_param('ssi', $username, $password, $zipcode);

    // Executing statement
    $stmt->execute();
}
```

With the OO API, substitute mysqli_stmt_init($db) with $db->stmt_init( ). This method returns a statement object, upon which you can invoke prepare( ), bind_param( ), and execute( ) methods.

Bound input and output parameters are associated with the specific variable, not the variable name. This matters when you call mysqli_stmt_bind_param( ) in a different scope than mysqli_stmt_execute( ). For instance, this works:

```
function execute_my_statement($stmt) {
    // Execute prepared statement
    mysqli_stmt_execute($stmt);
}

// Varibles defined in main scope
$username = 'rasmus';
$password = 'z.8cMpdFbNAPw';
$zipcode  = 94088;

// Prepare statement
$sql = 'INSERT INTO users VALUES(?, ?, ?)';
$stmt = mysqli_stmt_init($db);

if (mysqli_stmt_prepare($stmt, $sql)) {

    // Associate placeholders with data type and variable name
    // 'ssi' tells MySQL you're passing two strings and an integer
    mysqli_stmt_bind_param($stmt, 'ssi', $username, $password, $zipcode);

    execute_my_statement($stmt);
}
```

Even though you're calling mysqli_stmt_execute( ) inside execute_my_ statement( ), mysqli contains a reference to $username from the main scope. This allows the query to execute properly.

However, this also means the following *won't* work:

```
function execute_my_statement($stmt) {
    // Varibles defined in local scope
    $username = 'rasmus';
    $password = 'z.8cMpdFbNAPw';
    $zipcode  = 94088;

    // Execute prepared statement
    mysqli_stmt_execute($stmt);
}

// Prepare statement
$sql = 'INSERT INTO users VALUES(?, ?, ?)';
$stmt = mysqli_stmt_init($db);

if (mysqli_stmt_prepare($stmt, $sql)) {

    // Associate placeholders with data type and variable name
    // 'ssi' tells MySQL you're passing two strings and an integer
    mysqli_stmt_bind_param($stmt, 'ssi', $username, $password, $zipcode);
```

```
        execute_my_statement($stmt);
    }
```

In this example, you're binding $username in the main scope, but setting a *different* $username inside execute_my_statement( ). Just because both variables have the same name—$username—doesn't mean they're references to each other.

PHP 5: Binding Input Parameters with Multiple Queries

The previous example inserted only one piece of data into the database. Where prepared statements really shine, however, is when you need to execute the same query multiple times. In these cases, there's no need to reprepare or rebind the query. You can just load new information into the bound variables and execute the statement another time. Example 3-3 shows how to enter multiple users into the database.

Example 3-3. Querying with bound input parameters multiple times

```
$users = array(array('rasmus', 'z.8cMpdFbNAPw', 94088),
               array('zeev'  , 'asd34.23NNDeq',     0));

// Prepare statement
$sql = 'INSERT INTO users VALUES(?, ?, ?)';
$stmt = mysqli_stmt_init($db);
if (mysqli_stmt_prepare($stmt, $sql)) {

    // Associate placeholders with data type and variable name
    // 'ssi' tells MySQL you're passing two strings and an integer
    mysqli_stmt_bind_param($stmt, 'ssi', $username, $password, $zipcode);

    foreach ($users as $user) {
        // Place data into bound variables
        list($username, $password, $zipcode) = $user;

        // Execute prepared statement
        mysqli_stmt_execute($stmt);
    }
}
```

The initial setup in Example 3-3 is identical to previous examples, but instead of executing the statement once, mysqli_stmt_execute( ) lives inside a foreach loop. Every time the loop iterates, new values are placed in $username, $password, and $zipcode, and mysqli_stmt_execute( ) makes a new query. Even though mysqli_stmt_execute($stmt) hasn't changed, the query is different because the underlying data in the bound parameters has been updated.

This is where you can truly appreciate the benefit of using bound parameters. Not only is it significantly easier to re-execute a query using PHP, MySQL also executes them faster because it's already prepared the statement.

At present, you cannot bind array elements. It is tempting to omit the call to list and do the following:

```
mysqli_stmt_bind_param($stmt, 'ssi', $user[0], $user[1], $user[2]);

foreach ($users as $user) {
    // Execute prepared statement
    mysqli_stmt_execute($stmt);
}
```

This does not work. MySQLi will not grab elements from $user.

PHP 5: Binding Output Parameters

You can use bound parameters for more than just placing data into MySQL. You can also use them to retrieve data from MySQL.

Under the old MySQL extension, when you retrieved a row or column from the database, you needed to assign the result to a variable. This method still works with the mysqli extension, as shown earlier in the chapter.

However, mysqli also supports a new fetch method, mysqli_stmt_fetch( ). When you use mysqli_stmt_fetch( ), PHP variables are populated with MySQL table data, in a fashion similar to how mysqli_stmt_execute( ) pulls in values stored in PHP variables for a query, as shown in Example 3-4.

Example 3-4. Querying with bound output parameters

```
// Prepare statement
$sql = 'SELECT username FROM users';
$stmt = mysqli_stmt_init($db);
if (mysqli_stmt_prepare($stmt, $sql)) {
    // Bind result variables
    mysqli_stmt_bind_result($stmt, $username);

    // Execute prepared statement
    mysqli_stmt_execute($stmt);

    // Place query data into bound result variables
    while (mysqli_stmt_fetch($stmt)) {
        // Print results
        print "$username\n";
    }
}
rasmus
zeev
```

The query is prepared like the earlier examples, but before executing the prepared statement, you bind the output using mysqli_stmt_bind_result( ). The first parameter is the statement handle; the other parameters are the variables.

In this case, since the query returns only one column, $username is the only other argument. If the query returned multiple columns, then those variables would follow. For example, this query returns the username and the password:

```
// Prepare statement
$sql = 'SELECT username, password FROM users';
$stmt = mysqli_stmt_init($db);
if (mysqli_stmt_prepare($stmt, $sql)) {
    // Bind result variables
    mysqli_stmt_bind_result($stmt, $username, $password);
}
```

Since the query can return multiple rows, mysqli_stmt_fetch( ) is placed inside a while loop. Each time the function is called, another row is placed in the output parameters. When the data is exhausted, the function returns NULL.

Of course, there's an OO version of Example 3-4:

```
$sql = 'SELECT username FROM users';
$stmt = $db->stmt_init( );
if ($stmt->prepare($sql)) {
    // Bind result variables
    $stmt->bind_result($username);

    // Execute prepared statement
    $stmt->execute( );

    // Place query data into bound result variables
    while ($stmt->fetch( )) {
        // Print results
        print "$username\n";
    }
}
```

This example is similar to the OO code for handling bound input parameters, but now you also use $stmt->bind_result( ) and $stmt->fetch( ).

PHP 5: Bound Input and Output Parameters

You can bind both input and output parameters to the same query. For instance, the code in Example 3-5 gets all the usernames for people with a specific Zip Code.

Example 3-5. Querying with both bound input and bound output parameters

```
$zipcode = 94088;

// Prepare statement
$sql = 'SELECT username FROM users WHERE zipcode = ?';

$stmt = mysqli_stmt_init($db);
if (mysqli_stmt_prepare($stmt, $sql)) {

    // Associate placeholders with data type and variable name
    mysqli_stmt_bind_param($stmt, 'i', $zipcode);

    // Bind result variables
    mysqli_stmt_bind_result($stmt, $username);

    // Execute prepared statement
    mysqli_stmt_execute($stmt);

    // Place query data into bound result variables
    while (mysqli_stmt_fetch($stmt)) {
        // Print results
        print "$username\n";
    }
}
rasmus
```

This example combines code from Examples 3-3 and 3-4. After preparing the statement, you call both mysqli_stmt_bind_param( ) and mysqli_stmt_bind_result( ). When you execute the query, MySQLi obeys both settings.

The inner while fetches each row using mysqli_stmt_fetch( ) and prints out the data. Here, there's only one record—rasmus—because the dataset is quite small.

You can bind the same variables for both input and output. However, it often makes sense to use separate variables, so you can more easily distinguish input data from output.

Object-Oriented Interface

You've already seen a few examples showing how to use the object-oriented interface to mysqli with bound parameters. This section fills in the remaining details.

To complement the mysqli object, there's also a MySQLi statement object, mysqli_stmt. This object is returned by mysqli_stmt_init( ), and its methods are all the functions that begin with mysqli_stmt, such as mysqli_stmt_prepare( ) and mysqli_stmt_bind_param( ), but without the mysqli_stmt prefix.

Example 3-6 rewrites Example 3-5 using the OO interface.

Example 3-6. Querying with bound parameters and an OO interface

```
$zipcode = 94088;

// Prepare statement
$sql = 'SELECT username FROM users WHERE zipcode = ?';

$stmt = $db->stmt_init();
if ($stmt->prepare($sql)) {

    // Associate placeholders with data type and variable name
    $stmt->bind_param('i', $zipcode);

    // Bind result variables
    $stmt->bind_result($username);

    // Execute prepared statement
    $stmt->execute();

    // Place query data into bound result variables
    while ($stmt->fetch()) {
        // Print results
        print "$username\n";
    }
}
```

The call to `mysqli_stmt_init($db)` is now `$db->stmt_init()`. This method still has a leading `stmt` because it's a method of the `mysqli` object instead of a statement object.

The other calls now invoke methods on `$stmt`. The statement is prepared by calling `$stmt->prepare($sql)` and bound using `$stmt->bind_param('i', $zipcode)` and `$stmt->bind_result($username)`.

Since all the information about the statement is already stored in the object, you execute the query and fetch the data (`$stmt->execute()` and `$stmt->fetch()`) without passing any arguments.

Before and After: Subselects

Subselects are a popular database feature that's available in MySQL 4.1. A *subselect*, or a *subquery*, is a query that occurs within the context of another query. You then use the subselect's results in the main query.

Many developers like subselects because they allow them to chain queries together to winnow results. It's often possible to rewrite a query to eliminate a subselect; however, this is not always straightforward or efficient. Additionally, sometimes, without a subselect, you'll be forced to make multiple requests.

The following sections contain a few examples that show how a subselect can solve problems. Many of them use the following programs table:

```
mysql> DESCRIBE programs;
+------------+----------------+------+-----+---------+----------------+
| Field      | Type           | Null | Key | Default | Extra          |
+------------+----------------+------+-----+---------+----------------+
| id         | int(5) unsigned |     | PRI | NULL    | auto_increment |
| title      | varchar(50)    |      |     |         |                |
| channel_id | int(5) unsigned |     |     | 0       |                |
+------------+----------------+------+-----+---------+----------------+
3 rows in set (0.00 sec)

mysql> SELECT * FROM programs;
+----+-----------------+------------+
| id | title           | channel_id |
+----+-----------------+------------+
|  1 | Oprah           |         60 |
|  2 | Sex and the City|        201 |
|  3 | The Sopranos    |        201 |
|  4 | Frontline       |         13 |
+----+-----------------+------------+
4 rows in set (0.00 sec)
```

MySQL 4.0: Finding Related Entries

A common database-related task is finding rows that match a set of criteria. Normally, these specifications are known ahead of time:

```
// Find the names and address of all people
// who have an email address ending in "php.net".
SELECT name, email FROM users WHERE email LIKE '%.php.net';

// Find the title of all TV programs that air on channel 13
SELECT title
  FROM programs, channels
 WHERE channel.name = 'HBO'
   AND program.channel_id = channel.id;
```

Sometimes, as in the first case, you only need to query a single table. Other times, as in the second example, you need to link two tables together based on a common key to gather the information you want.

However, these links aren't always sufficient. For example, you know there's a show called The Sopranos and you want to discover all the other shows that air on the same channel, but you don't know which channel that is. One solution is to use two queries:

```
// Get channel_id:
$r = $db->query("SELECT channel_id FROM programs
                WHERE title = 'The Sopranos'");
$row = $r->fetch_assoc();
```

```
// Use channel_id to find programs:
$s = $db->query("SELECT title FROM programs
                 WHERE channel_id = $row[channel_id]");
while ($program = $s->fetch_assoc()) {
    print $program['title'] . "\n";
}
```
Sex and the City
The Sopranos

This is easy to understand, but it's a bit wasteful to make two queries for such a simple request. Another solution is to employ a self-join:

```
// All-in-one query using self-join:
$s = $db->query("SELECT p2.title
                 FROM programs AS p1,
                      programs AS p2
                 WHERE p1.title = 'The Sopranos'
                   AND p1.channel_id = p2.channel_id");
while ($program = $s->fetch_assoc()) {
    print $program['title'] . "\n";
}
```
Sex and the City
The Sopranos

It can seem a little odd at first to JOIN a table against itself, but it can actually come in quite handy. In this example, you're finding the set of shows that have a title of The Sopranos and cross-referencing them against all the shows have the same channel_id field.

In order to eliminate the ambiguity of which table you're referring to, you're forced to assign table aliases. The table you're using to locate the channel The Sopranos is on is p1, and the table in which you're searching for matching shows is p2. That's why you return p2.title.

To return all the rows in p2, use p2.*. This syntax is similar to *, which returns all rows, but qualifies it with a table name.

Since you're joining on the same column, an equivalent query is:

```
// All-in-one query using self-join and USING( )
$s = $db->query("SELECT p2.title
                 FROM programs AS p1 INNER JOIN programs AS p2
                 USING (channel_id)
                 WHERE p1.title = 'The Sopranos'");
while ($program = $s->fetch_assoc()) {
    print $program['title'] . "\n";
}
```
Sex and the City
The Sopranos

An INNER JOIN is identical to linking tables with a comma (,), and the USING( ) condition is shorthand for a list of columns to set as equal. Thus, USING(channel_id) is the same as p1.channel_id = p2.channel_id.

MySQL 4.1: Finding Related Entries

Still, that type of query can get hard to handle as the relationships become more complex. Many people find it easier to implement that request using a subselect:

```
// All-in-one query using subselect:
$s = $db->query("SELECT title FROM programs WHERE channel_id =
                    (SELECT channel_id FROM programs
                        WHERE title = 'The Sopranos' LIMIT 1)");

while ($program = $s->fetch_assoc()) {
    print $program['title'] . "\n";
}
Sex and the City
The Sopranos
```

MySQL starts off by parsing the SQL statement. When it reaches the second SELECT, it places what it already has on hold and executes the second query:

```
mysql> SELECT channel_id FROM programs WHERE title = 'The Sopranos' LIMIT 1;
+------------+
| channel_id |
+------------+
|        201 |
+------------+
1 row in set (0.00 sec)
```

That query returns a number (or NULL, if there are no matches). For the sake of example, assume it's 201. This then translates the original query into:

```
mysql> SELECT title FROM programs WHERE channel_id = 201;
+-----------------+
| title           |
+-----------------+
| Sex and the City|
| The Sopranos    |
+-----------------+
2 rows in set (0.00 sec)
```

MySQL can now execute the query and return your titles.

Notice how the subselect specifically adds a LIMIT clause to restrict the number of rows to 1. Since the results are used in the context of channel_id =, returning more than one number leads to a parser error because it's like doing channel_id = 201, 202.

When you expect your query will return multiple rows, switch from an equals sign (=) to IN( ):

```
mysql> SELECT title FROM programs WHERE channel_id IN(
          SELECT channel_id FROM programs WHERE title = 'The Sopranos');
```

```
+------------------+
| title            |
+------------------+
| Sex and the City |
| The Sopranos     |
+------------------+
2 rows in set (0.02 sec)
```

This allows you to find programs located in any of the channels returned by the subselect. Be careful, though—duplicate items are eliminated when you use IN( ). Sometimes this is good, but not always.

For instance, say you're implementing the backend of a TiVo or another DVR. You want to track all the shows that have been watched so you can suggest related programs the person might also be interested in viewing. This table, viewings, contains a list of program_ids. Each number is a key in the programs table from before and uniquely represents a program.

Here's one potential dataset:

```
mysql> SELECT * FROM viewings;
+------------+
| program_id |
+------------+
|          1 |
|          2 |
|          1 |
|          3 |
|          4 |
+------------+
5 rows in set (0.01 sec)
```

There are five shows, but program 1 was watched twice. Here's what happens if you look up the titles using IN( ):

```
mysql> SELECT title FROM programs WHERE id IN
       (SELECT program_id FROM viewings);
+------------------+
| title            |
+------------------+
| Oprah            |
| Sex and the City |
| The Sopranos     |
| Frontline        |
+------------------+
4 rows in set (0.01 sec)
```

There are only four records because the duplicate program ID of 1 isn't counted twice. To find out which show was so good as to merit a second viewing, you need to eliminate the subselect and return to a join:

```
mysql> SELECT title FROM programs INNER JOIN viewings
       ON viewings.program_id = programs.id;
```

```
+-----------------+
| title           |
+-----------------+
| Oprah           |
| Frontline       |
| Oprah           |
| Sex and the City|
| The Sopranos    |
+-----------------+
5 rows in set (0.01 sec)
```

Ah! Now you can see that someone really enjoys Oprah, so you're more likely to suggest related shows.

When Subselects Are Necessary

The previous examples showed different ways to rewrite your query. While using a subselect often made the query easier to write and understand, it was never necessary. There was always an alternative syntax that used a JOIN to eliminate the subselect, yet retained the same results.

That's not always the case. There are lots of examples where you just can't solve the problem in a single query without using a subselect. This normally occurs when you're using an aggregate function, such as COUNT( ).

Returning to the last problem, you've already seen how repeated entries in a table can cause problems when using IN( ), but they can give you trouble in other ways, too. For instance, you want to find the titles of the shows you've watched more than The Sopranos. Once again, the viewings table looks like this:

```
mysql> SELECT * FROM viewings;
+------------+
| program_id |
+------------+
|          1 |
|          2 |
|          1 |
|          3 |
|          4 |
+------------+
5 rows in set (0.01 sec)
```

To find the total number of times you've watched a show, you need to do a join against the programs table and count the number of matches:

```
mysql> SELECT COUNT(*) FROM viewings LEFT JOIN programs ON(program_id =
programs.id) WHERE programs.title = 'The Sopranos';
+---+
| c |
+---+
```

```
| 1 |
+---+
1 row in set (0.00 sec)
```

Place this result as a subselect inside the master query:

```
mysql> SELECT title, COUNT(*) AS c
          FROM viewings LEFT JOIN programs
            ON (program_id = programs.id)
       GROUP BY title
        HAVING c > (  SELECT COUNT(*)
                        FROM viewings
                   LEFT JOIN programs
                          ON (program_id = programs.id)
                       WHERE title = 'The Sopranos');
+-------+---+
| title | c |
+-------+---+
| Oprah | 2 |
+-------+---+
1 row in set (0.00 sec)
```

Once again, Oprah is the most popular show.

This question can't be rewritten to avoid a subselect, because the condition inside the subselect not only uses an aggregate function, such as COUNT( ) in this example, but also places restrictions upon the query using a WHERE clause. Since you only want the WHERE title = 'The Sopranos' condition to apply to the subselect's COUNT(*), it can't mix with the SELECT title, COUNT(*) in the rest of the query.

For more on aggregate functions and HAVING clauses, see the discussion in the section "User-Defined Functions" in Chapter 4.

Transactions

MySQL 4.0 supports database transactions. Transactions allow you to group together a sequence of database queries to ensure that MySQL either completes the entire set of actions or fails to perform any of them. There's no in-between state.

A perfect example demonstrating the importance of transactions is transferring money from a bank account. Removing money takes two steps: first, the program checks whether the account contains enough funds; if it does, it then subtracts the money from the account and places it in another.

You don't want a second withdrawal to occur in between checking the account balance and removing the funds, because the other transaction could completely empty the account, leaving no more money for your request. This is a big problem for banks.

Creating Transaction-Supported Tables

In order to support transactions, MySQL introduced a new database table format, called InnoDB. The original format, MyISAM, can't be used with transactions. If you're running MySQL 4.0 or higher, you should have support for InnoDB tables. To check, run the following MySQL query:

```
mysql> SHOW VARIABLES LIKE 'have_innodb';
+---------------+-------+
| Variable_name | Value |
+---------------+-------+
| have_innodb   | YES   |
+---------------+-------+
```

It should say YES. By default, MySQL enables InnoDB tables as of Version 4.0, so if this variable is set to NO, you should rebuild MySQL and remove the --without-innodb flag from your configuration.

 MySQL also supports transactions with Berkeley DB tables in MySQL 3.23, but that's not covered here.

To create an InnoDB table, add TYPE = InnoDB to the end of the CREATE statement. For example, to replicate the programs table:

```
CREATE TABLE   programs (id int(5) unsigned AUTO_INCREMENT,
                         title VARCHAR(50) not null,
                         channel_id int(5) unsigned not null,
                         primary key(id))
         TYPE = InnoDB;
```

This makes a programs table that supports transactions.

You can make MySQL convert an existing MyISAM table to the new format with the following command:

```
ALTER TABLE programs TYPE = InnoDB;
```

This converts programs to InnoDB. Substitute your table names for programs.

Using Transactions

To signal to MySQL that you want to begin a transaction, use the keyword BEGIN. (BEGIN WORK and START TRANSACTIONS are synonyms for BEGIN.) To end a transaction, use COMMIT. In PHP, you pass these keywords as part of your SQL inside of mysqli_query( ):

```
$user = array('rasmus', 'z.8cMpdFbNAPw');

mysqli_query($db, 'BEGIN');
```

```
foreach ($users as $user) {
    mysqli_query($db, "INSERT INTO users VALUES(
                        '$user[0]', '$user[1]')";
}
mysqli_query('COMMIT');
```

The SQL opens with BEGIN, and then PHP iterates through an array, creating a series of INSERTs. When the loop is done, COMMIT is sent.

This transaction will enter a group of user records into a database. It's unlikely to have any errors that require you to roll back the data. However, assume the users table requires that each username entry be UNIQUE. Then, this array causes a problem:

```
$users = array(array('rasmus', 'z.8cMpdFbNAPw'),
               array('zeev'  , 'asd34.23NNDeq'),
               array('rasmus', 'z.8cMpdFbNAPw'));
```

Since there are two entries in the array with a username of rasmus, MySQL issues an error when you attempt to enter the second rasmus into the table.

Here's the SQL to create that table:

```
CREATE TABLE    users(username VARCHAR(50) UNIQUE,
                      password VARCHAR(50))
        TYPE = InnoDB
```

Now you can structure your code to catch the error and revert the transaction, as in Example 3-7.

Example 3-7. Querying using transactions

```
$error = 0;

// Start transaction
mysqli_query($db, 'BEGIN');

// Prepare INSERT statement
$sql = 'INSERT INTO users VALUES(?, ?)';
$stmt = mysqli_stmt_init($db);
mysqli_stmt_prepare($stmt, $sql);
mysqli_stmt_bind_param($stmt, 'ss', $username, $password);

// Add each new user one-by-one
foreach ($users as $user) {

    list($username, $password) = $user;

    // Abort if there's an error
    if (!mysqli_stmt_execute($stmt)) {
        $error = mysqli_errno($db);
        break;
    }
}
```

Example 3-7. Querying using transactions (continued)

```
// Revert previous commits on error; otherwise, save
if ($error) {
    mysqli_query($db, 'ROLLBACK');
} else {
    mysqli_query($db, 'COMMIT');
}
```

The mysqli_query('BEGIN'); starts the transaction. The foreach( ) iterates over the $users array. Inside, the bound variables are set to the correct elements of $users and the query is executed. Since mysqli_stmt_execute( ) returns true on success and false on failure, there's no need to check the return value of mysqli_errno( ) for every request. Instead, call it when you know there's an error, set $error to the return code, and break out of the foreach.

Since mysqli_errno( ) always returns a positive number when there's an error, you can use the value of $error to decide whether to commit or roll back the transaction. When $error is positive, it evaluates as true and you should issue the ROLLBACK command to revert the transaction. When it's 0, pass mysqli_query( ) COMMIT to store the rows in the database.

AUTOCOMMIT

By default, MySQL automatically commits any command you issue, unless it's wrapped inside of a transaction. However, you can reverse this behavior for InnoDB tables, so that commands are presumed to be part of a transaction and are flushed *only* when COMMIT is sent.

Enable this feature with the following command:

```
// Disable AUTOCOMMIT
mysqli_autocommit($db, false);

// This SQL statement is identical to the above function
SET AUTOCOMMIT = 0;
```

Now your queries will be reflected in your current connection, but won't be saved unless you issue a COMMIT command. Example 3-8 is a modified version of the last script, Example 3-7, that uses this feature.

Example 3-8. Querying with AUTOCOMMIT disabled

```
$error = 0;

// Disable AUTOCOMMIT
mysqli_autocommit($db, false);

// Prepare INSERT statement
$sql = 'INSERT INTO users VALUES(?, ?)';
```

Example 3-8. Querying with AUTOCOMMIT disabled (continued)

```
$stmt = mysqli_stmt_prepare($db, $sql);
mysqli_stmt_bind_param($stmt, 'ss', $username, $password);

// Add each new user one-by-one
foreach ($users as $user) {

    list($username, $password) = $user;

    // Abort if there's an error
    if (!mysqli_stmt_execute($stmt)) {
        $error = mysqli_errno($db);
        break;
    }
}

// Save if not an error
if (!$error) {
    mysqli_query($db, 'COMMIT');
}
```

Since AUTOCOMMIT is disabled, there's no need to ROLLBACK the transaction at the end of the code.

You can check the current status of AUTOCOMMIT with:

```
mysql> SELECT @@AUTOCOMMIT;
+--------------+
| @@AUTOCOMMIT |
+--------------+
|            1 |
+--------------+
1 row in set (0.00 sec)
```

The double at signs (@@) tell MySQL to retrieve a MySQL-specific variable instead of a user-defined variable.

Before and After: Making Multiple Queries

In PHP 4, when you need to make more than one query in a row, you're forced to call mysql_query( ) once for each query. This often happens when you need distinct pieces of information from MySQL or when you want to create a fresh set of tables.

This isn't a big problem when you know your queries ahead of time, because it's easy to loop through and send them to MySQL one at a time. However, for some situations, this is not the case. For example, you're writing a PHP frontend to MySQL, such as phpMyAdmin (*http://www.phpmyadmin.net*), and want the ability to take a database dump and recreate the information.

Without the ability to send the entire dump at once, you're required to parse the data into individual statements. That's not as easy as it sounds, because you can't just split on the semicolon (;). For example, it's perfectly valid to have a line like INSERT INTO users VALUES('rasmus', 'pass;word');. Since pass;word is inside single quotes, MySQL knows it doesn't signal the end of a statement, but a simple split isn't smart enough to understand this. As a result, you're effectively forced to write a MySQL parser in PHP.

The restriction of one query per request is lifted in MySQLi. This actually wasn't a limitation in PHP, but a deficit in the protocol used by earlier versions of MySQL. Another benefit of MySQL 4.1's updated protocol is the ability to introduce a mysqli_multi_query( ) function for these types of cases.

While this is good news, it also introduces a greater potential for SQL injection attacks. An *SQL injection attack* is when a malicious person passes in data that alters your SQL so that you end up issuing a different (and probably more dangerous) SQL query than what you expected.

Here's an example that's supposed to return the bank account information for only a single user:

```
$sql = "SELECT account_number, balance FROM bank_accounts
        WHERE secret_code LIKE '$_GET[secret_code]'";
```

You know that it's important to use a secret code so that people can't access other people's information by incrementing a primary key ID number, because those numbers are easy to guess. However, you've forgotten to call mysql_real_escape_string( ) on $_GET['secret_code'], and this is trouble. A cracker can set secret_code to ' OR '1' LIKE '1, and that turns your query into:

```
SELECT account_number, balance FROM bank_accounts
 WHERE secret_code LIKE '' OR '1' LIKE '1';
```

Since any string always matches itself, this effectively alters the query to return *all* rows. If there's any positive to this exploit, it's that since MySQL only allows you to execute a single query at a time, you cannot radically alter the query.

However, now that you can issue multiple queries, you're vulnerable to something even worse. People can issue any query they want:

```
SELECT account_number, balance FROM bank_accounts
 WHERE secret_code LIKE '';
UPDATE bank_accounts
   SET balance = 1000000
 WHERE account_number = '12345678';
```

By altering secret_code to '; UPDATE bank_accounts SET balance = 1000000 WHERE account_number = '12345678';, you terminate the first query and append another. The second query isn't limited by the constraints of the first, so a query that's supposed to SELECT data now also UPDATEs it (or data in any other table).

To prevent this security vulnerability, mysqli forcibly disables mysqli_query( )'s ability to make multiple queries. Instead, there's an alternate set of functions for you to use.

mysql: Making Multiple Queries

In mysql, the best way to handle multiple queries is to place them in individual array elements. You can loop then through the array and issue the queries.

Example 3-9 creates a users table and populates it with rasmus and zeev accounts.

Example 3-9. Executing multiple queries with mysql_query( )

```
$queries = array(
    "DROP TABLE IF EXISTS users;",
    "CREATE TABLE users(username VARCHAR(50) UNIQUE,
                        password VARCHAR(50));",
    "INSERT INTO users VALUES('rasmus', 'z.8cMpdFbNAPw'),
                            ('zeev',    'asd34.23NNDeq');",
    "SELECT * FROM users WHERE username LIKE 'rasmus';");

foreach ($queries as $query) {
    if ($result = mysql_query($query, $db) and $result !== true) {
        while ($row = mysql_fetch_row($result)) {
            print "$row[0]\n";
        }
    }
}
```

It's important to quote the SQL statements properly because they often have embedded single and double quotation marks. In this case, the INSERT and SELECT statements both have single quotes.

The foreach iterates through each element and calls mysql_query( ). If everything goes okay, the function returns a true value. When there are rows to process, such as in a SELECT or DESCRIBE query, mysql_query( ) returns a resource. When the request was successful but there's no additional information, it just returns true.

This allows you to distinguish between queries where you can call mysql_fetch_row( ) by placing and $result !== true inside the conditional. You must use both and instead of && and !== instead of !=; otherwise, you get different results than expected because of operator precedence and type coercion issues.

Finally, the while loop retrieves each row and prints out the first column. Since only one of the four statements made in this example returns results and it returns only a single row, the entire output of this loop is rasmus.

Of course, as said earlier, none of this is necessary if your SQL isn't separated into individual statements.

mysqli: Making Multiple Queries

The mysqli extension solves many of the problems incurred when making multiple queries. Most importantly, you don't need to break the SQL apart. This not only eliminates the need for a MySQL parser, but also allows you to more easily place SQL inside your script without worrying about quotation marks.

The downside, however, is that the code to process a request is significantly more complex. Instead of a single function, mysql_query( ), four different functions are necessary to navigate through the results.

Use mysqli_multi_query( ) to send the query itself and mysqli_store_result( ) to load the results of each successive query into a position where they can be fetched. When you're done with a query, free it with mysqli_free_result( ) and move onto the next one using mysqli_next_result( ).

Example 3-10 is a revised version of Example 3-9 showing how these functions work in combination.

Example 3-10. Executing multiple queries with mysqli_multi_query( )

```
$query = <<<_SQL_
DROP TABLE IF EXISTS users;
CREATE TABLE users(username VARCHAR(50),
                   password VARCHAR(50));
INSERT INTO users VALUES('rasmus', 'z.8cMpdFbNAPw'),
                        ('zeev',   'asd34.23NNDeq');
SELECT * FROM users WHERE username LIKE 'rasmus';
_SQL_;

if (mysqli_multi_query($db, $query)) {
    do {
        if ($result = mysqli_store_result($db)) {
            while ($row = mysqli_fetch_row($result)) {
                print "$row[0]\n";
            }
            mysqli_free_result($result);
        }
    } while (mysqli_next_result($db));
}
```

Your SQL is no longer stored in an array, but as a string. This lets you use a heredoc to avoid the problem of single and double quotes.

The mysqli_multi_query( ) function takes a database link and a query, just like mysqli_query( ). If anything goes wrong, such as a parse error, it returns false; otherwise, it places the first result set into position for retrieval and returns true.

Since mysqli_multi_query( ) has already handled the first result, use a do/while loop instead of a while to iterate through all the data. Otherwise, the first call to mysqli_next_result( ) will actually load the second result.

Inside the loop, call mysqli_store_result( ) to transfer each result set to PHP. If the query doesn't return any rows, then mysqli_store_result( ) returns false. This actually happens for the first three queries in this example—the DROP, CREATE, and INSERT. Only the SELECT statement causes a non-false response.

This behavior is different from mysql_query( ) and is actually more useful because it allows you to eliminate the and $result !== true check from the code.

Now you can use the standard set of retrieval functions, such as mysqli_fetch_row( ), to process the data. This example just prints out the first column from every row retrieved.

Be sure to call mysqli_free_result( ) to release the memory when you're done with the result. Otherwise, it will pile up until the script finishes running. Since it's easy to make numerous queries using mysqli_multi_query( ), it's easy to quickly use up lots of RAM.

To check if there are additional results without advancing the counter by calling mysqli_next_result( ), call mysqli_more_results( ):

```
if (mysqli_multi_query($db, $query)) {
    do {
        if ($result = mysqli_store_result($db)) {
            while ($row = mysqli_fetch_row($result)) {
                print "$row[0]\n";
            }
            mysqli_free_result($result);

            // Add divider after all results except the last
            if (mysqli_more_results($db)) {
                print str_repeat('-', 10) . "\n";
            }
        }

    } while (mysqli_next_result($db));
}
```

The mysqli_more_results( ) function returns the same value as the next call to mysqli_next_result( ). This lets you add dividers or perform some other kind of processing after all statement results except the final one.

If you're put off by the complexity of this code, there's an alternative that combines the benefits of multiple queries with the simplicity of the earlier syntax. The section "MySQL Query Iterator" in Chapter 6 contains a MySQL multi-query iterator that encapsulates all the logic into a reusable class and lets you foreach through the results.

Securing Connections with SSL

You can now encrypt the connections between PHP and MySQL. Normally, MySQL does all communication in plain text because it's the fastest way to send data. However, MySQL 4.0 lets you use SSL encryption to prevent people from spying on traffic between PHP and MySQL, and MySQL 4.1 extends this to include replication over SSL.

An SSL-enabled version of MySQL doesn't require you to use SSL for all your connections. You can set different permission levels on your accounts, so you can place varying restrictions as you see fit. For some accounts, you may not want the hassle of dealing with SSL and authentication.

Once all your systems are configured, it's quite easy to use SSL with MySQLi. Getting everything up and running can be a bit of a struggle because you need to add OpenSSL support to both MySQL and PHP, create SSL certificates for MySQL, and also properly configure your MySQL user accounts and configuration files.

Here's a list of what you need to do:

1. Install OpenSSL if your system doesn't already have it.
2. Add SSL support to MySQL and reinstall.
3. Add SSL support to PHP, link against the new MySQL client, and reinstall.
4. Create SSL certificates for the MySQL server.
5. Add SSL certificate information to your *my.cnf* files.
6. Restart MySQL.
7. Edit the MySQL GRANT table to require SSL.
8. Connect to MySQL from PHP using SSL.

Before you can do anything, you need to have OpenSSL on your machine. Most systems come with OpenSSL preinstalled, but you can download a copy from *http://www.openssl.org/*.

The second step is to check whether your MySQL server already supports SSL. Issue the following command:

```
SHOW VARIABLES LIKE 'have_openssl';
```

If it returns YES, you're in luck; otherwise, you must reconfigure MySQL. Modify your previous configuration to add --with-openssl and --with-vio. (If you downloaded a prebuilt MySQL package, you will need to download the MySQL source and follow the installation instructions.) After you've rebuilt MySQL, install it.

Now add OpenSSL to PHP and get mysqli to enable its SSL support. This is done by adding the --with-openssl configuration option to PHP. Even if your copy of PHP already has SSL support, you still *must* remake PHP if your MySQL server didn't support SSL when you originally built PHP. When you're done, go ahead and reinstall PHP, restarting your web server if necessary.

Even though both PHP and MySQL now have SSL support, this doesn't mean they'll automatically use it. Before this can happen, you need to create SSL certificates for MySQL. See *http://dev.mysql.com/doc/mysql/en/Secure_create_certs.html* for a step-by-step guide if you're unfamiliar with OpenSSL and certificates.

Once the certificates are created, add the SSL certificate information to your *my.cnf* files. This allows MySQL to load in the configuration settings during startup. Here's an example:

```
[client]
ssl-ca=/usr/local/mysql/openssl/cacert.pem
ssl-cert=/usr/local/mysql/openssl/client-cert.pem
ssl-key=/usr/local/mysql/openssl/client-key.pem
[mysqld]
ssl-ca=/usr/local/mysql/openssl/cacert.pem
ssl-cert=/usr/local/mysql/openssl/server-cert.pem
ssl-key=/usr/local/mysql/openssl/server-key.pem
```

This adds the key, certificate, and certificate authority (CA) files to MySQL. You can also set a pathname to trusted SSL CA certificates using the ssl-capath configuration option and provide a list of ciphers using ssl-ciphers.

The next step is to restart the MySQL server. The have_openssl variable should now be YES.

Now the entire foundation is complete and you're ready to force SSL connections on your users. MySQL lets you handle this on a per-user basis with its GRANT tables, as you may want to allow some local users to make unencrypted connections. To require a basic SSL connection, add REQUIRE SSL to the end of your GRANT statement. For example:

```
GRANT ALL PRIVILEGES ON users.* TO 'ssl-user'@'localhost'
  IDENTIFIED BY 'password' REQUIRE SSL;
```

The web page at *http://dev.mysql.com/doc/mysql/en/Secure_GRANT.html* covers all the different ways you can make MySQL enforce an SSL connection and gives a few additional sample GRANT commands.

Everything is now complete and you're ready to make an SSL connection from PHP using `mysqli`. This can be done in two different ways, but both methods require you to use `mysqli_real_connect( )`.

The easiest way is to read the SSL settings from a *my.cnf* file:

```
$db = mysqli_init( );
mysqli_options($db, MYSQLI_READ_DEFAULT_FILE, '/etc/my.cnf');
mysqli_real_connect($db, 'localhost', 'ssl-user', 'password', 'database');
```

The `MYSQLI_READ_DEFAULT_FILE` option forces MySQL to read in the contents of the `client` group in */etc/my.cnf*. This allows you to set all your SSL options in a single place and use them from PHP, the `mysql` command-line tool, or other programs.

You can also specify the options using `mysqli_ssl_set( )`:

```
$db = mysqli_init( );
mysqli_ssl_set($db, '/usr/local/mysql/openssl/server-key.pem',
                    '/usr/local/mysql/openssl/server-cert.pem',
                    '/usr/local/mysql/openssl/cacert.pem',
                    NULL,
                    NULL);
mysqli_real_connect($db, 'localhost', 'ssl-user', 'password', 'database');
```

The `mysqli_ssl_set( )` function takes six arguments. The first is the database link and the next five are the SSL key, certificate, CA certificate, CA path, and cipher. If your encryption method doesn't require one or more of these parameters, pass `NULL` in their place.

This function always returns true. SSL errors are reported when you make the actual connection to MySQL.

Using `mysqli_ssl_set( )` overrides any variables set with the `MYSQLI_READ_DEFAULT_FILE` option, so you can still read in a configuration file for general settings, but alter your SSL information if necessary.

Both techniques automatically set the `MYSQLI_SSL_CLIENT` flag, so you don't need to add this to your call to `mysqli_real_connect( )`.

Porting Code and Migrating Databases

Although the new `mysqli` extension has many benefits over the older extension, they come at a cost. Depending upon your code, porting to the new extension can be a surprisingly tiresome task. If you've used a database abstraction layer—such as PEAR DB, ADOdb, or MDB—this task is simplified considerably. Even though you're only switching from one version of MySQL to another, the new extension is sufficiently different that quite a bit of work is necessary to make the switch.

However, you probably will want to use `mysqli` for your new projects, and that requires an upgrade to MySQL 4.1. Since an out-of-the-box MySQL 4.1 is incompatible with `mysql`, this presents a bit of a dilemma. You want the benefits of `mysqli` without worrying about legacy code.

Another option is just to make the switch to a database abstraction layer. This has some advantages and some disadvantages. The primary benefit is portability, but this comes at a cost of speed and features. For instance, you cannot bind output parameters with PEAR DB, nor does DB support all of the latest MySQLi options, such as `mysqli_multi_query( )` and `ssl_set( )`.

This section presents a variety of options for handling the conversion process. Each one has various positive and negative attributes. Some require more hours of work; others are faster to implement, but at a cost of execution speed. None of these solutions are bad in and of themselves, but, given certain circumstances, some should be preferable to others. In the end, you must weigh the trade-offs and make the decision for yourself.

Migration Paths

The biggest problem is that you're really making three migrations instead of one. You're migrating from:

- PHP 4 to PHP 5
- MySQL 3.2.x (or MySQL 4.0) to MySQL 4.1
- `mysql` to `mysqli`

All three migrations are non-trivial and require careful planning. Trying to do all three simultaneously is very risky. However, with preparation, there are a number of ways to handle the problem so the task does not become unmanageable.

Don't migrate anything

The fastest migration path is making a clean break between your old code and your new code. Legacy code runs under PHP 4, MySQL 3.2.x or MySQL 4.0.x, and `mysql`. New code runs under PHP 5, MySQL 4.1, and `mysqli`.

The advantage is no wasted time; however, you must replicate your entire setup—web server, database server, document trees—and run two parallel systems. (Alternatively, you can run one version of PHP as a CGI. See Appendix C for more details.) This presents additional administrative overhead because you have twice as many pieces of software to maintain.

Additionally, if you have even one piece of code that needs to run in both environments, you may end up making a majority of the changes anyway. Therefore, this solution is suggested only for people with discrete scripts that are written for a single project and not supported on an ongoing basis, except for minimal maintenance.

Migrate only to MySQL 4.1

The second easiest migration path is to keep separate systems like before but switch to a common MySQL 4.1 backend. This allows you to keep your databases in sync because both older PHP 4 projects and newer PHP 5–based projects can share the same database tables.

While your old projects cannot use the new `mysqli` extension, because they're still using PHP 4, they can still take advantage of server-level features in MySQL 4.1, such as subselects and transactions, that are not dependent on the client.

This solution does require a bit of work. In addition to installing MySQL 4.1, you must move your database tables to the new server. This process is not too difficult, but it's not backward compatible. MySQL 3.2.x uses the ISAM table format to store data; MySQL 4.0 and above use the MyISAM format. Although MySQL 4.0 supports both types of tables, MySQL 4.1 does not support the old format unless you specifically request it. Additionally, the InnoDB format used by MySQL for transactions is unavailable under most pre-4.1 versions of MySQL.

There is another downside. Specifically, MySQL 4.1 has a new password schema, so you must run MySQL with the `--old-passwords` flag if you want to use `mysql` with MySQL 4.1. The upgraded password system is more secure than earlier versions; however, it's incompatible with older MySQL clients, such as the one bundled with PHP 4. Therefore, MySQL provides an option to downgrade the authentication mechanism, to be backward compatible at the expense of some security.

This does not mean running MySQL 4.1 with `--old-passwords` is insecure. It's actually *more* secure than MySQL 4.0, but it's not as secure as a regular MySQL 4.1 configuration.

Migrate to MySQL 4.1 and PHP 5

A major disadvantage to the two earlier solutions is that you cannot run PHP 4 and PHP 5 as modules on the same web server. (You can set one up as a module and the other as a CGI, but that is not acceptable for most production environments.)

This means you need to run two versions of Apache (or whatever web server you're using). These servers must either have different hostnames or use different ports on the same hostname. Also, your old code cannot take advantage of any of the new features offered in PHP 5.

Luckily, a minimal port to PHP 5 is not difficult (assuming you don't make extensive use of DOM XML or XSLT functions; see Chapter 5 for more details). Thus, you may want to move all your code to PHP 5 but continue using the mysql extension for old projects and use mysqli only for new ones.

This allows you to avoid both the hassle of switching your entire code base over to mysqli and the pain of administering two sets of web servers and document hierarchies.

The disadvantage to this solution is that you're required to invest a good amount of time into migrating both code and data. Plus, you need to compile both extensions into PHP, which adds to the amount of memory taken up by your web server processes. Last, it can become confusing or annoying to track which projects use what version of the MySQL extensions.

Complete migration to MySQL 4.1, PHP 5, and mysqli

The final choice is a 100% migration of all three products. This is by far the most complex maneuver, especially if you're not using a database abstraction layer. Many mysql functions are altered in or removed from mysqli; although, to be fair, most of these functions are rather esoteric.

However, you gain significant benefits from this solution: faster execution times, stronger security, and cleaner code for all your programs. After expending this one-time cost, you never need to worry about the old code again, because all your scripts run under the same environment.

Making the right decision

After hashing through all those choices, you can see that the weaselly answer to "What should I do?" is "It depends." Unfortunately, sometimes the weaselly answer is also the truth.

Nevertheless, it's best to remember this is not an all-or-nothing decision that gets made once and is then forever set in stone. There's nothing wrong with, for example, trying to see if you can get by without porting all your old code to PHP 5. If in two months you decide that was a mistake, you can then go ahead and make the switch.

You can always stop your migration at any time, see if you're happy with your setup, and restart it later if need be. This approach is actually safer because it gives you time to discover bugs on a step-by-step basis. Additionally, it may actually be faster to migrate this way because it's easier to find bugs when you can isolate them to the latest level of changes.

That's why you're strongly encouraged to follow the path outlined next for the transition. This way, you can come back to the book and not worry about forgetting any steps.

Migration Plan of Attack

Due to the various incompatibilities between PHP 4 and PHP 5, mysql and mysqli, and MySQL 4.0 and MySQL 4.1, the easiest solution is to migrate your application and data in the following order:

1. Transfer your database tables to MySQL 4.1.2 (or higher), but continue to use mysql. This requires you to modify how MySQL 4.1 stores your password.
2. Port your code to PHP 5, but continue using mysql.
3. Switch to using the mysqli extension, but don't use any of the new features.
4. Take advantage of the new MySQL 4.1 features available in mysqli.

Since switching databases and porting code simultaneously is a recipe for disaster, don't try to do everything in one giant step. Instead, break the task down into bite-sized pieces, so you can ensure each individual step is successful. Otherwise, when you encounter a bug, it will be very difficult to track down.

This list is specifically ordered to avoid incompatibilities and ease your migration pain.

Step 1: Migrating from MySQL 3.2.x or MySQL 4.0.x to MySQL 4.1.2

The basic process for migrating from MySQL 3.2.x (or MySQL 4.0) to MySQL 4.1.2 is simple; however, there are many minor changes between the two versions that are not documented here, because they're relevant only to a small group of users.

"Section 2.5: Upgrading/Downgrading MySQL" in the MySQL Manual is the definitive source for all these differences. In addition to following the directions here, you should read this section to ensure that nothing slips through the cracks. In particular, developers using Windows or replication should be sure to consult the manual for changes specific to their setup. The material is available online at *http://www.mysql.com/doc/en/Upgrade.html*.

The material in this section assumes you not only have access to a command line, but are comfortable using it. An alternative solution is to use a web-based interface, such as phpMyAdmin (*http://www.phpmyadmin.net*). However, as of now, this product has experimental support for PHP 5 and MySQL 4.1. Therefore, you must figure out how to implement these steps in those products on your own.

Before you do anything, back up your databases. This allows you to restore your data in case anything happens during the upgrade process. See *http://www.mysql.com/doc/en/Backup.html* for how to store data.

Since MySQL 4.1 uses the MyISAM table type, you must upgrade your tables to the new format. If you're using MySQL 4.0.x, this is easy. You can use either of these two methods to upgrade the tables:

1. Run the `mysql_convert_table_format` script that comes with MySQL. This requires Perl and DBI, and you must set a few variables at the top of the script.

2. Issue the following SQL command for each table: ALTER TABLE *table_name* TYPE=MyISAM;. Substitute your table names for *table_name*.

If you're still using MySQL 3.2.x, it's more problematic because this version of MySQL doesn't understand the MyISAM format. The recommended MySQL solution is to first upgrade to MySQL 4.0. Once you've done this, you can use the methods just described. Alternatively, you can configure MySQL 4.1 to support the older ISAM format by passing in the `--with-isam` flag during compilation.

This option lets MySQL 4.1 read in the databases using the old format and lets you convert tables to MyISAM (or InnoDB). This is not a default configuration setting for MySQL 4.1, so you cannot use a prebuilt package or installer. Therefore, although it's more work to upgrade to MySQL 4.0 before 4.1, it allows you to avoid compiling MySQL yourself, which can be a major plus.

Before you can move onto MySQL 4.1, you also need to alter the MySQL GRANT tables. This lets MySQL store the securer passwords. Do this even if you're not planning on using `mysqli`, because it enables a few other features. There's another script available that makes all the necessary changes, so you need to:

1. Run the `mysql_fix_privilege_tables` script.

2. Since this script connects to MySQL as `root`, you need to provide the MySQL root password. On MySQL 4.0 systems, do `mysql_fix_privilege_tables password`. If you're upgrading directly to MySQL 4.1, do `mysql_fix_privilege_tables --password=password`.

3. Shut down and restart the MySQL server.

See *http://www.mysql.com/doc/en/Upgrading-grant-tables.html* for more details.

Now you are finally ready to switch over to MySQL 4.1.2 or higher. (MySQL 4.1.0 and 4.1.1 won't work correctly with PHP 5 in some cases.) Go to the MySQL web site, download the server, and follow the directions for installing it. Remember, if you're upgrading directly from MySQL 3.2.x, you must compile your own version of MySQL to enable ISAM support.

Shut down the old version of MySQL and restart the new one. If you want to support PHP 4 or PHP 5 with mysql, add the --old-passwords flag. The MySQL Manual has more information on this topic at *http://www.mysql.com/doc/en/Password_hashing.html*.

Step 2: Porting to PHP 5

When porting PHP 4 code to PHP 5, make migrating to MySQLi your *last* step, not your first. You can still use the older MySQL extension with PHP 5, so it's not necessary to switch to MySQLi to run PHP 5. As you'll see, the only XML extension in PHP 5 that's backward compatible with PHP 4 is SAX. DOM, XSLT, and XPath all require you to alter your code. All other major PHP 4 extensions continue to work as-is under PHP 5. Therefore, unlike with your XML code, you have the luxury of controlling when you should port your MySQL code.

It makes sense to convert to mysqli as the final step of your migration process. You can use your web site under PHP 5 without mysqli; that's not true for other extensions. This strategy minimizes the initial downtime and gets a working version of your site up for testing while you migrate to MySQLi.

Since the rest of this book covers migrating to PHP 5, the specific details of the migration process are omitted here to prevent infinite recursion.

Step 3: Migrating to mysqli

A two-pronged migration strategy is best because there are both API changes and new features in mysqli. The first step is to make sure your existing code is compatible with the new mysqli API. This finally allows you to deploy your current site under PHP 5 and MySQL 4.1, but without the old mysql extension.

Once that's done, you should then work new features into your code base. It's tempting to upgrade everything at once, but this always ends up taking more time than expected.

The largest change in the API is that there is no longer a concept of the "current database." Many mysql functions allow you to omit a database handle, automatically defaulting to the last connection. This feature has been eliminated. Although it was convenient, it made it very difficult to update the functions to support new MySQL features without breaking backward compatibility or requiring you to pass the database handle anyway.

Therefore, you're now required to always pass a database connection. Additionally, this handle is now the *first* function parameter. It was previously the final parameter, so it could be optional. This location mimics the MySQL API and makes the argument order more consistent.

Besides altering these functions, another set of functions have been eliminated entirely. In most cases, these are the more obscure mysql functions, such as mysql_field_table( ). Many can be easily replicated with a simple SQL query; others require a few queries.

The two "most used" missing functions are mysql_pconnect( ) and mysql_escape_string( ). Switch these to mysqli_connect( ) and mysqli_real_escape_string( ), respectively.

In addition to mysql_connect( ), whose new API has already been detailed, the functions in Table 3-3 have all been modified to require a database handle as their first argument.

Table 3-3. MySQL functions with a changed argument list

mysql	mysqli
mysql_connect([string hostname [:port][:/path/to/socket] [, string username [, string password [, bool new [, int flags]]]]])	mysqli_connect([string hostname [,string username [,string password [,string database_name [,int port [,string socket]]]]]])
mysql_select_db(string database_name [, int link_identifier])	mysqli_select_db(int link_identifier, string database_name)
mysql_query(string query [, int link_identifier])	mysqli_query(int link_identifier, string query [,int resultmode])
mysql_fetch_field(resource result [, int field_offset])	mysqli_fetch_field(object result)
mysql_change_user(string user, string password [, string database [, resource link_identifier]])	mysqli_change_user(int link_identifier, string user, string password, string database)
mysql_real_escape_string(string to_be_escaped [, int link_identifier])	mysqli_real_escape_string(int link_identifier, string to_be_escaped)
mysql_affected_rows([int link_identifier])	mysqli_affected_rows(int link_identifier)
mysql_close([int link_identifier])	mysqli_close(int link_identifier)
mysql_error([int link_identifier])	mysqli_error(int link_identifier)
mysql_errno([int link_identifier])	mysqli_errno(int link_identifier)
mysql_get_host_info([int link_identifier])	mysqli_get_host_info (int link_identifier)

Table 3-3. MySQL functions with a changed argument list (continued)

mysql	mysqli
mysql_get_proto_info([int link_identifier])	mysqli_get_proto_info(int link_identifier)
mysql_get_server_info([int link_identifier])	mysqli_get_server_info(int link_identifier)
mysql_info([int link_identifier])	mysqli_info(int link_identifier)
mysql_insert_id([int link_identifier])	mysqli_insert_id(int link_identifier)
mysql_ping([int link_identifier])	mysqli_ping(int link_identifier)
mysql_stat([int link_identifier])	mysqli_stat(int link_identifier)
mysql_thread_id([int link_identifier])	mysqli_thread_id(int link_identifier)

Table 3-4 contains a list of functions not transferred to mysqli and their replacement versions. In many cases these functions were already deprecated, so your code probably won't contain many instances of these functions.

Table 3-4. Functions not ported to mysqli

mysql	mysqli
mysql_create_db($database, $db);	mysqli_query($db, "CREATE DATABASE $database");
mysql_drop_db($database, $db);	mysqli_query($db, "DROP DATABASE $database");
mysql_escape_string($string);	mysqli_real_escape_string($string);
mysql_field_flags($result, $i);	$fields = mysqli_fetch_field($result); $fields[$i]->flags;
mysql_field_len($result, $i)	$fields = mysqli_fetch_field($result); $fields[$i]->max_length;
mysql_field_name($result, $i)	$fields = mysqli_fetch_field($result); $fields[$i]->name;
mysql_field_table($result, $i)	$fields = mysqli_fetch_field($result); $fields[$i]->table;
mysql_field_type($result, $i)	$fields = mysqli_fetch_field($result); $fields[$i]->type;
mysql_db_name($result, $i)	mysqli_data_seek($result, $i); $row = mysqli_fetch_row($result);
mysql_db_query($database, $query, $db);	mysqli_select_db($db, $database); mysqli_query($db, $query);
mysql_list_dbs($db);	mysqli_query($db, "SHOW DATABASES");

Table 3-4. Functions not ported to mysqli (continued)

mysql	mysqli
mysql_list_fields($database, $table, $db)	mysqli_use_db($db, $database); mysqli_query($db, "SHOW COLUMNS FROM $table");
mysql_list_processes($db)	mysqli_query($db, "SHOW PROCESSLIST");
mysql_list_tables($database, $db)	mysqli_query($db, "SHOW TABLES FROM $database");
mysql_pconnect($hostname, $username, $password);	mysqli_connect($hostname, $username, $password);
mysql_result($result, $column);	$row = mysqli_fetch_row($result); $row[$column];
mysql_tablename($result, $i)	mysqli_data_seek($r, $i); $row = mysqli_fetch_row($r);
mysql_unbuffered_query( )	mysqli_real_query( ); and mysqli_use_result( );

Adding new features

Once all that is finally complete, take a deep breath. Now you can move on to the fun part. Go back over your applications and locate places where the new features can improve your code.

In particular, bound parameters can significantly speed up queries and also reduce the potential for SQL injection attacks. You'll probably also discover places where using a subselect can reduce the complexity of your PHP script because you've moved the logic into MySQL.

CHAPTER 4
SQLite

Substituting text files for a database is like cutting a fish with a hammer. You might get it to work, but it's going to be a really messy process. When your application needs a server-side storage mechanism but you can't rely upon the presence of a specific database, turn to SQLite. It correctly handles locking and concurrent accesses, the two big headaches with home-brewed flat files.

Since the SQLite database is bundled with PHP 5, now every PHP 5 script can read, write, and search data using SQL. SQLite differs from most databases because it is not a separate application. Instead, SQLite is an extension that reads from and writes to regular files on the hard drive. Any PHP users who have permission to manipulate files can use SQLite to edit a database, just like they can use GD to edit images.

Although the name SQLite hints at a less than full-featured product, SQLite actually supports almost all of SQL92, the SQL standard specification. Besides the usual INSERTs and SELECTs, with SQLite you can also use transactions, query using subselects, define your own functions, and invoke triggers.

SQLite actually performs most actions more quickly than many other popular databases. In particular, SQLite excels at SELECTing data. If your application does an initial (or periodic) data INSERT and then reads many times from the database, SQLite is an excellent choice. The PHP web site uses SQLite to handle some forms of searches.

Unfortunately, SQLite has some downsides. Specifically, when you update the database by adding new data, SQLite must lock the entire file until the alteration completes. Therefore, it does not make sense in an environment where your data is constantly changing. SQLite does not have any replication support, because there's no master program to handle the communication between the master database and its slaves.

Additionally, SQLite has no concept of access control, so the GRANT and REVOKE keywords are not implemented. This means you cannot create a protected table that only certain users are allowed to access. Instead, you must implement access control by using the read and write permissions of your filesystem.

SQLite is not for sites that are flooded with heavy traffic or that require access permissions on their data. But for low-volume personal web sites and small business intranet applications, SQLite lets you do away with the burden of database administration. SQLite is also perfect for log file analysis scripts and other applications that benefit from a database but whose authors don't want to require the user to install one. SQLite is bundled with PHP 5, so unless it has been specifically omitted, it's part of every PHP 5 installation.

The SQLite home page (*http://www.sqlite.org/*) has more details about SQLite's features, limitations, and internals. A list of PHP's SQLite functions is online at *http://www.php.net/sqlite*.

This chapter starts off with SQLite basics: creating databases, passing SQL queries to SQLite, and retrieving results—everything you need to start using SQLite. It then moves on to alternative SQLite retrieval functions and interfaces, including a nifty object-oriented interface. After covering how to talk with SQLite, this chapter shows how to improve SQLite performance with indexes and how to gracefully handle errors. It closes with a few advanced features: transactions and user-defined functions, which help keep your data consistent and extend SQLite, respectively.

SQLite Basics

It's easy to get up and running with SQLite. Its design eliminates the need for any configuration variables, such as a database server name or a database username and password. All you need is the name of a file where the data is stored:

```
$db = sqlite_open('/www/support/users.db');
sqlite_query($db, 'CREATE TABLE users(username VARCHAR(100),
                                       password VARCHAR(100))');
```

This creates a users table stored in the database file located at */www/ support/users.db*. When you try to open a database file that doesn't already exist, SQLite automatically creates it for you; you don't need to execute a special command to initialize a new database.

If you cannot seem to get SQLite to work, make sure you have both read and write permission for the location on the filesystem where you're trying to create the database.

SQLite has even fewer data types than PHP—everything's a string. While you *can* define a column as INTEGER, SQLite won't complain if you then INSERT the string PHP into that column. This feature (the SQLite manual declares this a feature, not a bug) is unusual in a database, but PHP programmers frequently use this to their advantage in their scripts, so it's not a completely crazy idea. A column's type matters only when SQLite sorts its records (what comes first: 2 or 10?) and when you enforce UNIQUEness (0 and 0.0 are different strings, but the same integer).

The table created in this example has two columns: username and password. The columns' fields are all declared as VARCHARs because they're supposed to hold text. Although it doesn't really matter what type you declare your fields, it can be easier to remember what they're supposed to hold if you give them explicit types.

Inserting Data

Add new rows to the database using INSERT and sqlite_db_query( ):

```
$username = sqlite_escape_string($username);
$password = sqlite_escape_string($password);

sqlite_query($db, "INSERT INTO users VALUES ('$username', '$password')");
```

You must call sqlite_escape_string( ) to avoid the usual set of problems with single quotes and other special characters. Otherwise, a password of abc'123 will cause a parser error. Don't use addslashes( ) instead of sqlite_escape_string( ), because the two functions are not equivalent.

Retrieving Data

To retrieve data from an SQLite database, call sqlite_query( ) with your SELECT statement and iterate through the results:

```
$r = sqlite_query($db, 'SELECT username FROM users');
while ($row = sqlite_fetch_array($r)) {
    // do something with $row
}
```

By default, sqlite_fetch_array( ) returns an array with the fields indexed as both a numeric array and an associative array. For example, if this query returned one row with a username of rasmus, the preceding code would print:

```
Array (
    [0] => rasmus
    [username] => rasmus
)
```

As you can see, sqlite_fetch_array( ) works like mysqli_fetch_array( ).

When you're using user-entered data in a WHERE clause, in addition to calling sqlite_escape_string( ), you must filter out SQL wildcard characters. The easiest way to do this is with strtr( ):

```
$username = sqlite_escape_string($_GET['username']);
$username = strtr($username, array('_' => '\_', '%' => '\%'));

$r = sqlite_query($db,
                "SELECT * FROM users WHERE username LIKE '$username'");
```

Use sqlite_num_rows( ) to find the total number of rows returned by your query without iterating through the results and counting them yourself:

```
$count = sqlite_num_rows($r);
```

You can call sqlite_num_rows( ) without retrieving the results from SQLite. Remember, this function takes the query result handle, like sqlite_fetch_array( ).

If speed is a concern, use sqlite_array_query( ). This retrieves all the data and puts it into an array in a single request:

```
$r = sqlite_array_query($db, 'SELECT * FROM users');
foreach ($r as $row) {
    // do something with $row
}
```

However, if you have more than 50 rows and only need sequential access to the data, use sqlite_unbuffered_query( ):

```
$r = sqlite_unbuffered_query($db, 'SELECT * FROM users');
while ($row = sqlite_fetch_array($r)) {
    // do something with $row
}
```

This is the most efficient way to print items in an XML feed or rows in an HTML table because the data flows directly from SQLite to your PHP script without any overhead tracking behind the scenes. However, you can't use it with sqlite_num_row( ) or any function that needs to know the "current" location within the result set.

When you are done with the connection, call sqlite_close( ) to clean up:

```
sqlite_close($db);
```

Technically, this is not necessary, since PHP will clean up when your script finishes. However, if you open many SQLite connections, calling sqlite_close( ) when you're finished reduces memory usage.

SQLite Versus MySQL

The SQLite function names are similar to the MySQL functions, but not identical. Table 4-1 provides a side-by-side comparison of the two.

Table 4-1. Comparison of major MySQL and SQLite function names

MySQL	SQLite
mysqli_connect( )	sqlite_connect( )
mysqli_close( )	sqlite_close( )
mysqli_query( )	sqlite_query( )
mysqli_fetch_row( )	sqlite_fetch_array( )
mysqli_fetch_assoc( )	sqlite_fetch_array( )
mysqli_num_rows( )	sqlite_num_rows( )
mysqli_insert_id( )	sqlite_last_insert_rowid( )
mysqli_real_escape_string( )	sqlite_escape_string( )

Alternate SQLite Result Types

SQLite has many different functions for retrieving data. The ones you've already seen are not the only ones at your disposal, and you can control whether sqlite_fetch_array( ) returns numeric arrays, associative arrays, or both.

By default, when sqlite_fetch_array( ) returns data, it provides you with an array containing numeric *and* associative keys. This is a good thing, because it lets you refer to a column either by its position in the SELECT or by its name:

```
$r = sqlite_query($db, 'SELECT username FROM users');
while ($row = sqlite_fetch_array($r)) {
    print "user: $row[username]\n";  // this line and...
    print "user: $row[0]\n";         // this line are equivalent
}
```

This is also a bad thing because it can catch you unawares. For example:

```
$r = sqlite_query($db, 'SELECT * FROM users');
while ($row = sqlite_fetch_array($r)) {
    foreach ($row as $column) {
        print "$column\n";           // print each retrieved column
    }
}
```

This actually displays every column *twice*! First it prints the value stored in $row[0], and then it prints the same value referenced by its column name. If you have a generalized table-printing routine where you don't know the number of fields in advance, you might fall prey to this bug.

Additionally, if you retrieve a large dataset from SQLite, such as an entire web page or an image, then each result takes up twice as much memory because there are two copies stashed in the array.

Therefore, SQLite query functions take an optional parameter that controls the results. Pass SQLITE_ASSOC for only column names, SQLITE_NUM for only column positions, and SQLITE_BOTH for the combination. These arguments are constants, not strings, so you do not place them in quotation marks. For example:

```
// numeric
$row = sqlite_fetch_array($r, SQLITE_NUM);

// associative
$row = sqlite_fetch_array($r, SQLITE_ASSOC);

// both (the default value)
$row = sqlite_fetch_array($r, SQLITE_BOTH);
```

SQLite returns column names in the same mixed case as you CREATEd them. This is not true of all databases. Some like to use all uppercase letters; others turn everything into lowercase. When porting applications from one of these databases to SQLite, use the sqlite.assoc_case configuration parameter to maintain compatibility without rewriting your code. The default value is 0, for mixed case; changing it to 1 turns the strings in your associative arrays to uppercase, whereas 2 sets them to lowercase. Modifying the column names slows down SQLite slightly, but PHP's strtolower( ) is significantly worse in this regard.

Object-Oriented Interface

The SQLite extension allows you to interact with SQLite in an object-oriented manner. SQLite's OO interface turns your database connection into an object and lets you call methods on it. When using this interface, there's no need to pass in a database handle to any SQLite functions, because the object knows what database connection it should use.

Additionally, the SQLite OO interface lets you iterate directly over queries inside a foreach without needing to call fetch_array( ). PHP will automagically request the appropriate row from SQLite and then stop the loop when you've read all the rows.

Using the SQLiteDatabase Object

To use the OO interface, instantiate a new SQLiteDatabase object and call methods on it. Example 4-1 uses this interface to connect to the database */www/support/users.db* and SELECT all the rows from the users table.

Example 4-1. Using the SQLite object-oriented interface

```
$db = new SQLiteDatabase('/www/support/users.db');

// one at a time
$r = $db->query('SELECT * FROM users');
while ($row = $r->fetch()) {
    // do something with $row
}

// all at once
$r = $db->arrayQuery('SELECT * FROM users');
foreach ($r as $row) {
    // do something with $row
}

unset($db);
```

All procedural SQLite functions are available under the object-oriented interface, but their names are not identical. For one, you must remove the leading sqlite_ from the function name. Also, names use studlyCaps instead of underscores.

Additionally, you don't pass in the database link identifier, since that's stored in the object. So, sqlite_query($db, $sql) becomes $db->query($sql), and so forth.

The major exception to these rules is sqlite_close( ). To end the connection when using the OO interface, delete the object by using unset( ).

Table 4-2 contains a list of frequently used SQLite functions and their object equivalents.

Table 4-2. SQLite functions

Procedural name	Object-oriented name
$db = sqlite_open($table)	$db = new SQLiteDatabase($table)
sqlite_close($db)	unset($db)
$r = sqlite_query($db, $sql)	$r = $db->query($sql)
$r = sqlite_query_array($db, $sql)	$r = $db->arrayQuery($sql)
$r = sqlite_query_unbuffered($db, $sql)	$r = $db->unbufferedQuery($sql)
sqlite_fetch_array($r)	$r->fetch( )
sqlite_fetch_single($r)	$r->fetchSingle( )
$safe = sqlite_escape_string($s)	$safe = $db->escapeString($s)
$id = sqlite_last_insert_rowid($r)	$id = $db->lastInsertRowid($r)

Object Iterators

SQLite takes advantage of a new PHP 5 feature that lets you access rows from your database query as though they're just elements from an array. This feature is called iteration and is the subject of Chapter 6.

Don't confuse this with sqlite_array_query( ). SQLite is not prefetching all the rows and storing them as keys inside an array; instead, upon each loop iteration, it returns a new row as if the row already lived in your results array:

```
// one at a time
$r = $db->query('SELECT * FROM users');
foreach ($r as $row) {
    // do something with $row
}
```

You can also embed the query directly inside the foreach:

```
// one at a time
foreach ($db->query('SELECT * FROM users') as $row) {
    // do something with $row
}
```

While this interface hides many of the messy details of database result retrieval, SQLite must still make the requests and transfer the data from the database. Therefore, this syntax works only in foreach. You cannot use a for loop or pass $db->query( ) into other array functions, such as array_map( ).

When iterating over an SQLite result, it's usually best to use the unbuffered_query( ) function or unbufferedQuery( ) method instead of the simple query( ) method. Since you rarely take advantage of the additional benefits provided by query( ), unbuffered_query( ) gives you an efficiency gain at no cost.

```
// one at a time
$r = $db->unbufferedQuery('SELECT * FROM users');
foreach ($r as $row) {
    // do something with $row
}
```

Indexes, Error Handling, and In-Memory Tables

Now that you know the basics, it's time to cover the features needed to create robust applications using SQLite. Features such as creating primary and other keys, using in-memory tables, and error handling are all necessary to keep your site up and running in a responsive manner.

Indexes

Adding an *index*, also called a *key*, is the easiest way to improve application performance. When SQLite searches a database without keys, it needs to look at every single row in the table to check for matches. However, after you apply an index to the search fields, SQLite can often avoid this time-consuming process. Instead, it consults a specially constructed record that allows SQLite to quickly look up a field's location within the table.

If you know ahead of time that the data in a particular field in your database is going to be unique (i.e., each value will appear in only one record for that field), then you should declare the field UNIQUE in your CREATE TABLE SQL statement. SQLite automatically indexes UNIQUE fields.

```
CREATE TABLE users (username TEXT UNIQUE, password TEXT);
```

In a web application, a username field is often unique, whereas a password field is not. When username is UNIQUE, SQLite creates a key, since SQLite needs to scan the column to protect against duplicate entries every time you insert a record. This prevents the database from having two users named rasmus. Also, you often query against fields that are important enough to be UNIQUE:

```
SELECT * FROM users WHERE username LIKE 'rasmus';
```

To add an index to any existing SQLite table, issue the CREATE INDEX statement:

```
CREATE INDEX indexname ON tablename(fieldname);
```

Here, indexname is the name of the index. It can be anything, but *tablename_ fieldname*_index is a good way to protect against reusing the same index name. For example:

```
CREATE INDEX users_username_index ON users(username);
```

Creating a plain-vanilla INDEX imposes no UNIQUEness constraints on your data. This is helpful because there are non-unique fields, such as locations or dates, where you still need quick search capabilities:

```
SELECT * FROM stores WHERE state LIKE 'New York';

SELECT * FROM purchases WHERE date LIKE '2004-07-22';
```

You can add a UNIQUE key to a pre-existing table:

```
CREATE UNIQUE INDEX indexname ON tablename(fieldname);
```

To remove an index, issue the DROP INDEX command:

```
DROP INDEX indexname;
```

Indexes make your database files larger. Other than that, there's usually no harm in keeping an index around, even if you're not using it.

Primary Keys

A *primary key* is a special kind of index. When you place primary key status upon a column in your table, the field serves as a unique identifier for a row. Therefore, if you're interested in gathering information about a specific row in the database, the best way to retrieve it is by using its primary key.

A field with primary key status must be an integer. SQLite assigns the number 1 to the first row put into the table, 2 to the second, and so on. If you delete a line from the table, SQLite preserves the hole in the database and places any new records at the end instead of filling up the empty row.

To get SQLite to automatically create this strictly increasing set of values, first define a column in your table as an INTEGER PRIMARY KEY. Extending the previous example:

```
CREATE TABLE users (userid   INTEGER PRIMARY KEY,
                    username TEXT UNIQUE,
                    password TEXT );
```

Then, when you add a new row to the table, pass NULL as the value of the primary key:

```
INSERT INTO users VALUES (NULL, 'rasmus', 'z.8cMpdFbNAPw');
```

If you want to assign a specific number to a row as its primary key, pass that number instead of NULL. To find the value of the primary key of the last added row, call sqlite_last_insert_rowid( ) (or lastInsertRowid( ) when using the OO interface). For example:

```
$db = new SQLiteDatabase('/www/support/users.db');
$sql = "INSERT INTO users VALUES (NULL, '$username', '$password');";
$db->query($sql);
$rowid = $db->lastInsertRowid( );
```

The $rowid variable holds the primary key assigned to your INSERT.

This method is better than writing a query that retrieves the largest valued key; it's possible that between inserting your initial row and making this request, another user has altered the table.

Error Handling

Just like the mysqli extension, SQLite error handling differs depending on whether you use the procedural or object-oriented interface. With the procedural interface, you must check the return value of each SQLite call and then consult the message in a special SQLite error variable. Alternatively, the SQLite object tosses an SQLiteException whenever it encounters dragons.

Procedural error handling

Here is a good way to structure your procedural code to check for SQLite errors:

```
$db = sqlite_open($database, 0666, $sqlite_error) or die ($sqlite_error);

if ($r = sqlite_query($db, $sql)) {
    // row iteration code here
} else {
    die (sqlite_error_string(sqlite_last_error($db)));
}
```

There are three different ways to access SQLite errors. When you initially try to connect to an SQLite database, the third parameter to sqlite_open() (in this case $sqlite_error) is a variable passed by reference. If SQLite cannot open the database, it will return false and store the error message in $sqlite_error.

The second parameter to sqlite_open() is the *mode*, which is an octal number that describes the file permissions SQLite uses when creating a new database. Currently, the SQLite extension always uses a mode of 0666, regardless of what's passed in during sqlite_open(). In other words, this value is ignored completely; however, it may be respected in future versions of the extension. This mode means the database is readable and writable by all users, including the web server.

Once your connection is established, SQLite still returns false upon errors, but it no longer uses $sqlite_error. Instead, it has a pair of error-reporting functions: sqlite_last_error() and sqlite_error_string().

The first function, sqlite_last_error(), returns the SQLite error code for the most recent error. Since the error code is a number, it's not very helpful for humans. To convert the number to an actual error message, pass it to sqlite_error_string().

In the previous example, any error triggers a die(). More user-friendly applications require gentler error handling. Using error_log() in combination with a polite, generic message to users may be the best solution.

You cannot "save up" error checking while you complete a series of queries. SQLite resets the value returned by sqlite_last_error() after every query, so old error messages will be removed before you view them. SQLite even resets the message after an error-free query, so a query with an error followed by valid query leaves you with an error message of not an error.

Object-oriented error handling

When you use the object-oriented interface to the SQLite extension, you need to process exceptions or risk a fatal error. Exceptions are a method of error processing that eliminates the need to check return values of functions. They're described in more detail in Chapter 7.

SQLite doesn't always throw exceptions instead of returning NULL. In fact, the opposite it true: it throws exceptions only from its constructor. Therefore, while you need to catch that single exception, you still need to rely on traditional error handling for other errors.

Example 4-2 demonstrates this.

Example 4-2. Catching SQLite exceptions

```
$database = 'sqlite.db';
$sql      = 'INVALID SQL';
try {
    $db = new SQLiteDatabase($database);
} catch (SQLiteException $error) {
    print "Message: ".$error->getMessage()."\n";
    print "File:".$error->getFile()."\n"; die;
}

if ($r = $db->query($sql)) {
    // row iteration code here
} else {
    die (sqlite_error_string($db->lastError()));
}
```

When SQLite has an error, it throws an SQLiteException. After you catch the exception, learn more about the specific error by calling getMessage() and find out which file caused the error with getFile().

For example, if you try to create an SQLite database file in a location where you do not have write permission, the code inside the catch block prints:

```
Message: sqlite_factory(): unable to open database: /sbin/sqlite.db
File: /www/docroot/sqlite.php
```

When you detect an error outside of the constructor, as in the query() method in Example 4-2, use the lastError() method to retrieve the error code. To convert this number to a human-understandable message, use sqlite_error_string(). The function sqlite_error_string() is not an object method, because it is static and does not vary between database instances.

In-Memory Tables

For extra-fast access, SQLite supports storing tables in RAM instead of on disk. Unfortunately, these tables do not persist across requests, so you cannot create them once and then refer to them again and again; instead, they need to be created each time a page loads. Therefore, these tables are best used in applications that load in lots of data up front and then make a series of requests, such as a report generation script.

To tell SQLite to use an in-memory database, pass the token `:memory:` as your database name:

```
sqlite_open(':memory:');
sqlite_query('CREATE TABLE...');
```

Besides the special database name, there's no difference between using in-memory and on-disk tables. You interact with them using the same set of PHP and SQL commands.

Transactions

SQLite supports database transactions. Transactions are good for ensuring database consistency, but they serve a second purpose in SQLite: speed. When a set of queries are grouped together inside a transaction, SQLite executes them significantly faster than if they were performed individually. The more queries you throw at SQLite simultaneously, the larger the percentage increase in speed.

When SQLite creates a connection or makes a query, it does a certain amount of setup; likewise, when it closes a connection or completes a query, it again must perform a sequence of housecleaning tasks. These duties are relatively expensive, but SQLite needs to do this only once per transaction, regardless of how many queries are inside the transaction. This translates into a performance improvement.

However, there's a downside to using transactions in SQLite: when you wrap all your calls into a transaction, SQLite locks the entire database file, and the locked file cannot be accessed by other users. (More finely grained locking capabilities are a benefit of using a "real" database instead of SQLite.) If you're more concerned about overall system responsiveness than with optimizing for a specific action, benchmark your site to evaluate whether using transactions in this manner is appropriate in your script.

To signal to SQLite that you want to begin a transaction, use the keyword `BEGIN`; to end a transaction, use `COMMIT`. In PHP, pass these keywords as part of your SQL inside of `sqlite_query( )`:

```
$users = array(array('rasmus', 'z.8cMpdFbNAPw'),
               array('zeev'  , 'asd34.23NNDeq'));

$sql = 'BEGIN;';
foreach ($users as $user) {
    $sql .= "INSERT INTO users
                VALUES('${user[0]}', '${user[1]}');";
}
```

```
$sql .= 'COMMIT;';

sqlite_query($db, $sql);
```

The SQL opens with BEGIN, and then PHP iterates through an array, appending a series of INSERTs to $sql. When the loop is done, COMMIT is appended. SQL statements are separated by semicolons (;). This lets SQLite know to move from one statement to another. Unlike the MySQL extensions, it is always acceptable to combine multiple SQL statements in a line, even if you're not within a transaction.

You can also spread out a transaction over multiple calls to sqlite_query( ) like this:

```
$users = array(array('rasmus', 'z.8cMpdFbNAPw'),
               array('zeev'  , 'asd34.23NNDeq'));

sqlite_query($db, 'BEGIN;');

foreach ($users as $user) {
        // Assume data is already escaped
    $sql = "INSERT INTO users
                VALUES('${user[0]}', '${user[1]}');";
    sqlite_query($db, $sql);
}

sqlite_query($db, 'COMMIT;');
```

It is more efficient to make just a single query; however, spreading your queries out gives you the opportunity to undo, or *roll back*, a transaction.

For instance, here's a modification of the previous example that aborts the transaction if an error is found:

```
function add_users($db, $users) {
    $error = false;

    // Start transaction
    sqlite_query($db, 'BEGIN;');

    // Add each new user one-by-one
    foreach ($users as $user) {
        $sql = "INSERT INTO users
                    VALUES('${user[0]}', '${user[1]}');";
        sqlite_query($db, $sql);

        // Abort if there's an error
        if (sqlite_last_error($db)) {
            $error = true;
            break;
        }
    }
}
```

```
    // Revert previous commits on error; otherwise, save
    if ($error) {
        sqlite_query($db, 'ROLLBACK;');
    } else {
        sqlite_query($db, 'COMMIT;');
    }

    return !$error;
}
```

This function does the same loop through $users, but now it checks sqlite_last_error( ) after every INSERT. If there's an error, the function returns a true value, so $error gets set and you break out of the loop. When there are no errors, sqlite_last_error( ) returns 0.

Instead of automatically committing the transaction, check $error. If an error is found, reverse the transaction by executing the ROLLBACK command. Issuing a ROLLBACK instructs SQLite to revert the status of the database to its condition before BEGIN was sent.

Here is an example that triggers a rollback:

```
$db = sqlite_open('/www/support/users.db');

$users = array(array('rasmus', 'z.8cMpdFbNAPw'),
               array('zeev'  , 'asd34.23NNDeq'),
               array('rasmus', 'z.8cMpdFbNAPw'));

add_users($db, $users);
```

Assume the users table requires that each username entry be UNIQUE. Since there are two entries in the array with a username of rasmus, SQLite issues an error when you attempt to enter the second rasmus into the table.

You could ignore the error and proceed, but as things currently stand, the entire set of users is skipped. A more sophisticated example would examine the specific value returned by sqlite_last_error( ) and take different actions on a case-by-case basis. This would let you skip over a minor error like this but also let you revert the transaction if a more drastic error occurred.

User-Defined Functions

In addition to all the built-in SQL functions, such as lower( ) and upper( ), you can extend SQLite to include functions of your own written in PHP. These are known as *user-defined functions*, or *UDFs* for short. With a UDF, you embed logic into SQLite and avoid doing it yourself in PHP. This way, you take advantage of all the features inherent in a database, such as sorting and finding distinct entries.

There are two types of UDFs: standard and aggregate. Standard UDFs are one-to-one: when given a single row of data, they return a single result. Functions that change case, calculate cryptographic hashes, and compute the sales tax on an item in a shopping cart are all standard functions. In contrast, aggregate functions are many-to-one: when using an aggregate function, SQLite passes it multiple rows and receives only a single value.

Although it is not a UDF, the most popular aggregate function is count( ), which returns the number of rows passed to it. Besides count( ), most aggregate functions are related to statistics: finding the average, standard deviation, or the maximum or minimum value of a set of data points.

Standard Functions

UDFs are good for chopping up strings so you can perform nonstandard collations and groupings. For example, you want to sort through a list of URLs, maybe from a referrer log file, and create a list of unique hostnames sorted alphabetically. So, *http://www.example.com/directory/index.html* and *http://www.example.com/page.html* would both map to one entry: *http://www.example.com*.

To do this in PHP, you need to retrieve all the URLs, process them inside your script, and then sort them. Plus, somewhere in all that, you need to do the deduping. However, if it weren't for that pesky URL-conversion process, this could all be done in SQL using the DISTINCT and ORDER BY keywords.

With a UDF like the one shown in Example 4-3, you foist all that hard work back onto SQLite where it belongs.

Example 4-3. Retrieving unique hostnames using an SQLite UDF

```
// CREATE table and INSERT URLs
$db = sqlite_open('/www/support/log.db');
$sql = 'CREATE TABLE access_log(url);';

$urls = array('http://www.example.com/directory/index.html',
              'http://www.example.com/page.html');

foreach ($urls as $url) {
    $sql .= "INSERT INTO access_log VALUES('$url');";
}
sqlite_query($db, $sql);


// UDF written in PHP
function url2host($url) {
    $parts = parse_url($url);
    return "$parts[scheme]://$parts[host]";
}
```

Example 4-3. Retrieving unique hostnames using an SQLite UDF (continued)

```
// Tell SQLite to associate PHP function url2host() with the
// SQL function host(). Say that host() will only take 1 argument.
sqlite_create_function($db, 'host', 'url2host', 1);

// Do the query
$r = sqlite_query($db, 'SELECT DISTINCT host(lower(url)) AS clean_host
                        FROM access_log ORDER BY clean_host;');

// Loop through results
while ($row = sqlite_fetch_array($r)) {
    print "$row[clean_host]\n";
}
```

http://www.example.com

To use a UDF, you first write a regular function in PHP. The function's arguments are what you want to pass in during the SELECT, and the function should return a single value. The url2host() function takes a URL; calls the built-in PHP function parse_url() to break the URL into its component parts; and returns a string containing the scheme, ://, and the host. So, http://www.example.com/directory/index.html gets broken apart into many pieces. http is stored into $parts['scheme'] and www.example.com goes into $parts['host'].* This creates a return value of http://www.example.com.

The next step is to register url2host() with SQLite using sqlite_create_function(). This function takes four parameters: the database handle, the name you want the function to be called inside SQLite, the name of your function written in PHP, and the number of arguments your function expects. The last parameter is optional, but if you know for certain that your function accepts only a specific number of parameters, providing this information helps SQLite optimize things behind the scenes. In this example, the SQL function is host(), while the PHP function is url2host(). These names can be the same; they're different here to make the distinction between them clear.

Now you can use host() inside any SQL calls using that database connection. The SQL in Example 4-3 SELECTs host(lower(url)) AS clean_host. This takes the URL stored in the url column, converts it to lowercase, and calls the UDF host().

The function is not permanently registered with the database, and goes away when you close the database. If you want to use it when you reopen the database, you must reregister it. Also, the function is registered only for that database; if you open up a new database using sqlite_connect(), you need to call sqlite_create_function() again.

---

* The other portions of the URL are stored in different variables.

The returned string is then named AS clean_host; this lets you refer to the results later on in the SQL query and also access the value in PHP using that name. Since you're still in SQLite, you can take advantage of this to sort the list using ORDER BY host. This sorts the results in alphabetical order, starting at a.

Now that's cool, but it's not *that* cool. What *is* cool is SQLite's ability to call UDFs in the ORDER BY clause. If you use the default alphabetical sort, *http:// php.example.org* and *http://www.example.org* won't be near each other, because "p" and "w" aren't next to each other in the alphabet. Yet both hosts are located under the example.org domain, so it makes sense that they should be listed together. Not surprisingly, another UDF saves the day.

```
function reverse_host($url) {
    list ($scheme, $host) = explode('://', $url);
    return join('.',array_reverse(explode('.',$host)));
}

sqlite_create_function($db, 'reverse', 'reverse_host', 1);
```

The reverse_host( ) function takes a URL and chops it into two bits, the scheme and host, by explode( )ing on ://. You can do this because the previous UDF, host( ), has specifically created strings in this manner. Next, $host is passed through a series of three functions that splits it up into its component parts, reverses those parts, and then glues them back together. This flips around the pieces of the host separated by periods, but doesn't actually reverse the text. So, www.example.org becomes org.example.www and not gro.elpmaxe.www or www.elpmaxe.gro.

This reversed hostname is perfect for sorting. When you alphabetize org. example.www, it nicely sits next to all its brethren in the .org top-level domain, then sorts by the other hosts inside example.org, and finally orders the remaining subdomains. And that's exactly what you want.

You then register reverse_host( ) in the exact same way you registered url2string( ), using sqlite_create_function( ).

Once that's done, you can call reverse( ) inside your SQL query:

```
$r = sqlite_query($db, 'SELECT DISTINCT host(lower(url)) AS clean_host
                        FROM access_log ORDER BY reverse(clean_host);');
```

Given the following list of URLs as input:

```
http://www.example.com
http://php.example.org
http://www.example.org
```

you get the following as output:

```
http://www.example.com
http://php.example.org
http://www.example.org
```

The URL containing php.example.com has filtered down in the list below www.example.com, even though php comes before www in the alphabet.

In contrast, Example 4-4 shows what you need to do to implement this in PHP without UDFs.

Example 4-4. Sorting unique hostnames without using SQLite UDFs

```
function url2host($url) {
    $parts = parse_url($url);
    return "$parts[scheme]://$parts[host]";
}

function reverse_host($url) {
    list ($scheme, $host) = explode('://', $url);
    return join('.',array_reverse(explode('.',$host)));
}

function host_sort($a, $b) {
    $count_a = $GLOBALS['hosts'][$a];
    $count_b = $GLOBALS['hosts'][$b];

    if ($count_a < $count_b) { return  1; }
    if ($count_a > $count_b) { return -1; }

    return strcasecmp(reverse_host($a), reverse_host($b));
}

$hosts = array();

$r = sqlite_unbuffered_query($db, 'SELECT url FROM access_log');
while ($url = sqlite_fetch_single($r)) {
    $host = url2host($url);
    $hosts[$host]++ ;
}

uksort($hosts, 'host_sort');
```

This process breaks down into many steps:

1. Make a database query for urls.
2. Retrieve url into $url using sqlite_fetch_single( ).
3. Convert $url into a host and store it in $host.
4. Place $url as a new element in the $hosts array and increment that element by 1. This tracks the number of times each URL has appeared.
5. Perform a user-defined key sort on the $hosts array.

The sqlite_fetch_single( ) function returns the first (and in this case only) column from the result as a string. This allows you to skip the step of saving the result as an array and then extracting the element, either by using list or as the 0th index.

Doing $hosts[$host]++ is a old trick that allows you to easily count the number of times each key appears in a list.

Since uksort( ) only passes array keys to the sorting function, host_host( ) is not very elegant, because it requires using a global variable to determine the number of hits for each element.

Overall, compared to a UDF, this method requires more memory, execution time, and lines of code, because you're replicating database functionality inside PHP.

User-Defined Aggregate Functions

As discussed earlier, most aggregate functions are statistical functions, such as AVG( ) or STDEV( ). People usually use aggregate functions to return a single row from their query, but that's not a requirement. You can use them to link together a set of related rows, to compact your query and return one row per group.

This extension to the earlier referrer log sorting example shows how to use an aggregate function to provide the total number of hits per hostname, in addition to everything in the previous section:

```
SELECT DISTINCT host(lower(url)) AS clean_host, COUNT(*) AS hits
FROM access_log GROUP BY clean_host ORDER BY hits DESC, reverse(clean_host)
```

The COUNT(*) function sums the total number of rows per host. However, this won't work without adding the GROUP BY host clause. GROUPing rows allows COUNT(*) to know which sets of entries belong together. Whenever you have an aggregate function—such as COUNT( ), SUM( ), or any function that takes a set of rows as input and returns only a single value as its output—use GROUP BY when you want your query to return multiple rows. (If you're just doing a basic SELECT COUNT(*) FROM host to find the total number of rows in the table, there's no need for any GROUPing.)

COUNT(*) is aliased to hits, which allows you to refer to it in the ORDER BY clause. Then, to sort the results first by total hits, from most to least, and then alphabetically within each total, use ORDER BY hits DESC, reverse(host). By putting hits first, you prioritize it over reverse(clean_host) and the DESC keyword flips the sorting order to descending (the default is ascending).

Using that query, this set of sites:

```
http://www.example.org
http://www.example.org
```

```
http://www.example.com
http://php.example.org
```

and this PHP code:

```
while ($row = sqlite_fetch_array($r)) {
    print "$row[hits]: $row[clean_host]\n";
}
```

gives:

```
2: http://www.example.org
1: http://www.example.com
1: http://php.example.org
```

Furthermore, to restrict results to sites with more hits than a specified amount, use a HAVING clause:

```
SELECT DISTINCT host(lower(url)) AS clean_host, COUNT(*) AS hits
        FROM access_log
        GROUP BY clean_host
        HAVING hits > 1
        ORDER BY hits DESC, reverse(clean_host)
```

You cannot use WHERE here, because WHERE can only operate on data directly from a table. Here the restriction hits > 1 compares against the result of a GROUP BY, so you need to employ HAVING instead.

You can define your own aggregate functions for SQLite in PHP. Unlike standard UDFs, you actually need to define two functions: one that's called for each row and one that's called after all the rows have been passed in.

The code in Example 4-5 shows how to create a basic SQLite user-defined aggregate function that calculates the average of a set of numbers.

Example 4-5. Averaging numbers using an SQLite aggregate function

```
// CREATE table and INSERT numbers
$db = sqlite_open('/www/support/data.db');
$sql = 'CREATE TABLE numbers(number);';
$numbers = array(1, 2, 3, 4, 5);
foreach ($numbers as $n) {
    $sql .= "INSERT INTO numbers VALUES($n);";
}
sqlite_query($db, $sql);

// average_step() is called on each row.
function average_step(&$existing_data, $new_data) {
    $existing_data['total'] += $new_data;
    $existing_data['count']++;
}

// average_final() computes the average and returns it.
function average_final(&$existing_data) {
```

Example 4-5. Averaging numbers using an SQLite aggregate function (continued)

```
    return $existing_data['total'] / $existing_data['count'];
}

sqlite_create_aggregate($db, 'average', 'average_step', 'average_final');

$r = sqlite_query($db, 'SELECT average(number) FROM numbers');
$average = sqlite_fetch_single($r);
print $average;
```

3

First, you define the two aggregate functions in PHP, just as you do for regular UDFs. However, the first parameter for both functions is a variable passed by reference that is used to keep track of the UDF's state. In this example, you need to track both the running sum of the numbers and how many rows have contributed to this total. That's done in average_step( ).

In average_final( ), the final sum is divided by the number of elements to find the average. This is the value that's returned by the function and passed back to SQLite (and, eventually, to you).

To formally create an aggregate UDF, use sqlite_create_aggregate( ). It works like sqlite_create_function( ), but you pass both PHP function names instead of just one.

Binary Data

SQLite is not binary safe by default. Requiring PHP to automatically protect against problems caused by binary data causes a significant reduction in speed, so you must manually encode and decode data when it might be anything other than plain text. If your UDFs only operate on text, this isn't a problem.

Inside a UDF, use sqlite_udf_binary_decode( ) to convert data stored in SQLite into usable strings in PHP:

```
function udf_function_encode($encoded_data) {
    $data = sqlite_udf_binary_decode($encoded_data);
    // rest of the function...
}
```

When you're finished, if the return value might also be binary unsafe, re-encode it using sqlite_udf_binary_encode( ):

```
function udf_function_decode($encoded_data) {
    // rest of the function...
    return sqlite_udf_binary_encode($return_value);
}
```

CHAPTER 5

XML

PHP 5 has a completely new set of XML extensions that address major problems in PHP 4's XML extensions. While PHP 4 allows you to manipulate XML, its XML tools are only superficially related. Each tool covers one part of the XML experience, but they weren't designed to work together, and PHP 4 support for the more advanced XML features is often patchy. Not so in PHP 5. The new XML extensions:

- Work together as a unified whole
- Are standardized on a single XML library: libxml2
- Fully comply with W3 specifications
- Efficiently process data
- Provide you with the right XML tool for your job

Additionally, following the PHP tenet that creating web applications should be easy, there's a new XML extension that makes it simple to read and alter XML documents. The aptly named SimpleXML extension allows you to interact with the information in an XML document as though these pieces of information are arrays and objects, iterating through them with foreach loops and editing them in place merely by assigning new values to variables.

XML Extensions in PHP 5

PHP 5 has five major XML extensions. Each one has different features, advantages, and costs:

DOM
> The 800-pound gorilla of XML. You can do everything and the <kitchen-sink> with DOM, but navigating through your documents can be cumbersome.

SAX

PHP's original XML extension. SAX is a streaming, or event-based, parser that uses less memory than DOM, but frequently requires more complex PHP code.

SimpleXML

A new PHP 5–only extension that excels at parsing RSS files, REST results, and configuration data. If you know the document's format ahead of time, SimpleXML is the way to go. However, SimpleXML supports only a subset of the XML specification.

XPath

This extension allows you to query XML documents like you're searching a database, to find the subset of information that you need and eliminate the unnecessary portions.

XSLT

A way to take XML documents and transform them into HTML or another output format. It uses XML-based stylesheets to define the templates. XSLT is easily shared among different applications, but has a quirky syntax.

Most web developers are familiar with XML basics. However, PHP 5 makes it easier to use some less well-known parts of XML, including XPath and XML Namespaces. XPath is a powerful but underutilized way to search XML documents and extract information. With XML Namespaces, you can safely combine pieces of XML from multiple sources into a single XML document and still uniquely identify every element. If you're not familiar with XML or the advanced bits like XPath and XML Namespaces, you might want to make a quick detour to the XML introduction in Appendix A.

This chapter starts by introducing DOM and SimpleXML, the two major XML extensions in PHP 5. This introduction shows how to create, save, and interact with DOM and SimpleXML objects. These two approaches to working with XML are similar, but they have different aims. DOM is rigorous and works with any XML, whereas SimpleXML aims to make common XML tasks very easy, at the cost of not being useful for some types of XML.

Some programmers like DOM because it requires you to be highly disciplined. Additionally, they believe that when your requests are very explicit, it makes code easier to understand and reduces the possibility for mistakes.

Other people believe the opposite. They think that DOM is too heavyweight for general XML processing because even the most basic tasks require multiple levels of dereferencing. To them, these levels only clutter up code and make it hard to understand exactly what's going on.

In this book, XML examples are given in *both* DOM and SimpleXML, so you can get a feel for when you should (or prefer to) use one versus the other.

When porting code, it's nice to learn about new features by reading text describing them and by scanning a table listing the differences between the old and new versions. However, that's not practicable here—the major overhaul of the XML extensions means that often the new way to do an XML processing task is completely different from the old way. It's easier to understand what needs to be done by examining a few short before-and-after examples. By comparing the two, you can review your own code and make similar modifications. Once that's done, you can then double back and fill in the missing parts by looking at the other material.

Therefore, instead of listing all the new methods you can use to manipulate XML, the majority of this chapter contains code showing how to solve a series of common XML tasks. The examples are as follows:

- Reading XML into a tree
- Reading XML from a stream
- Creating new XML documents
- Searching XML with XPath
- Changing XML into HTML or other output formats with XSLT
- Validating XML to ensure it conforms to a specification

These sections are all presented in a before-and-after format. First, you see how it was done in PHP 4. Then, you see updated code showing what changes, if any, you need to make to your code for it to work under PHP 5.

To make things consistent, the examples all use the same XML documents. These documents represent a basic XML address book. Example 5-1 shows the standard version.

Example 5-1. Example XML address book

```
<?xml version="1.0"?>
<address-book>
    <person id="1">
        <!--Rasmus Lerdorf-->
        <firstname>Rasmus</firstname>
        <lastname>Lerdorf</lastname>
        <city>Sunnyvale</city>
        <state>CA</state>
        <email>rasmus@php.net</email>
    </person>
```

Example 5-1. Example XML address book (continued)

```
    <person id="2">
        <!--Zeev Suraski-->
        <firstname>Zeev</firstname>
        <lastname>Suraski</lastname>
        <city>Tel Aviv</city>
        <state></state>
        <email>zeev@php.net</email>
    </person>
</address-book>
```

Example 5-2 is a version that uses namespaces.

Example 5-2. Example namespaced XML address book

```
<?xml version="1.0"?>
<ab:address-book
    xmlns:ab="http://www.example.com/address-book/">
    <ab:person id="1">
        <!--Rasmus Lerdorf-->
        <ab:firstname>Rasmus</ab:firstname>
        <ab:lastname>Lerdorf</ab:lastname>
        <ab:city>Sunnyvale</ab:city>
        <ab:state>CA</ab:state>
        <ab:email>rasmus@php.net</ab:email>
    </ab:person>

    <ab:person id="2">
        <!--Zeev Suraski-->
        <ab:firstname>Zeev</ab:firstname>
        <ab:lastname>Suraski</ab:lastname>
        <ab:city>Tel Aviv</ab:city>
        <ab:state></ab:state>
        <ab:email>zeev@php.net</ab:email>
    </ab:person>
</ab:address-book>
```

Installing XML and XSLT Support

PHP 5 uses libxml2 and libxslt as the underlying foundation for its XML support. By hooking into these tools, PHP developers don't need to write their own XML processors, which gives them more time to work on PHP.

Originally written for the GNOME project, libxml2 is a standalone library that can be used by other programs, including languages like PHP. Written in C, libxml2 runs on Linux, Windows, Mac OS X, FreeBSD, and many other operating systems. The official libxml2 web site is at *http://www.xmlsoft.org/*.

libxml2 offers several benefits over other XML parsers: speed, licensing, and standards. While other XML parsers might be faster in certain specialized circumstances, libxml2 is overall one of the fastest parsing engines available.

libxml2 also implements most XML specifications. In addition to the basic XML standard, libxml2 also supports XML Namespaces, XPath, XPointer, XInclude, XML Catalogs, Relax NG, and XML Schemas Part 2. Additional standards are being added on a regular basis. libxml2 also integrates with libxslt to support XSLT.

PHP 5 requires libxml2 2.5.10 or higher. If you are running Unix or Mac OS X, find the version of libxml2 on your machine by running xml2-config --version:

```
% xml2-config --version
```

2.5.10

If this program cannot be found or the version number is lower than 2.5.10, you must install (or upgrade) libxml2 on your machine. The latest version of libxml2 is available at *http://www.xmlsoft.org/downloads.html*.

By default, PHP 5 enables DOM, SAX, and SimpleXML; however, if your copy of libxml2 is in a nonstandard location, use --with-libxml-dir=DIR to help PHP during the configuration process.

For instance, on Mac OS X, the fink package manager installs files in */sw* by default:

```
--with-libxml-dir=/sw
```

PHP 5 also uses libxslt for XSLT processing. Check your version by running xslt-config --version:

```
% xslt-config --version
```

1.0.32

PHP requires a minimum version of libxslt 1.0.18. It *does not* automatically enable XSLT support; you must add it yourself:

```
--with-xsl
```

You can also set an installation directory for libxslt:

```
--with-xsl=/sw
```

Windows distributions of PHP come with libxml2 and libxslt DLLs. However, to enable XSLT support, uncomment this line from your *php.ini* file by removing the leading semicolon (;):

```
;extension=php_xsl.dll
```

DOM

DOM is one of PHP 5's two major XML processing extensions. This section introduces DOM, providing an overview of how it organizes information. It also demonstrates how to turn XML documents into DOM objects and vice versa.

About DOM

There is only one way to read XML into a tree using PHP 4: DOM. DOM, short for Document Object Model, is a W3C standard describing a platform- and language-neutral interface for interacting with XML and other structured documents. DOM then provides a series of utility functions to recurse through the branches and pick out the nodes and data that you want.

It's easier to parse XML into a tree than to use a streaming parser such as SAX. When you read XML into a tree, you can move through the document in a way that is similar to navigating PHP data structures such as multidimensional arrays or objects that have subobjects. However, if your document is large, DOM can use lot of memory.

PHP 5's DOM utilities have undergone a complete rewrite. If you used the DOM functions in PHP 4, you know that PHP's DOM support has largely been sketchy and incomplete. The original implementation did not conform at all to the W3C naming conventions, thus partially defeating the purpose of a language-neutral API. Although PHP 4.3 unveiled an improved and more compliant set of DOM functions, there are still holes and memory leaks.

On top (or perhaps because) of all this, a large "EXPERIMENTAL" tag had seemingly been permanently placed upon PHP 4's DOM functions. When the warning "The behavior of this extension—including the names of its functions and anything else documented about this extension—may change without notice in a future release of PHP. Use this extension at your own risk" appears at the top of documentation, it does not engender comfort.

Happily, all that has changed in PHP 5. The new DOM extension not only has updated internals, but you now interact with it in the standard way, and it has a few new features, such as validation. Still, the entire DOM specification is quite large and complex, and not all features are available yet. But what has been implemented is done correctly and is consistent with other languages.

Unfortunately, if you've written any applications that use the old DOM extension, they won't work with PHP 5. You must update them.

Turning XML Documents into DOM objects

Before you can do anything DOM-related in PHP 5, you need to create a new instance of the DOM object, called DOMDocument:

```
$dom = new DOMDocument;
```

Now you can load XML into $dom. DOM differentiates between XML stored as a string and XML stored in a file. To read from a string, call loadXML( ); to read from a file, call load( ):

```
$dom = new DOMDocument;

// read from a string
$dom->loadXML('<string>I am XML</string>');

// read from a file
$dom->load('address-book.xml');
```

The DOM load( ) method, like all XML input and output methods, actually works for more than just files. It really works with streams, so it can read from HTTP or write to FTP. See Chapter 8 for more information about streams.

If DOM encounters problems reading the XML—for example, the XML is not well-formed, your file does not exist, or you try to pass in an array instead of a string—DOM emits a warning. In some cases, such as a failure of the DOM extension to create a new DOM object or safe_mode blocking off access to the file, it returns false instead.

This example tries to load a string that's invalid XML:

```
$dom = new DOMDocument;

// read non well-formed XML document
$dom->loadXML('I am not XML');
```

It causes DOM to give a PHP Warning that begins like this:

PHP Warning: DOMDocument::loadXML( ): Start tag expected, '<' not found

Whitespace is considered significant in XML, so spaces between tags are considered text elements. For example, there are *five* elements inside the person element:

```
<person>
        <firstname>Rasmus</firstname>
        <lastname>Lerdorf</lastname>
</person>
```

It looks like there are only two elements, firstname and lastname, but there are actually three additional text nodes. They're hard to see because they're whitespace. They occur between the opening person tag and the opening firstname tag, the closing firstname tag and opening lastname tag, and the closing lastname and closing person tag.

However, removing the whitespace makes the document hard for humans to read. Happily, you can tell DOM to ignore whitespace:

```
$dom = new DOMDocument;

// Whitespace is no longer significant
$dom->preserveWhiteSpace = false;

$dom->loadXML('<string>I am XML</string>');
```

Setting the preserveWhiteSpace attribute to false makes DOM skip over any text nodes that contain only spaces, tabs, returns, or other whitespace.

DOM Nodes

DOM organizes XML documents into nodes. You can use DOM to retrieve the text stored in a node, find a node's children, insert another node at that location, and so forth.

Figure 5-1 shows how DOM represents the beginning of the address book.

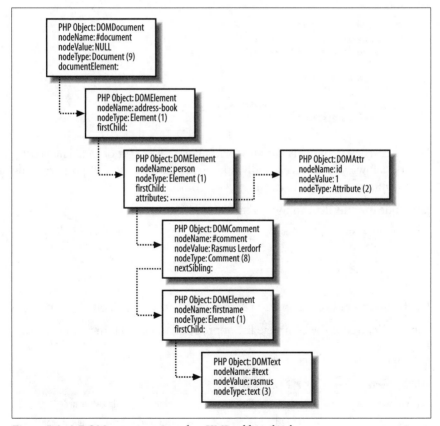

Figure 5-1. A DOM representation of an XML address book

Accessing the root element

The root element of an XML document is stored as the `documentElement` property of a DOM object:

```
$dom = new DOMDocument;
$dom->preserveWhiteSpace = false;
$dom->load('address-book.xml');

$root = $dom->documentElement;
```

The `$root` variable now holds a pointer to the document root.

Navigating through nodes

DOM has a whole set of tree iteration properties that allow you to explicitly move from one element to another. In PHP 4, these are object methods, but they're object properties in PHP 5.

The easiest way to process all of a node's children is with a `foreach` upon its `childNodes`. For example, to process all the `person` elements in the address book:

```
$dom = new DOMDocument;
$dom->preserveWhiteSpace = false;
$dom->load('address-book.xml');

$root = $dom->documentElement;

foreach ($root->childNodes as $person) {
    process($person);
}
```

The `childNodes` attribute is not an array, but a `DOMNodeList` object. The `item( )` method allows you to access individual items, and the `length` property tells you the number of items in the list.

This code is equivalent to the `foreach` loop:

```
$people = $root->childNodes;

for ($i = 0; $i < $people->length; $i++) {
    process($people->item($i));
}
```

The first element lives in position 0, the second in 1, and so on.

Table 5-1 contains the complete list of properties and what they do.

Table 5-1. DOM iteration properties

PHP 5 property	PHP 4 method	Description
parentNode	parent_node( )	The node above the current node
childNodes	child_nodes( )	A list of nodes below the current node

Table 5-1. DOM iteration properties (continued)

PHP 5 property	PHP 4 method	Description
firstChild	first_child( )	The "first" node below the current node
lastChild	last_child( )	The "last" node below the current node
previousSibling	previous_sibling( )	The node "before" the current node
nextSibling	next_sibling( )	The node "after" the current node

Determining node types

libxml2 has 21 different types of nodes. The most frequently encountered types are elements, attributes, and text. The nodeType method returns a number describing the node.

For instance, the documentElement is always an element:

```
$root = $dom->documentElement;

print $root->nodeType;
```

    1

Table 5-2 lists libxml2's node types.

Table 5-2. libxml2's numeric node types

Node type	Number
Element	1
Attribute	2
Text	3
CDATA section	4
Entity reference	5
Entity	6
PI (Processing Instruction)	7
Comment	8
Document	9
Document type	10
Document fragment	11
Notation	12
HTML document	13
DTD	14
Element declaration	15
Attribute declaration	16
Entity declaration	17
Namespace declaration	18

Table 5-2. libxml2's numeric node types (continued)

Node type	Number
XInclude start	19
XInclude end	20
DocBook document	21

Accessing text nodes

DOM never makes any assumptions about how your data is organized or what you wish to do with it. If you have a snippet of XML that looks like this:

```
<firstname>Rasmus</firstname>
```

DOM does not assume that your primary interest is the string Rasmus. To DOM, Rasmus is just the text portion of a child node associated with the node for the firstname element.

Here's how to access Rasmus:

```
// load in XML
$rasmus = newDOMDocument;
$rasmus->loadXML('<firstname>Rasmus</firstname>');

// two DOM longhand ways
$rasmus->firstChild->firstChild->nodeValue;
$rasmus->firstChild->firstChild->data;

// the first element of the children method
$rasmus->childNodes->item(0)->nodeValue;

// a DOM shorthand way of saying the same thing
$rasmus->firstChild->nodeValue;

// a PHP 5 shorthand method
// *NOT* portable across DOM implementations
$rasmus->textContent;

// yet another way, because this is the root element
$rasmus->documentElement->nodeValue;
```

DOM does not couple the element with the text wrapped by its tags. Therefore, you must ask the node for its first child. This gives you the text node holding PHP. However, you can't print the node, because it's an object, not a string. To access the text portion of a text node, you need to grab its nodeValue.

PHP 5's DOM implementation has a special attribute textContent that's equivalent to firstChild->nodeValue. This attribute name is shorter, but it is not portable, because it's not part of the DOM standard.

Accessing element nodes

DOM stores an element's name in the `tagName` property. This code loops through a person element from the address book and prints out the names of all the elements and the values of their first children:

```
$dom = new DOMDocument;
$dom->preserveWhiteSpace = false;
$dom->load('address-book.xml');

$person = $dom->documentElement->firstChild;

foreach ($person->childNodes as $field) {
    if ($field->nodeType == 1) {
        print "$field->tagName: {$field->firstChild->nodeValue}\n";
    }
}
```

```
firstname: Rasmus
lastname: Lerdorf
city: Sunnyvale
state: CA
email: rasmus@php.net
```

The $person object holds the person node, and its children are the address book fields.

Inside the foreach, you need to check the nodeType to make sure you have an element node. All elements in libxml2 have a nodeType of 1. Skipping this check processes the comment node because DOM does not ignore comments.

Turning DOM Objects into XML Documents

To take a DOM document and convert it back into XML, you have two options: save( ) and saveXML( ). The first method saves a document to a file; the other returns a string representation of the document, which you can print out or store in a variable.

```
$dom->save('address-book.xml');
```

```
print $dom->saveXML( );
```

As always, you must have write permission for the directory in which you're saving the file.

If you disable the preserveWhiteSpace attribute, your XML ends up as a single line:

```
$dom = new DOMDocument;
$dom->preserveWhiteSpace = false;
```

```
$dom->load('address-book.xml');
print $dom->saveXML();
```

```
<address-book><person id="1"><!--Rasmus Lerdorf--><firstname>Rasmus</fi
rstname><lastname>Lerdorf</lastname><city>Sunnyvale</city><state>CA</st
ate><email>rasmus@php.net</email></person><person id="2"><!--Zeev Suras
ki--><firstname>Zeev</firstname><lastname>Suraski</lastname><city>Tel A
viv</city><state/><email>zeev@php.net</email></person></address-book>
```

To prevent this, set the `formatOutput` attribute to true:

```
$dom = new DOMDocument;
$dom->preserveWhiteSpace = false;
$dom->formatOutput = true;

$dom->load('address-book.xml');
print $dom->saveXML();
```

```
<?xml version="1.0"?>
<address-book>
  <person id="1">
<!--Rasmus Lerdorf-->
    <firstname>Rasmus</firstname>
    <lastname>Lerdorf</lastname>
    <city>Sunnyvale</city>
    <state>CA</state>
    <email>rasmus@php.net</email>
  </person>
  <person id="2">
<!--Zeev Suraski-->
    <firstname>Zeev</firstname>
    <lastname>Suraski</lastname>
    <city>Tel Aviv</city>
    <state/>
    <email>zeev@php.net</email>
  </person>
</address-book>
```

Now the elements are indented. However, since libxml2 does not indent comments, those nodes remain on the left.

SimpleXML

SimpleXML has been described as "the mostest bestest thing ever." While it's hard to live up to such grand praise, SimpleXML does do a remarkable job of making it—dare I say—simple to interact with XML. When you want to read a configuration file written in XML, parse an RSS feed, or process the result of a REST request, SimpleXML excels at these tasks. It doesn't work well for more complex XML-related jobs, such as reading a document where you don't know the format ahead of time or when you need to access processing instructions or comments.

Turning XML Documents into SimpleXML Objects

There are two ways to read XML under SimpleXML. If your XML document is stored as a string in a PHP variable, use simplexml_load_string( ). If it's in a file, call simplexml_load_file( ) instead. For instance:

```
// Variable
$xml = simplexml_load_string('<xml>I am XML</xml>');

// Local file
$people = simplexml_load_file('address-book.xml');
```

SimpleXML Elements

SimpleXML turns elements into object properties. The text between the tags is assigned to the property. If more than one element with the same name lives in the same place (such as multiple <people>s), then they're placed inside a list.

Element attributes become array elements, where the array key is the attribute name and the key's value is the attribute's value.

Figure 5-2 shows SimpleXML's view of the start of the address book.

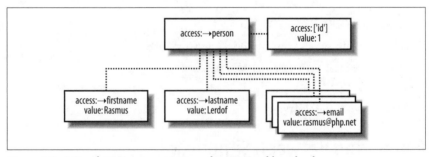

Figure 5-2. A SimpleXML representation of an XML address book

To access a single value, reference it directly using object method notation. Here's the same snippet from the DOM section:

```
<firstname>Rasmus</firstname>
```

If you have this in a SimpleXML object, $firstname, here's all you need to do to access Rasmus:

```
$firstname
```

SimpleXML assumes that when you have a node that contains only text, you're interested in the text. Therefore, print $firstname does what you expect it to: it prints Rasmus.

Iteration methods, like foreach, are the best choice for cycling through multiple elements. Code for this is shown in later examples.

Unlike DOM, attributes are not stored as separate nodes. Instead, attributes are stored as array elements. For example, this prints out the id attribute for the first person element:

```
$ab = simplexml_load_file('address-book.xml');

// the id attribute of the first person
print $ab->person['id'] . "\n";
```

which gives you:

1

Turning SimpleXML Objects into XML Documents

The asXML( ) method converts a SimpleXML object back into an XML string:

```
// display the XML
print $ab->asXML( );
```

The asXML( ) method can save the XML to a file by passing the location of the output file as an argument:

```
// save the XML
$ab->asXML('address-book');
```

This method also works on subnodes. For instance:

```
$ab = simplexml_load_file('address-book.xml');
print $ab->person->firstname->asXML( );
```

```
<firstname>Rasmus</firstname>
```

Converting Between SimpleXML and DOM Objects

Using SimpleXML is usually easier than using DOM, but sometimes DOM's comprehensiveness lets you do something that's either hard or impossible in SimpleXML.

For example, you cannot discover the name of the root element in Simple-XML, but that's no problem in DOM, as shown in Example 5-3.

Example 5-3. Converting between SimpleXML and DOM objects

```
$ab = simplexml_load_file('address-book.xml');

// Find the name of the root node
$name = dom_import_simplexml($ab)->tagName;

print $name;
```

address-book

SimpleXML gobbles up the root element, so there's no way to derive its name using SimpleXML. However, the `dom_import_simplexml( )` function takes a SimpleXML object and converts it to a DOM document. Under DOM, reference the object's `tagName` property and you're done.

These conversion features are particularly useful when you're using SimpleXML as a generic XML document parser, because SimpleXML doesn't really support XML document introspection. In contrast, DOM excels at this task.

Alternatively, you can perform the reverse transformation, as shown in Example 5-4.

Example 5-4. Converting between DOM and SimpleXML objects

```
$ab = new DOMDocument;
$ab->load('address-book.xml');

// Find the email address of the first person
$email = simplexml_import_dom($ab)->person->email;

print $email;
```

rasmus@php.net

Use the `simplexml_import_dom( )` function to turn a DOM object into a SimpleXML object.

Don't worry about the performance overhead of these functions. Since SimpleXML and DOM both use `libxml2` as their underlying XML engine, no additional XML parsing occurs when you convert an object. This makes it efficient to switch between the two interfaces.

Before and After: Reading XML into a Tree

The most common XML task is reading an XML document and printing out its contents. DOM and SimpleXML store XML documents in trees. This allows you to easily maneuver though the document to find information because if you know where your node is located, you can access it directly.

Reading an Address Book

The following programs take an XML document, read it into a tree, and then find a set of nodes. They all use the example address book from Example 5-1 as their data, search for all the people nodes, and then print out everyone's first and last name.

The first two versions use DOM, one written in PHP 4 and the other in PHP 5. There is also a SimpleXML version, which is considerably shorter.

PHP 4 and DOM

Example 5-5 demonstrates the PHP 4 DOM extension.

Example 5-5. Reading XML with PHP 4 and DOM

```
$dom = domxml_open_file('address-book.xml');

foreach ($dom->get_elements_by_tagname('person') as $person) {
    $firstname = $person->get_elements_by_tagname('firstname');
    $firstname_text = $firstname[0]->first_child();
    $firstname_text_value = $firstname_text->node_value();

    $lastname = $person->get_elements_by_tagname('lastname'));
    $lastname_text = $lastname[0]->first_child();
    $lastname_text_value = $lastname_text->node_value();

    print "$firstname_text_value $lastname_text_value\n";
}
```

Rasmus Lerdorf
Zeev Suraski

Under PHP 4, DOM method names use underscores (_) to separate words, such as get_elements_by_tagname( ) and first_child( ).

To find all elements with a given name, use get_elements_by_tagname( ). This returns an array of elements through which you can iterate. You foreach through each of the <person>s. Within this loop, there are two steps: retrieving the email element and then printing out the value.

The $person DOM object is just a subtree, or a portion, of the original DOM object, but it is also a full-featured node of its own. Therefore, you can still call $person->get_elements_by_tagname('firstname') to find all firstname elements, just as you earlier called $dom->get_elements_by_tagname('person') to locate persons. However, in this case, you only look through the elements in $person instead of the entire XML document.

Since get_elements_by_tagname( ) returns an array of DOM objects but the array contains only one element, it's referenced with $firstname[0].

You can't directly call a method on a returned object; therefore, it takes two lines to grab an element's text. You must do $firstname_text = $firstname[0]->first_child( ) and then $firstname_text_value = $firstname_text->node_value( ).

PHP 5 and DOM

DOM in PHP 5 uses objects instead of resources, as shown in Example 5-6.

Example 5-6. Reading XML with PHP 5 and DOM

```
$dom = newDOMDocument;
$dom->load('address-book.xml');

foreach ($dom->getElementsByTagname('person') as $person) {
    $firstname = $person->getElementsByTagname('firstname');
    $firstname_text_value = $firstname->item(0)->firstChild->nodeValue;

    $lastname = $person->getElementsByTagname('lastname');
    $lastname_text_value = $lastname->item(0)->firstChild->nodeValue;

    print "$firstname_text_value $lastname_text_value\n";
}
```

Rasmus Lerdorf
Zeev Suraski

This is similar to the PHP 4 example. Method names, however, are altered to use the studlyCaps naming convention. So, get_elements_by_tagname( ) is getElementsByTagname( ).

Such a trivial change seems designed merely to frustrate programmers. However, the DOM standard uses studlyCaps and so do the DOM methods in every other language, including C, Java, Perl, and Python. Therefore, the methods were renamed to bring them into line with this convention.

The getElementsByTagname( ) method now returns a DOM node list instead of an array. Therefore, you access the elements using the item( ) method. For example:

```
// PHP 4
$firstname[0];

// PHP 5
$firstname->item(0);
```

Two changes result from PHP 5's improved object model. You no longer need to use a temporary variable to hold an object before accessing one of its methods. So, to find the $firstname_text_value, you can write $firstname->

item(0)->firstChild->nodeValue. Also, the firstChild and nodeValue properties are no longer methods, so they don't take ( )s.

Another way to read XML with PHP 5 and DOM is to create a custom class. Since the DOMDocument is now a PHP object, you can extend it and create your own methods. Example 5-7 creates an addressBook class that contains a printNames( ) method.

Example 5-7. Reading XML with PHP 5 and DOM by subclassing DOMDocument

```
class addressBook extends DOMDocument {

    public function printNames() {
        foreach ($this->getElementsByTagname('person') as $person) {
            $firstname = $person->getElementsByTagname('firstname');
            $firstname_text_value = $firstname->item(0)->firstChild->nodeValue;

            $lastname = $person->getElementsByTagname('lastname');
            $lastname_text_value = $lastname->item(0)->firstChild->nodeValue;

            print "$firstname_text_value $lastname_text_value\n";
        }
    }
}

$ab = new addressBook;
$ab->load('address-book.xml');
$ab->printNames();
```

Rasmus Lerdorf
Zeev Suraski

The addressBook class has access to all the methods and properties of DOMDocument, so you interact with it just like a standard DOM object.

You can also create new methods, such as printNames( ). The only difference between the code inside printNames( ) and the previous example is that you now refer to the DOM object as $this.

This makes it very easy to write a set of DOM manipulation methods that help you navigate through the object while keeping your ability to invoke a particular DOM method when necessary.

PHP 5 and SimpleXML

The SimpleXML version is the shortest, as shown in Example 5-8.

Example 5-8. Reading XML with PHP 5 and SimpleXML

```
$sx = simplexml_load_file('address-book.xml');

foreach ($sx->person as $person) {
```

Example 5-8. Reading XML with PHP 5 and SimpleXML (continued)

```
    $firstname_text_value = $person->firstname;
    $lastname_text_value = $person->lastname;

    print "$firstname_text_value $lastname_text_value\n";
}
```

Rasmus Lerdorf
Zeev Suraski

When you use SimpleXML, there's no need to call a method to retrieve a set of elements with the same tag name. Instead, you can directly iterate over them using foreach. Here, the iteration occurs over $sx->person, which holds all the person nodes.

You can also directly print SimpleXML objects:

```
    foreach ($sx->person as $person) {
        print "$person->firstname $person->lastname\n";
    }
```

Rasmus Lerdorf
Zeev Suraski

PHP interpolates SimpleXML objects inside of quoted strings and retrieves the text stored in them.

Reading an Address Book with Namespaces

Reading namespaced elements is similar to reading global elements, but in addition to the element's local name, you must also provide the namespace.

The following examples use Example 5-2's revised XML address book, which places everything in a namespace.

PHP 4 and DOM

There is no easy way to get all namespaced elements in PHP 4 if you just use DOM. The best way to solve this problem is to use DOM in conjunction with XPath. See "Before and After: Searching XML with XPath," later in this chapter, for more details.

PHP 5 and DOM

PHP 5 has a special DOM method to retrieve elements within a namespace: getElementsByTagnameNS( ). To search a namespaced document, replace the calls to getElementsByTagname( ) with getElementsByTagnameNS( ). Pass the namespace URL as the first argument and the element's local name as the second argument, as shown in Example 5-9.

Example 5-9. Reading namespaced XML with PHP 5 and DOM

```
$ab = 'http://www.example.com/address-book/';
$dom = new DOMDocument;
$dom->load('address-book-ns.xml');

foreach ($dom->getElementsByTagnameNS($ab, 'person') as $person) {
    $firstname = $person->getElementsByTagnameNS($ab, 'firstname');
    $firstname_text_value = $firstname->item(0)->firstChild->nodeValue;

    $lastname = $person->getElementsByTagnameNS($ab, 'lastname');
    $lastname_text_value = $lastname->item(0)->firstChild->nodeValue;

    print "$firstname_text_value $lastname_text_value\n";
}
```

Rasmus Lerdorf
Zeev Suraski

XML documents use a namespace prefix to handle the problem of bulky URLs. Since DOM methods use the actual name instead of a prefix, using a variable as a surrogate prefix makes code easier to read and ensures requests always use the same namespace.

Besides the modified getElementsByTagNameNS( ) method, this code is identical to the non-namespaced version in Example 5-6.

PHP 5 and SimpleXML

SimpleXML assumes that if you're reading an XML document with namespaces, then they were probably forced upon you by some namespace tyrant and you're wishing that the namespaces would just disappear. So it does its best to grant your request.

The code to read the namespaced version of the address book is almost identical to the non-namespaced version in Example 5-7, except that you specify the namespace with the children( ) method. This tells SimpleXML to look for elements inside a namespace. In Example 5-10, this method is used inside the foreach to find person elements.

Example 5-10. Reading namespaced XML with PHP 5 and SimpleXML

```
$ab = 'http://www.example.com/address-book/';
$sx = simplexml_load_file('address-book-ns.xml');

foreach ($sx->children($ab)->person as $person) {
    $firstname_text_value = $person->firstname;
    $lastname_text_value = $person->lastname;

    print "$firstname_text_value $lastname_text_value\n";
}
```

Rasmus Lerdorf
Zeev Suraski

The children( ) method takes a single argument, the namespace URL. The code $sx->children($ab)->person is equivalent to $sx->person, except that the call to children($ab) makes SimpleXML return only person elements inside of the http://www.example.com/address-book/ namespace.

Once the namespace has been set, SimpleXML remembers it and assumes any further children also live in that namespace. Therefore, you can access $person->firstname without calling children( ) again, but it is okay to do so:

```
$sx = simplexml_load_file('address-book-ns.xml');
$ab = 'http://www.example.com/address-book/';

foreach ($sx->children($ab)->person as $person) {
    $firstname_text_value = $person->children($ab)->firstname;
    $lastname_text_value = $person->children($ab)->lastname;

    print "$firstname_text_value $lastname_text_value\n";
}
```

Before and After: Searching XML with XPath

Except for the simplest documents, it's rarely easy to access the data you want one element at a time. As your XML files become increasingly complex and your parsing desires grow, using XPath is easier than filtering the data inside a foreach.

In PHP 4 and PHP 5, there is an XPath class that takes a DOM object as its constructor. You can then search the object and receive DOM nodes in reply. SimpleXML also supports XPath, and it's easier to use because its integrated into the SimpleXML object.

Whether you're using XPath with DOM or SimpleXML, both extensions support XML Namespaces. Therefore, you can find elements or attributes that live inside a namespace.

Reading an Address Book

Everything that can be done with the traditional DOM methods can also be done using XPath. The examples in this section also show how to search the address book.

PHP 4 and DOM

To create an XPath query under PHP 4, you must start with a DOM object and pass it off to an XPath context.

Here's how to retrieve the email addresses of everyone in the address book:

```
$dom = domxml_open_file('address-book.xml');

$xpath = xpath_new_context($dom);
$emails = $xpath->xpath_eval('/address-book/person/email');

// Can also be:
// $emails = xpath_eval($xpath, '/address-book/person/email');

foreach ($emails->nodeset as $e) {
    $tmp = $e->first_child();
    $email = $tmp->node_value();
    // do something with $email
}
```

After creating a new DOM object, call xpath_new_context( ) to initialize the XPath context. Query this context using xpath_eval( ), passing the XPath query as the first parameter (in this example, it's /people/person/email). This function returns an array of matching DOM nodes, which are stored in the array's nodeset element. Iterate through nodeset to act upon each node in turn.

By default, xpath_eval( ) operates upon the entire XML document. Search a subsection of the tree by passing in the subtree as a final parameter to xpath_eval( ). For instance, to gather all the first and last names of people in the address book, retrieve all the people nodes and query each node individually, as in Example 5-11.

Example 5-11. Using XPath with PHP 4 and DOM

```
$dom = domxml_open_file('address-book.xml');

$xpath = xpath_new_context($dom);
$person = $xpath->xpath_eval('/address-book/person');

foreach ($person->nodeset as $p) {
    $fn = $xpath->xpath_eval('firstname', $p);
    $tmp = $fn->nodeset[0]->first_child;
    $firstname = $tmp->node_value();

    $ln = $xpath->xpath_eval('lastname', $p);
    $tmp = $ln->nodeset[0]->first_child();
    $lastname = $tmp->node_value();

    print "$firstname $lastname\n";
}
```

Example 5-11. Using XPath with PHP 4 and DOM (continued)

Rasmus Lerdorf
Zeev Suraski

Inside the foreach, call xpath_eval( ) to retrieve the firstname and lastname nodes. Now, in addition to the XPath query, also pass $people to the method. This makes the search local to the node.

PHP 5 and DOM

DOM supports XPath queries, but again you do not perform the query directly on the DOM object itself. In keeping with PHP 5's superior OO capabilities, instead of the using the xpath_new_context( ) function, you create a DOMXPath object:

```
$dom = newDOMDocument;
$dom->load('address-book.xml');
$xpath = new DOMXPath($dom);
$email = $xpath->query('/address-book/person/email');
```

Instantiate DOMXPath by passing in a DOMDocument to the constructor. To execute the XPath query, call query( ) with the query text as your argument. This returns an iterable DOM node list of matching nodes. The email example is now:

```
$dom = newDOMDocument;
$dom->load('address-book.xml');
$xpath = new DOMXPath($dom);
$emails = $xpath->query('/address-book/person/email');

foreach ($emails as $e) {
    $email = $e->firstChild->nodeValue;
    // do something with $email
}
```

The fundamental logic is the same for this example and the PHP 4 DOM version; however, this code is cleaner. The XPath querying method no longer places the node list in a nodeset array element, so you iterate directly over the returned list.

Also, the PHP 4 example requires a temporary variable, $tmp, to hold $e->firstChild. With PHP 5, you can access $e->firstChild->nodeValue directly.

The more complex example, where you retrieve firstname and lastname, is significantly shorter than the PHP 4 version, as shown in Example 5-12.

Example 5-12. Using XPath with PHP 5 and DOM

```
$dom = newDOMDocument;
$dom->load('address-book.xml');
$xpath = new domXPath($dom);
$person = $xpath->query('/address-book/person');
```

Example 5-12. Using XPath with PHP 5 and DOM (continued)

```
foreach ($person as $p) {
    $fn = $xpath->query('firstname', $p);
    $firstname = $fn->item(0)->firstChild->nodeValue;

    $ln = $xpath->query('lastname', $p);
    $lastname = $ln->item(0)->firstChild->nodeValue;

    print "$firstname $lastname\n";
}
```

Rasmus Lerdorf
Zeev Suraski

Again, the temporary variable is eliminated, as well as the need to reference nodeset. However, the syntax to restrict query to a subset of the tree is the same as that in the email example—you still pass the subtree in as a second parameter.

PHP 5 and SimpleXML

In contrast to DOM, all SimpleXML objects have an integrated query( ) method. Calling this method queries the current object using XPath and returns a SimpleXML object containing the matching nodes, so you don't need to instantiate another object to use XPath. The method's one argument is your XPath query.

To find all the matching email addresses in Example 5-1's sample address book:

```
$s = simplexml_load_file('address-book.xml');
$emails = $s->xpath('/address-book/person/email');

foreach ($emails as $email) {
    // do something with $email
}
```

This is shorter because there's no need to dereference the firstNode or to take the nodeValue.

SimpleXML handles the more complicated example, too. Since xpath( ) returns SimpleXML objects, you can query them directly, as in Example 5-13.

Example 5-13. Using XPath with PHP 5 and SimpleXML

```
$s = simplexml_load_file('address-book.xml');
$people = $s->xpath('/address-book/person');

foreach($people as $p) {
    list($firstname) = $p->xpath('firstname');
    list($lastname) = $p->xpath('lastname');
```

Example 5-13. Using XPath with PHP 5 and SimpleXML (continued)

```
    print "$firstname $lastname\n";
}
```

Rasmus Lerdorf
Zeev Suraski

Since the inner XPath queries return only one element, use list to grab it from the array.

Reading an Address Book with Namespaces

When your elements and attributes live inside an XML namespace, you must indicate this in your XPath request. To refer to a namespaced element in XPath, append a namespace prefix and colon to the local name.

The revised XPath query to find email addresses is as follows:

```
/ab:address-book/ab:person/ab:email
```

Of course, this assumes that your XPath processor knows to map the prefix ab to the namespace http://www.example.com/address-book/. Sometimes this is done automatically; other times, you must do this in your program.

In PHP, every XPath extension provides a function that lets you associate prefixes and namespace URLs. In PHP 4, you have to call this function to register all namespaces. In PHP 5, both DOM and SimpleXML will automatically register any namespaces used in the document with their prefix.

Of course, you are always free to register another prefix for a namespace. This is a good idea if you don't produce all the XML documents you're consuming. If your data provider alters their namespace prefix, their document is still valid because a validator ignores prefixes and only examines the actual namespace URL. However, if you're relying on a specific prefix in your code, your application will break.

Regardless of whether you're using PHP 4 or PHP 5, to use XPath to find elements living in the default namespace, you must *always* manually assign a prefix to the namespace inside your program and then use that prefix in your XPath query. This is not a limitation of PHP, but a design "feature" of the XPath specification.

Example 5-14 modifies Example 5-2 to use a default namespace instead of the prefix ab.

Example 5-14. Example default namespaced XML address book

```
<address-book
    xmlns="http://www.example.com/address-book/">
    <person id="1">
```

Example 5-14. Example default namespaced XML address book (continued)

```
        <!--Rasmus Lerdorf-->
        <firstname>Rasmus</firstname>
        <lastname>Lerdorf</lastname>
        <city>Sunnyvale</city>
        <state>CA</state>
        <email>rasmus@php.net</email>
    </person>

    <person id="2">
        <!--Zeev Suraski-->
        <firstname>Zeev</firstname>
        <lastname>Suraski</lastname>
        <city>Tel Aviv</city>
        <state></state>
        <email>zeev@php.net</email>
    </person>
</address-book>
```

If you encounter an XML document like this, you *cannot* use the following XPath query:

```
/address-book/person/email
```

This query searches for non-namespaced elements, and your elements live in a namespace, even if they do not explicitly indicate this. You should create a prefix to use with the http://www.example.com/address-book/ namespace and use that in your queries. The code for this is shown in the following examples.

PHP 4 and DOM

Example 5-15 shows how to find first and last names in a namespaced XML document in PHP 4.

Example 5-15. Using XPath with PHP 4, DOM, and namespaces

```
$dom = domxml_open_file('address-book-ns.xml');
$xpath = new domXPath($dom);
$xpath->xpath_register_ns('ab', 'http://www.example.com/address-book/');
$person = $xpath->query('/ab:address-book/ab:person');

foreach ($person as $p) {
    $fn = $xpath->query('ab:firstname', $p);
    $firstname = $fn[0]->firstChild->nodeValue;

    $ln = $xpath->query('ab:lastname', $p);
    $lastname = $ln[0]->firstChild->nodeValue;

    print "$firstname $lastname\n";
}

Rasmus Lerdorf
Zeev Suraski
```

There are two differences between this version and the non-namespaced one. First, there's a call to xpath_register_ns() to associate ab with the namespace. Second, wherever there are XPath queries, all elements are prefixed with ab: (for example, /ab:address-book/ab:person).

PHP 5 and DOM

In PHP 5, there are few differences between Example 5-16 and the non-namespaced version because the DOMXPath object automatically registers ab as a prefix.

Example 5-16. Using XPath with PHP 5, DOM, and namespaces

```
$dom = newDOMDocument;
$dom->load('address-book-ns.xml');
$xpath = new DOMXPath($dom);
$person = $xpath->query('/ab:address-book/ab:person');

foreach ($person as $p) {
    $fn = $xpath->query('ab:firstname', $p);
    $firstname = $fn->item(0)->firstChild->nodeValue;

    $ln = $xpath->query('ab:lastname', $p);
    $lastname = $ln->item(0)->firstChild->nodeValue;

    print "$firstname $lastname\n";
}
```

Rasmus Lerdorf
Zeev Suraski

As you can see, the changes occur only in the XPath query syntax.

To register a namespace, call the DOMXPath object's registerNamespace() method. For example, this registers ab:

```
$xpath->registerNamespace('ab', 'http://www.example.com/address-book/');
```

PHP 5 and SimpleXML

SimpleXML also registers namespaces for you, so it too requires minimal modifications, as shown in Example 5-17.

Example 5-17. Using XPath with PHP 5, SimpleXML, and namespaces

```
$s = simplexml_load_file('address-book-ns.xml');
$people = $s->xpath('/ab:address-book/ab:person');

foreach($people as $p) {
    list($firstname) = $p->xpath('ab:firstname');
    list($lastname) = $p->xpath('ab:lastname');
```

Example 5-17. Using XPath with PHP 5, SimpleXML, and namespaces (continued)

```
    print "$firstname $lastname\n";
}
```

Rasmus Lerdorf
Zeev Suraski

You cannot currently register namespaces using SimpleXML. This means that the only way to access elements in the default namespace is to invoke a cumbersome XPath expression.

Example 5-18 shows how to query the address book when the elements live inside a default namespace, as in Example 5-14.

Example 5-18. Using XPath with PHP 5, SimpleXML, and default namespaces

```
$s = simplexml_load_file('address-book-ns.xml');
$ab = 'http://www.example.com/address-book/';
$people = $s->xpath("/*[local-name( )='address-book' and
                        namespace-uri( )='$ab']
                     /*[local-name( )='person'          and
                        namespace-uri( )='$ab']");

foreach($people as $p) {
    list($firstname) = $p->xpath("*[local-name( )='firstname' and
                                    namespace-uri( )='$ab']");
    list($lastname)  = $p->xpath("*[local-name( )='lastname'  and
                                    namespace-uri( )='$ab']");

    print "$firstname $lastname\n";
}
```

Rasmus Lerdorf
Zeev Suraski

This complex XPath expression uses the local-name( ) and namespace-uri( ) XPath functions to search for nodes based on the namespace URL, instead of the more concise syntax that uses namespace prefixes.

For more on XPath, see "XPath" in Appendix A.

Reading XML as Events with SAX

SAX is the original XML extension available with PHP. It's also the best supported, since expat has been bundled with PHP since the release of PHP 4. PHP's SAX support in PHP 5 and PHP 4 is the same. The only difference is a behind-the-scenes change.

Since PHP 5 unbundles expat in favor of libxml2, a compatibility layer maps SAX calls from one parser to the other. Therefore, your SAX applications should work exactly as they did under expat. Theory, however, doesn't always equal reality. There are a few differences that can slip you up.

Here's a list of the major incompatibilities:

Namespace parsing with `xml_parser_create_ns( )`
> The `xml_parser_create_ns( )` function, which is a namespace-aware version of `xml_parser_create( )` has problems with default namespaces under old versions of `libxml2`. Therefore, this function is disabled unless you build PHP using `libxml2` Version 2.6 or greater.

Fallback handling with `xml_set_default_handler( )`
> With expat, all events that lack a handler are processed by the default handler. With `libxml2`, you must define a specific handler for each event. The default handler only handles comments and internal entities, such as `&amp;`.

External entity handling with `xml_set_external_entity_ref_handler( )`
> This function works under `libxml2`. Under expat, the default handler captures external entities like `<!ENTITY rasmus SYSTEM "rasmus.ent">`.

Before and After: Creating New XML Documents

If you want to create a new XML document, you have two choices. Since XML is text, you can always print it yourself using `print`. The other option is to use DOM.

With DOM you assemble an entire XML document by calling methods in PHP. When you're done, tell DOM to convert your DOM object into XML.

At first, it is much easier to create XML yourself and avoid DOM. Just as extracting information from a DOM object requires multiple steps, adding new nodes to a DOM tree isn't easy. However, using DOM does have some benefits:

- Your XML is always well-formed and without syntax errors.
- DOM correctly outputs your document in any one of many different character encodings.
- You can easily validate your object against a schema.

SimpleXML does not allow you to create XML documents.

Creating an Address Book

The code examples in this section create the address book from Example 5-1 and populate it with the first entry.

PHP 4 and DOM

Example 5-19 shows how to create an address book in PHP 4.

Example 5-19. Creating XML with PHP 4 and DOM

```
// create a new document
$dom = domxml_new_doc('1.0');

$people = $dom->append_child($dom->create_element('address-book'));

$person = $people->append_child($dom->create_element('person'));
$person->set_attribute('id', 1);
$person->append_child($dom->create_comment('Rasmus Lerdorf'));

$e = $person->append_child($dom->create_element('firstname'));
$e->append_child($dom->create_text_node('Rasmus'));

$e = $person->append_child($dom->create_element('lastname'));
$e->append_child($dom->create_text_node('Lerdorf'));

$e = $person->append_child($dom->create_element('city'));
$e->append_child($dom->create_text_node('Sunnyvale'));

$e = $person->append_child($dom->create_element('state'));
$e->append_child($dom->create_text_node('CA'));

$e = $person->append_child($dom->create_element('email'));
$e->append_child($dom->create_text_node('rasmus@php.net'));

echo $dom->dump_mem(true);
```

This prints:

```
<?xml version="1.0"?>
<address-book>
  <person id="1">
<!--Rasmus Lerdorf-->
    <firstname>Rasmus</firstname>
    <lastname>Lerdorf</lastname>
    <city>Sunnyvale</city>
    <state>CA</state>
    <email>rasmus@php.net</email>
  </person>
</address-book>
```

The create_element( ) method creates a new XML element. However, it's not actually attached to the DOM tree: the element is just floating out in the ether, waiting to be placed into a document. The next call, append_child( ), attaches the node to the tree under the object. Similarly, the comment is created using create_comment( ) and is then added to the node.

Therefore, adding new text elements is largely a repetitive process of create and append. For each entry in the address book, both an element and a text node must be created. Those objects are then passed to append_child( ), to insert them into the DOM tree.

PHP 5 and DOM

In PHP 5, DOM objects are real PHP objects. This means there are now two ways to interact with DOM. The first way is similar to PHP 4's: you create new nodes by calling methods on a DOM object. However, you can also instantiate nodes as actual PHP objects.

Example 5-20 shows how to make the address book using the PHP 5 DOM syntax.

Example 5-20. Creating XML with PHP 5 and DOM

```
$dom = new DOMDocument('1.0', 'utf-8');

$people = $dom->appendChild($dom->createElement('address-book'));
$person = $people->appendChild($dom->createElement('person'));
$person->setAttribute('id', 1);

$person->appendChild($dom->createComment('Rasmus Lerdorf'));
$person->appendChild($dom->createElement('firstname', 'Rasmus'));
$person->appendChild($dom->createElement('lastname', 'Lerdorf'));
$person->appendChild($dom->createElement('city', 'Sunnyvale'));
$person->appendChild($dom->createElement('state', 'CA'));
$person->appendChild($dom->createElement('email', 'rasmus@php.net'));

$dom->formatOutput = true; // indent elements
print $dom->saveXML();

<?xml version="1.0" encoding="utf-8"?>
<address-book>
  <person id="1">
<!--Rasmus Lerdorf-->
    <firstname>Rasmus</firstname>
    <lastname>Lerdorf</lastname>
    <city>Sunnyvale</city>
    <state>CA</state>
    <email>rasmus@php.net</email>
  </person>
</address-book>
```

The DOMDocument constructor takes two optional arguments: the XML version number and the document encoding. At the time of this writing, most people use XML 1.0 (the W3C released 1.1 on February 4, 2004), and so the default value for this parameter is 1.0. Typical encoding types include UTF-8,

UTF-16, and ISO-8859-1 (aka ISO-Latin-1), but you aren't restricted to these three. You can't set the encoding of a DOM document in PHP 4.

Other methods act like they do in PHP 4, but they do not have underscores in their names.

The createElement( ) method has one new feature. If you pass in only one argument, it makes an element with that name. This behavior is similar to how create_element( ) works in PHP 4. However, if you pass in two arguments, the second parameter makes DOMElement create a text element with that string and append it as a child.

DOM supports the full set of XML items: elements, attributes, text nodes, comments, CDATA sections, PIs, and so forth. It also lets you create document fragments, which are identical to DOM objects but don't require the XML stored inside of them to be well-formed. XML, for instance, limits a document to a single root node, but a document fragment can have multiple roots. You might want this setup if you're planning on appending this fragment inside of a XML document, where its layout is valid.

Creating a DOM node of another type, such as a comment, is identical to the earlier example. You just substitute createComment( ) for createElement( ). Table 5-3 lists the all these functions, what they are called in PHP 4, and what they look like in an XML document.

Table 5-3. DOM node-creation functions

Description	PHP 4	PHP 5 method	PHP 5 class
Element	create_ element(name)	createElement(name)	new DOMElement(name)
Attribute	create_ attribute(name, value)	createAttribute (name, value)	new DOMAttribute (name, value)
Text	create_text_ node(text)	createTextNode(text)	new DOMText(text)
Comment	create_ comment(comment)	createComment (comment)	new DOMComment(comment)
CDATA	create_cdata_ section(CDATA)	createCDATASection (CDATA)	new DOMCDATASection(CDATA)
Processing instruction	create_ processing_ instruction (target, pi)	createProcessing Instruction (target[, pi])	new DOMProcessing Instruction (target[, pi])
Document fragment	N/A	createDocument Fragment( )	new DOMDocumentFragment

CDATA sections are similar to text nodes, but inside a CDATA section you don't need to escape entities and other markup characters, because they're treated as literal text.

The object-oriented alternative looks like Example 5-21.

Example 5-21. Creating XML with PHP 5 and DOM using OO

```
$dom = new DOMDocument('1.0', 'utf-8');

$people = $dom->appendChild(new DOMElement('address-book'));
$person = $people->appendChild(new DOMElement('person'));
$person->appendChild(new DOMAttr('id', 1));

$person->appendChild(new DOMComment('Rasmus Lerdorf'));
$person->appendChild(new DOMElement('firstname', 'Rasmus'));
$person->appendChild(new DOMElement('lastname', 'Lerdorf'));
$person->appendChild(new DOMElement('city', 'Sunnyvale'));
$person->appendChild(new DOMElement('state', 'CA'));
$person->appendChild(new DOMElement('email', 'rasmus@php.net'));

$dom->formatOutput = true; // indent elements
print $dom->saveXML();
```

In this version, it's easier to see when you're creating an object and what its type is. The appendChild( ) method is now used even to add new attributes. Instead of calling setAttribute( ), you now append a new DOMAttr object.

Before and After: Transforming XML with XSLT

PHP 4 has a separate XSLT extension that relies on the Sablotron XSLT parsing library. In PHP 5, that's replaced by integrated XSLT support with the DOM functions. Also, libxslt has replaced Sablotron as the processor of choice.

PHP 4

In PHP 4, the XSLT extension uses resources instead of objects:

```
$xml = 'data.xml';
$xsl = 'stylesheet.xsl';

$xslt = xslt_create();
$results = xslt_process($xslt, $xml, $xsl);

if (!$results) {
    error_log("XSLT Error: #".xslt_errno($xslt).": ".xslt_error($xslt));
```

```
}

    xslt_free($xslt);
```

You pass xslt_process( ) the filenames of your XML and XSLT documents, and it loads the XML from disk. You can also read in from a variable (using the weird argument syntax), but not from a DOM object.

PHP 5

Using XSLT in PHP 5 involves two main steps: preparing the XSLT object and then triggering the actual transformation for each XML file.

To begin, load in the stylesheet using DOM. Then, instantiate a new XSLTProcessor object, and import the XSLT document by passing in your newly created DOM object to the importStylesheet( ) method.

```
// Load XSL template
$xsl = newDOMDocument;
$xsl->load('stylesheet.xsl');

// Create new XSLTProcessor
$xslt = new XSLTProcessor( );
// Load stylesheet
$xslt->importStylesheet($xsl);
```

Now the transformer is up and running. You can transform any DOM object in one of three ways: into a string, into a file, or back into another DOM object.

```
// Load XML input file
$xml = newDOMDocument;
$xml->load('data.xml');

// Transform to string
$results = $xslt->transformToXML($xml);

// Transform to a file
$results = $xslt->transformToURI($xml, 'results.txt');

// Transform to DOM object
$results = $xslt->transformToDoc($xml);
```

When you call transformToXML( ) or transformToDoc( ), the extension returns the result string or object. In contrast, transformToURI( ) returns the number of bytes written to the file, not the actual document.

These methods return false when they fail, so to accurately check for failure, write:

```
if (false === ($results = $xslt->transformToXML($xml))) {
    // an error occurred
}
```

Using = = = prevents a return value of 0 from being confused with an actual error.

Setting Parameters

You can pass data from PHP into your XSLT stylesheet with the setParameter( ) method. This allows you to do things such as filter data in your stylesheet based on user input.

For example, the program in Example 5-22 allows you to find people based on their city.

Example 5-22. Setting XSLT parameters from PHP

```
// This could also come from $_GET['city'];
$city = 'Tel Aviv';

$dom  = new DOMDocument;
$$dom->load('address-book.xml');
$xsl  = new DOMDocument;
$xsl->load('stylesheet.xsl');

$xslt = new XSLTProcessor( );
$xslt->importStylesheet($xsl);
$xslt->setParameter(NULL, 'city', $city);
print $xslt->transformToXML($dom);
```

The program uses the following stylesheet:

```
<?xml version="1.0" ?>
<xsl:stylesheet version="1.0"
  xmlns:xsl="http://www.w3.org/1999/XSL/Transform">

<xsl:template match="@*|node( )">
  <xsl:copy>
    <xsl:apply-templates select="@*|node( )"/>
  </xsl:copy>
</xsl:template>

<xsl:template match="/address-book/person">
  <xsl:if test="city=$city">
    <xsl:copy>
      <xsl:apply-templates select="@*|node( )"/>
    </xsl:copy>
  </xsl:if>
</xsl:template>
</xsl:stylesheet>
```

The program and stylesheet combine to produce the following results:

```
<?xml version="1.0"?>
<address-book>
```

```
    <person id="2">
        <!--Zeev Suraski-->
        <firstname>Zeev</firstname>
        <lastname>Suraski</lastname>
        <city>Tel Aviv</city>
        <state/>
        <email>zeev@php.net</email>
    </person>
</address-book>
```

The PHP script does a standard XSLT transformation, except that it calls
`$xslt->setParameter(NULL, 'city', $city)`. The first argument is the
parameter's namespace, the second is the parameter's name, and the third is
the parameter's value.

Here, the value stored in the PHP variable $city—in this case, Tel Aviv—is
assigned to the XSLT parameter city, which does not live under a
namespace. This is equal to placing the following in an XSLT file:

```
<xsl:param name="city">Tel Aviv</xsl:param>
```

You usually access a parameter inside a stylesheet like you do a PHP variable, by placing a dollar sign ($) in front of its name. The stylesheet example
creates a template that matches /address-book/person nodes.

Inside the template, you test whether city=$city; in other words, is the city
child of the current node equal to the value of the city parameter? If there's a
match, the children are copied along; otherwise, the records are eliminated.

In this case, city is set to Tel Aviv, so Rasmus's record is removed and
Zeev's remains.

Calling PHP Functions from Stylesheets

XSLT parameters are great when you need to communicate from PHP to
XSLT. However, they're not very useful when you require the reverse. You
can't use parameters to extract information from the stylesheet during the
transformation. Ideally, you could call PHP functions from a stylesheet and
pass information back to PHP.

PHP 4 solves this using a Sablotron feature known as scheme handlers.
Scheme handlers aren't available in PHP 5, because PHP doesn't use the
Sablotron XSLT processor. However, there's a new method that duplicates
this functionality: registerPHPFunctions( ). Here's how it's enabled:

```
$xslt = new XSLTProcessor();
$xslt->registerPHPFunctions();
```

This allows you to call any PHP function from your stylesheets. It's not
available by default, because it presents a security risk if you're processing
stylesheets controlled by other people.

Both built-in and user-defined functions work. Inside your stylesheet, you must define a namespace and call the function() or functionString() methods:

```
<?xml version="1.0" ?>
<xsl:stylesheet version="1.0"
    xmlns:xsl="http://www.w3.org/1999/XSL/Transform"
    xmlns:php="http://php.net/xsl"
    xsl:extension-element-prefixes="php">

<xsl:template match="/">
    <xsl:value-of select="php:function('strftime', '%c')" />
</xsl:template>

</xsl:stylesheet>
```

At the top of the stylesheet, define the namespace for PHP: http://php.net/xsl. This example sets the namespace prefix to php. Also, set the extension-element-prefixes value to php so XSLT knows these are functions.

To call a PHP function, reference php:function(). The first parameter is the function name; additional parameters are the function arguments. In this case, the function name is strftime and the one argument is %c. This causes strftime to return the current date and time.

Example 5-23 uses this stylesheet, stored as *stylesheet.xsl*, to process a single-element XML document.

Example 5-23. Transforming XML with PHP 5, XSLT, and PHP functions

```
$dom  = new DOMDocument;
$dom->loadXML('<blank/>');
$xsl  = new DOMDocument
$xsl->load('stylesheet.xsl');

$xslt = new XSLTProcessor();
$xslt->importStylesheet($xsl);
$xslt->registerPHPFunctions();
print $xslt->transformToXML($dom);
```

Mon Jul 22 19:10:21 2004

This works like standard XSLT processing, but there's an additional call to registerPHPFunctions() to activate PHP function support.

You can also return DOM objects. This example takes the XML address book and mangles all the email addresses to turn the hostname portion into three dots. Everything else in the document is left untouched:

```
function mangle_email($nodes) {
    return preg_replace('/([^@\s]+)@([-a-z0-9]+\.)+[a-z]{2,}/is',
                        '$1@...',
                        $nodes[0]->nodeValue);
```

```
        }

        $dom  = new DOMDocument;
        $dom->load('address-book.xml');
        $xsl  = new DOMDocument
        $xsl->load('stylesheet.xsl');

        $xslt = new XSLTProcessor();
        $xslt->importStylesheet($xsl);
        $xslt->registerPhpFunctions();
        print $xslt->transformToXML($dom);
```

Inside your stylesheet, create a special template for /address-book/person/email elements:

```
        <?xml version="1.0" ?>
        <xsl:stylesheet version="1.0"
          xmlns:xsl="http://www.w3.org/1999/XSL/Transform"
          xmlns:php="http://php.net/xsl"
          xsl:extension-element-prefixes="php">

        <xsl:template match="@*|node()">
          <xsl:copy>
            <xsl:apply-templates select="@*|node()"/>
          </xsl:copy>
        </xsl:template>

        <xsl:template match="/address-book/person/email">
          <xsl:copy>
            <xsl:value-of select="php:function('mangle_email', node())" />
          </xsl:copy>
        </xsl:template>
        </xsl:stylesheet>
```

The first template ensures that the elements aren't modified, while the second passes the current node to PHP for mangling. In the second template, the mangle_email() function is passed the current node, represented in XPath as node(), instead of a string. Be sure not to place the node inside quotation marks, or you'll pass the literal text node().

Nodes becomes DOM objects inside PHP and always arrive in an array. In this case, mangle_email() knows there's always only one object and it's a DOMText object, so the email address is located in $nodes[0]->nodeValue.

When you know that you're only interested in the text portion of a node, use the functionString() function. This function converts nodes to PHP strings, which allows you to omit the array access and nodeValue dereference:

```
        function mangle_email($email) {
            return preg_replace('/([^@\s]+)@([-a-z0-9]+\.)+[a-z]{2,}/is',
                               '$1@...',
                               $email);
```

```
}
```

```
// all other code is the same as before
```

The new stylesheet template for /address-book/person/email is:

```
<xsl:template match="/address-book/person/email">
  <xsl:copy>
    <xsl:value-of
        select="php:functionString('mangle_email', node( ))" />
  </xsl:copy>
</xsl:template>
```

The mangle_email( ) function now processes $email instead of $nodes[0]-> nodeValue because the template now calls the functionString( ) function.

The function( ) and functionString( ) methods are incredibly useful, but using them undermines the premise of XSL as a language-neutral transformation engine. When you call PHP from XSLT, you cannot easily reuse your stylesheets in projects that use Java, Perl, and other languages, because they cannot call PHP. Therefore, you should consider the trade-off between convenience and portability before using this feature.

Validating Against a Schema

Schemas are a way to define a specification for your XML documents. In PHP 4, there is no built-in way to validate an XML document against any type of schema. The PEAR XML_DTD package (available at *http://pear.php.net/ package/XML_DTD*) provides a way to validate XML files against a Document Type Definition (DTD). However, because it uses SAX, it is not easy to combine DTD validation with DOM.

PHP 5 allows you to validate files against DTDs, XML Schema, and RelaxNG schema. The DOM extension supports all three types, while SimpleXML provides only an XML Schema validator.

PHP 5 and DOM

Validating any file using DOM is a similar process, regardless of the underlying schema format. To validate, call a validation method on a DOM object. It returns true if the file passes. If there's an error, it returns false and prints a message to the error log. There is no method for "capturing" the error message.

```
$file = 'address-book.xml';
$schema = 'address-book.xsd';
$ab = new DOMDocument;
$ab->load($file);
```

```
if ($ab->schemaValidate($schema)) {
    print "$file is valid.\n";
} else {
    print "$file is invalid.\n";
}
```

If the schema is stored in a string, use DOMDocument::schemaValidateSource( ) instead of schemaValidate( ).

Table 5-4 lists all the validation methods.

Table 5-4. DOM schema validation methods

Method name	Schema type	Data location
schemaValidate	XML Schema	File
schemaValidateSource	XML Schema	String
relaxNGValidate	RelaxNG	File
relaxNGValidateSource	RelaxNG	String
validate	DTD	N/A

All of the validation methods behave in a similar manner, so you only need to switch the method name in the previous example to switch to a different validation scheme.

Both XML Schema and RelaxNG support validation against files and strings. You can validate a DOM object only against the DTD defined at the top of the XML document.

CHAPTER 6

Iterators and SPL

Iteration is a key component of PHP programming. Whenever you loop through the elements of an array, the rows in a database, the files in a directory, or the lines of an HTML table, that's iteration.

Iteration takes many forms in PHP, but the most popular two are foreach and while loops. For example:

```
foreach ($array as $key => $value) {
    // iterate through array elements
}

reset($array);
while (list($key, $value) = each($array)) {
    // iterate through array elements
}
```

Although both of these constructs solve the same problem, foreach is shorter and easier. Iteration using a while loop can also introduce subtle bugs into your code, like in this example:

```
// $path is valid and readable
$dir = opendir($path);
while ($file = readdir($dir)) {
    print "$file\n";
}
closedir($dir);
```

This code opens and iterates through files in a directory. When there are no more files, readdir( ) returns false, the while ends, and the directory is closed. It works perfectly.

It works perfectly, that is, until someone places a file named *0* in the directory. Then, $file is set to 0, and the loop terminates early because while (0) evaluates as false. Oops.

The correct way to read files from a directory is as follows:

```
while (false !== ($file = readdir($dir))) {
    print "$file\n";
}
```

You need to do a strict equality check using the === operator. Even == gives you the wrong results because PHP autoconverts $file from a string to a Boolean.

Since there's no reason for you (or anyone else) to remember this, PHP 5 has an improved foreach that iterates through certain types of objects in a controlled manner. These objects are called iterators.

Iterators help eliminate problems in your code. For instance, the Standard PHP Library (SPL) extension provides a DirectoryIterator:

```
foreach (new DirectoryIterator($path) as $file) {
    print "$file\n";
}
```

This example produces the same results as the earlier code that uses the directory functions, but this code is shorter and safer because you cannot forget the === comparison.

SPL contains both standalone iterators and iterators meant to be chained together in a sequence. For example, you can pipe the output of a DirectoryIterator to an iterator that discards files that don't end in .html. This design helps you create a series of modular iterators that you can quickly combine to solve tasks.

SPL is bundled with PHP 5 and enabled by default, so it's essentially part of PHP 5 itself. Table 6-3 at the end of this chapter has a complete overview of all the different classes with Iterator in their name, including some not covered in this chapter.

Despite all these useful iterators, you're bound to want additional ones. Fortunately, iterators don't have to be coded in C. You can easily code iterators in PHP, for looping through LDAP or IMAP listings, or even cycling through results fetched from Amazon.com using REST.

You can also embed an iterator inside a class using aggregation. When the object is iterated inside a foreach loop, the embedded iterator is used, effectively turning your objects into iterators.

For example, you can iterate over SQLite query results without explicitly fetching each row:

```
$db = new SQLiteDatabase($database);
foreach($db->query($sql) as $row) {
    // operate on $row
}
```

The SQLiteResult class has a built-in iterator that calls the object's fetch( ) method during iteration, and you can do the same for your own PHP classes. Normally, when you iterate over an object with foreach, PHP cycles through the object's properties. In PHP 5, you can override this behavior and make PHP loop over whatever you decide.

This chapter starts with iteration basics, by first showing how to iterate through a directory using PHP 4 and then comparing that to PHP 5's DirectoryIterator iterator. Afterward, there's a version of DirectoryIterator written in PHP.

The next iterator discussed in this chapter simplifies an example from earlier in the book: handling the results of MySQL multi-queries. Without an iterator, navigating through multi-query results is tricky, but this challenge is made simple using MySQLiQueryIterator.

Iterators don't have to work alone. You can combine them to filter and limit results. SPL has *meta-iterators*, or iterators that need to be fed another iterator to be useful.

For instance, using the FilterIterator in conjunction with a DirectoryIterator allows you to eliminate files that don't end in *.html* from your directory output.

Then there's the LimitIterator, which allows you to "page" through an iterator's results, using the same syntax as the SQL LIMIT clause. Combining it with the SimpleXMLIterator lets you redeploy your database logic onto XML documents.

After regular iterators, the chapter moves on to recursive iterators. Normal iterators only work for a single list of items, but it's quite common to have lists within lists. Directories contain files, but they can also contain other directories. To recurse through multiple levels, you need to upgrade your iterator to handle this complexity.

SPL's RecursiveDirectoryIterator class solves this task. Again, this iterator is recreated in PHP, to demonstrate the additional methods.

Once that's complete, there's a slight shift as this chapter moves back to traditional array and object iteration. PHP 5 brings a few changes to these old favorites to account for property access restrictions.

The chapter then shows how to implement the IteratorAggregate method. This lets a class return a custom iterator that you control, instead of using PHP's default behavior.

Finally, the last section lists all the SPL classes and interfaces, so you can get a bird's-eye view of the material and see what else SPL has to offer.

Before and After: Using Iterators

This section shows you how to use and write basic iterators. It begins by comparing directory iteration with and without an iterator and then shows you how to write a DirectoryIterator in PHP.

All the directory iteration examples process the set of files shown in Figure 6-1.

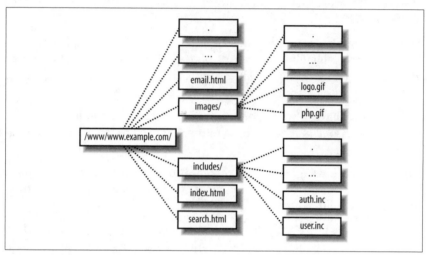

Figure 6-1. Files located in /www/www.example.com/

PHP 4: Reading Files in a Directory

In PHP 4, you read files by using opendir( ), readdir( ), and closedir( ):

```
$dir = opendir('/www/www.example.com/');
while (false !== ($file = readdir($dir))) {
    print "$file\n";
}
closedir($dir);

.
..
email.html
images
includes
index.html
search.html
```

The opendir( ) function returns a directory handle. Then, you usually pass the handle to readdir( ) inside a while loop. When iteration is complete, you clean up with closedir( ).

As noted in the introduction, this looks simple, but you can run into problems if you're not careful. The check inside the while cannot be `$f = readdir($d)`, because then a file named *0* would terminate the loop.

The results from the preceding code include files of all types, including directories. To filter out directories, call `is_file( )` on the results:

```
$d = '/www/www.example.com/';

$dir = opendir($d);
while (false !== ($file = readdir($dir))) {
    if (is_file($d . DIRECTORY_SEPARATOR . $file)) {
        print "$file\n";
    }
}
closedir($dir);
email.html
index.html
search.html
```

Again, this check requires more subtlety than it should. If you don't use the PHP constant `DIRECTORY_SEPARATOR` and instead hardcode a slash, your script will break if it's run on a Windows machine.

PHP 5: Reading Files in a Directory

A better solution is to use the directory iterator class, `DirectoryIterator`. This class is part of SPL, so you don't need to `include` it before you use it.

`DirectoryIterator` takes a pathname as its constructor and then lets you loop through the files in the path:

```
$dir = new DirectoryIterator('/www/www.example.com/');
foreach ($dir as $file) {
    print "$file\n";
}
.
..
email.html
images
includes
index.html
search.html
```

This code produces the same output as the more complex while loop that uses the directory functions.

Also, eliminating directories doesn't require the use of a special PHP constant:

```
$dir = new DirectoryIterator('/www/www.example.com/');
foreach ($dir as $file) {
    if (! $file->isDir()) {
```

```
        print "$file\n";
    }
}
email.html
index.html
search.html
```

Using the isDir( ) method neatly sidesteps the platform-specific issue since this detail is handled only once, inside the iterator itself.

DirectoryIterator Methods

The isDir( ) method is not the only method of the DirectoryIterator class. Other methods return the file's full path, the current path, and determine whether the file is a "dot." In Unix and Mac OS X, every directory automatically contains two special files named dot (.) and dot dot (..), which are links to the current directory and parent directory, respectively. If you're not careful, they can wreak havoc upon directory processing.

Table 6-1 lists some of the major DirectoryIterator methods.

Table 6-1. Important DirectoryIterator methods

Name	Return type	Description
getPath( )	String	Returns the opened path (e.g., */www/www.example.com*)
getFilename( )	String	Returns the current filename (e.g., *index.html*)
getPathname( )	String	Returns the current path and file (e.g., */www/www.example.com/index.html*)
isDir( )	Boolean	Determines whether the current file is a directory
isDot( )	Boolean	Determines whether the current file is a dot file (i.e., "." or "..")

Implementing the Iterator Interface

In the previous example, an SPL class was used as an iterator. However, it's also useful to write your own iterators. This isn't difficult—iterators are just PHP classes that implement the Iterator interface.

The Iterator interface is a set of five methods: rewind( ), valid( ), key( ), current( ), and next( ). (The names are similar to the old PHP array iteration functions, but they don't act identically, so don't confuse them.) These methods tell PHP how to pull the next item from your list, when there are no additional items, how to reset the list and start over from the beginning, and so forth.

When iterating over an object using foreach( ), the methods are called like this:

```
$it = new MyIterator; // MyIterator is an class that implements Iterator
for ($it->rewind(); $it->valid(); $it->next()) {
    $key = $it->key();
    $value = $it->current();
    // code inside the foreach starts here:
    print "$key: $value\n";
}
unset($it);
```

You must implement all five methods. However, depending on how your class operates, some of them can be empty.

Table 6-2 describes what each method does and what values they need to return. You cannot pass any information to these methods; instead, you must store data in object properties.

Table 6-2. Iterator interface methods

Method	Description	Returns
rewind()	Resets iterator list to its start	Void (nothing)
valid()	Says if there are additional items left in the list	true if additional items; false otherwise
next()	Moves iterator to the next item in the list	Void (nothing)
key()	Returns the key of the current item	Mixed
current()	Returns the current item	Mixed

Example 6-1 demonstrates an implementation of DirectoryIterator in PHP.

Example 6-1. Implementing DirectoryIterator in PHP

```
// Class is called MyDirectoryIterator to prevent a
// namespace clash with SPL's DirectoryIterator.
class MyDirectoryIterator implements Iterator {

    protected $dir;
    protected $path;

    protected $key;
    protected $file;
    protected $valid;

    public function __construct($path) {
        $this->dir = opendir($path);
        $this->path = $path;
    }

    public function __destruct() {
        closedir($this->dir);
    }
```

Example 6-1. Implementing DirectoryIterator in PHP (continued)

```
    protected function readDir( ) {
        return ($this->file = readdir($this->dir)) !== false;
    }

    public function rewind( ) {
        rewinddir($this->dir);
        $this->key = 0;
        $this->valid = $this->readDir( );
    }

    public function valid( ) {
        return $this->valid;
    }

    public function key( ) {
        return $this->key;
    }

    public function current( ) {
        return $this->file;
    }

    public function next( ) {
        $this->key++;
        $this->valid = $this->readDir( );
    }
}
```

The constructor takes a pathname, just as DirectoryIterator does, and stores the directory handle in a protected property named $dir. It also saves the path, but this property isn't used right now—it's for an example later in the chapter. (If only all programs could be written with this kind of uncanny foresight.) The destructor closes the handle using closedir( ) when the iterator is used up.

The rewind( ) method calls rewinddir( ) on the handle to restore the internal directory pointer to the start. It also sets the count to 0. Since there's no natural notion of a key for a directory file, this class mimics the behavior of DirectoryIterator. The first file is given a key of 0, the next gets a key of 1, and so forth. Last, it reads in a file by calling readDir( ) and sets $valid to the result.

The readDir( ) method calls the PHP function readdir( ) and saves the result in the $file property. If this function returns false, then readDir( ) also returns false; otherwise, readDir( ) returns true. Although it's still necessary to strictly check the return value of readdir( ), you can isolate this comparison to a single location within your entire code base. When common code isn't duplicated again and again, it's easier to repair bugs because you can fix them all at once.

Using the PHP directory functions, there's no way to check if a directory has another file without trying to retrieve the file. Therefore, valid( ) just returns the value of the valid property that's set in readDir( ).

The key( ) and current( ) methods return the value stored in the object properties count and current. Since rewind( ) is called before either of these are accessed, they will always be set.

The next( ) method is quite similar to rewind( ). It also reads in a new file and sets $valid accordingly, but instead of resetting $key to 0, it increments it by 1.

Use MyDirectoryIterator exactly how you use DirectoryIterator:

```
$dir = new MyDirectoryIterator('/www/www.example.com/');
foreach ($dir as $file) {
    print "$file\n";
}
.

..
email.html
images
includes
index.html
search.html
```

With this implementation, you can't add additional methods, such as isDir( ), to the class, because the class returns the filename instead of a file object, just like DirectoryIterator. However, you can modify MyDirectoryIterator to create a MyFile object that allows you to call methods on $file.

MySQL Query Iterator

Iterators are for more than just directories. You can also apply them to database queries. In Chapter 3, you saw MySQL's new mysqli_multi_query( ) function, which is used to send multiple queries at once. However, processing involves a minimum of four functions and a do/while loop. Yikes!

Despite these complexities, the essential action is iteration: in this case, you're iterating through database results. The iteration requires more steps than a normal query, but in its essence, it's just iteration.

This is the perfect task to encapsulate inside an Iterator. The MySQLiQueryIterator takes a nasty string of code:

```
if (mysqli_multi_query($db, $query)) {
        do {
```

```
        if ($result = mysqli_store_result($db)) {
            while ($row = mysqli_fetch_row($result)) {
                print "$row[0]\n";
            }
            mysqli_free_result($result);
        }
    } while (mysqli_next_result($db));
}
```

and transforms it into something clear and simple:

```
foreach (new MySQLiQueryIterator($db, $query) as $result) {
    if ($result) {
        while ($row = mysqli_fetch_row($result)) {
            print "$row[0]\n";
        }
    }
}
```

Example 6-2 demonstrates the code for MySQLiQueryIterator.

Example 6-2. Implementing a MySQL multi-query iterator

```
class MySQLiQueryIterator implements Iterator {
    protected $link;
    protected $query;
    protected $key;
    protected $valid;
    protected $result;

    public function __construct($link, $query) {
        $this->link = $link;
        $this->query = $query;
    }

    public function rewind() {
        $this->key = 0;
        if (mysqli_multi_query($this->link, $this->query)) {
            $this->result = mysqli_store_result($this->link);
            $this->valid = true;
        } else {
            $this->result = false;
            $this->valid = false;
        }
    }

    public function valid() {
        // mysqli_more_results() is one ahead of Iterator valid()
        $valid = $this->valid;
        $this->valid = mysqli_more_results($this->link);
        return $valid;
    }

    public function key() {
```

Example 6-2. Implementing a MySQL multi-query iterator (continued)

```
            return $this->key;
    }

    public function current() {
            return $this->result;
    }

    public function next() {
            if ($this->result) { mysqli_free_result($this->result); }
            $this->key++;
            if (mysqli_next_result($this->link)) {
                    $this->result = mysqli_store_result($this->link);
            } else {
                    $this->result = false;
            }
    }
}
```

This iterator takes the MySQL multi-query methods and redistributes them throughout the different interface methods.

The constructor stores the database handle and the SQL query. Unlike `MyDirectoryIterator`, this iterator assumes you already have an open connection to the database because it's common to make many database queries in a single page.

The `rewind()` method sets the key to 0 and executes the query using `mysqli_multi_query()`. If the query succeeds, the method saves the output of `mysqli_store_result()` in the `result` property and sets the `valid` property to true; if it fails, then both properties are set to `false`.

Next, the `valid()` method returns the result from `mysqli_more_results()`, but there's a catch. The `Iterator` interface wants to know if the *current* element is valid, but `mysqli_more_results()` tells you if the *next* element is valid.

The solution is to return one value "behind" `mysqli_more_results()` by storing the old value in a temporary variable, fetching the new results, and then returning the old value. This allows you to fetch new data without causing an off-by-one error.

The `key()` and `current()` methods aren't very exciting, as they only return the values stored in their properties. These methods should never alter the iterator's state, because it's legal to call them multiple times inside the block.

Finally, the `next()` method fetches an additional row using `mysqli_store_result()`. However, before it does this, it releases the old result data and increments the key.

Here's an example of the iterator in action:

```
$db = mysqli_connect('db.example.org');

$query = >>>_SQL_
DROP TABLE IF EXISTS users;
CREATE TABLE users(username VARCHAR(50) UNIQUE,
                   password VARCHAR(50));
INSERT INTO users VALUES('rasmus', 'z.8cMpdFbNAPw');
INSERT INTO users VALUES('zeev',    'asd34.23NNDeq');
SELECT username FROM users;
_SQL_;

foreach (new MySQLiQueryIterator($db, $query) as $result) {
        if ($result) {
                while ($row = mysqli_fetch_row($result)) {
                    print "$row[0]\n";
                }
        }
}
rasmus
zeev
```

The SQL creates a new users table and populates it with two rows, one for rasmus and another for zeev. This SQL and the database connection are then passed to MySQLiQueryIterator.

The iterator executes the query and returns the results bit by bit. When $result is false, it means that line of the query didn't return any rows. This is common because some queries—CREATE, DROP, and INSERT, for instance—don't return rows.

You could modify the iterator to automatically consume these results and only return data that's fetchable. However, the example's design allows you to track every single query. This is useful when, for example, you're doing a bulk INSERT of data and want to track your progress by printing out every 10th row. This would be impossible if the iterator didn't return all results.

When $result is true, you can operate on the result handle using any MySQL retrieval function you want. This example fetches each row and prints out the first column, which contains usernames.

Chaining Iterators

An important iterator feature is the ability to chain them together so they can act as a series of filters. For example, you can use iterators to restrict results to words that match a particular regular expression or to return only the first 10 results.

I call these types of iterators meta-iterators. SPL comes with two meta-iterators: FilterIterator, to filter results, and LimitIterator, to limit results.

Filtering Results with FilterIterator

FilterIterator is an abstract class that implements all the methods of a regular Iterator. However, it has a twist—you must define an accept( ) method that controls whether an item should be returned or filtered out from the results.

Unlike DirectoryIterator, which is directly instantiable, you cannot create a new FilterIterator. Instead, you must extend it and implement accept( ).

Here's an example that filters by a Perl-compatible regular expression:

```
class RegexFilter extends FilterIterator {

    protected $regex;

    public function __construct(Iterator $it, $regex) {
        parent::__construct($it);
        $this->regex = $regex;
    }

    public function accept() {
        return preg_match($this->regex, $this->current());
    }

}
```

RegexFilter takes two arguments in its constructor: an Iterator to filter and a regular expression pattern to use as a filter. The first parameter is passed on to the parent FilterIterator constructor, because it handles the iteration for your class.

The regular expression (regex for short) is stored in a protected property, $regex, for use inside the accept( ) method. This method must return true for items you wish to return and false for the ones that should be removed.

Handily, preg_match( ) returns the number of times the pattern matches the string. This number is always 0 or 1. (For multiple matches, use preg_match_all( ).) Since 1 evaluates as true and 0 as false, you can directly pass along preg_match( )'s return value.

Because $regex is a Perl-compatible regular expression, you must place pattern delimiters around your regex. The regular expression is checked against the value of $this->current( ). Alternatively, you could check it against $this->key( ), depending on how you want the iterator to work.

This example allows you to use RegexFilter inline with a foreach loop and DirectoryIterator:

```
$dir = new DirectoryIterator('/www/www.example.com/') {
$filtered_dir = new RegexFilter($dir, '/html$/i');

foreach ($filtered_dir as $file);
    print "$file\n";
}
email.html
index.html
search.html
```

You pass RegexFilter two arguments, an iterator and the regular expression pattern. This example returns files ending with html and eliminates the others. The regular expression uses the /i modifier to do a case-insensitive check.

When you only want to iterate over the objects once, you can create both RegexFilter and DirectoryIterator inside the foreach:

```
foreach (new RegexFilter(
         new DirectoryIterator('/www/www.example.com/'), '/html$/i')
         as $file) {
    print "$file\n";
}
email.html
index.html
search.html
```

Limiting Results with LimitIterator

Another useful meta-iterator is LimitIterator. This Iterator, which behaves just like the SQL LIMIT clause, allows you to filter nondatabase listings with the same logic you use with a database.

This example returns only the third and fourth files in the directory:

```
foreach(new LimitIterator(
        new DirectoryIterator('/www/www.example.com/'), 2, 2)
        as $file) {
    print "$file\n";
}
email.html
images
```

Unlike FilterIterator, LimitIterator doesn't require you to implement a method; therefore, it's directly instantiable. You don't need to extend it.

Its constructor takes three arguments: the iterator, the start position, and the number of items to return. Items start at position 0, so the third is at position 2. That's why this example passes 2, 2 as the second and third parameters.

Of course, you can chain three Iterators in combination. For example, to find only the first file ending in html in the */www/www.example.com/* directory:

```
foreach(new LimitIterator(new RegexFilter(
        new DirectoryIterator('/www/www.example.com/'), '/html$/i'), 0, 1)
        as $file) {
    print "$file\n";
}
email.html
```

It's important to order the Iterators correctly, or you won't get the results you expect. Don't switch RegexFilter and LimitIterator:

```
foreach(new RegexFilter(new LimitIterator(
        new DirectoryIterator('/www.www.example.com/'), 0, 1), '/html$/i')
        as $file) {
    print "$file\n";
}
```

This prints nothing! LimitIterator returns only one record—the file named ".". Then, FilterIterator comes along, sees that the record doesn't end in html, and eliminates it. This leaves you with no results.

SimpleXML Iterator

The SimpleXML iterator allows you to use SimpleXML objects with the other iterator classes. This allows you to easily construct an SQL-like interface to XML files.

For instance, suppose you have an XML address book like the one in Example 5-1. However, instead of containing only 2 records, it contains hundreds of records, and you want to display the records in groups of 10.

One solution is to place the information into a database. Another is to use XPath. A third is to combine a SimpleXMLIterator with a LimitIterator:

```
$ab = file_get_contents('address-book.xml');
$page = 0;
$limit = 10;

foreach (new LimitIterator(new SimpleXMLIterator($ab),
        $page * $limit, $limit) as $person) {

    print "$person->firstname $person->lastname: $person->email\n";
}
```

The SimpleXMLIterator takes a string of XML and creates an iterable SimpleXML object. Here, it's parsing *address-book.xml*.

This iterator is then passed to a LimitIterator that restricts the output to only the $limit number of records beginning at $page * $limit. When $page is 0, it returns the first 10 records; when $page is 1, you get records 11 through 20.

The $person item can be treated like a SimpleXMLElement, so $person-> firstname returns the text stored in the firstname element.

Before and After: Recursive Directory Iteration

The previous iterator examples handle only a flat list of items, but frequently your lists contain other lists. For instance, a directory can have other directories inside it, those child directories can contain additional directories, and so on.

Solve this problem with a recursive iterator, an iterator that works with multilevel lists. The following examples demonstrate directory iteration for subdirectories.

PHP 4: Recursively Reading Files in a Directory

In PHP 4, the easiest way to process all the files in a directory and its children is to call a function recursively:

```
function iterate_dir($path) {
    $files = array();
    if (is_dir($path) & is_readable($path)) {
        $dir = dir($path);
        while (false !== ($file = $dir->read())) {
            // skip . and ..
            if (('.' == $file) || ('..' == $file)) {
                continue;
            }
            if (is_dir("$path/$file")) {
                $files = array_merge($files, iterate_dir("$path/$file"));
            } else {
                array_push($files, $file);
            }
        }
        $dir->close();
    }
    return $files;
}

$files = iterate_dir('/www/www.example.com');
foreach ($files as $file) {
  print "$file\n";
}
email.html
```

```
logo.gif
php.gif
auth.inc
user.inc
index.html
search.html
```

This function loops through every file in the current directory. If the file is a directory, the function recursively calls itself and passes the subdirectory name as the argument. These results are then merged back into a master list of files stored in the $files array. When a file is not a directory, it's added to the list using array_merge( ).

Repeatedly calling iterate_dir( ) is slow, but it allows you to order the files so that children live under their parents.

Prepending $path to the filename before it's merged into the $files array modifies the example output to include the full path:

```
function iterate_dir($path) {

    // same as before

    if (is_dir("$path/$file")) {
        $files = array_merge($files, iterate_dir("$path/$file"));
    } else {
        array_push($files, "$path/$file");
    }

    // same as before
}

$files = iterate_dir('/www/www.example.com');
foreach ($files as $file) {
    print "$file\n";
}
/www/www.example.com/email.html
/www/www.example.com/images/logo.gif
/www/www.example.com/images/php.gif
/www/www.example.com/includes/auth.inc
/www/www.example.com/includes/user.inc
/www/www.example.com/index.html
/www/www.example.com/search.html
```

PHP 5: Recursively Reading Files in a Directory

PHP 5 replaces that complicated work with a RecursiveDirectoryIterator. Use it like this:

```
$dir = new RecursiveIteratorIterator(
        new RecursiveDirectoryIterator('/www/www.example.com/'));
foreach ($dir as $file) {
```

```
    print "$file\n";
}
```
email.html
logo.gif
php.gif
auth.inc
user.inc
index.html
search.html

No, that's not a typo—there really is a class named
RecursiveIteratorIterator. This class is an Iterator for classes that implement the RecursiveIterator interface. Think of PHP as automatically
implementing an IteratorIterator as part of foreach, but to ensure children are properly traversed, you need to use this SPL class.

Also, if you look closely, this output is different than that returned by the
PHP 4 example. Something has filtered out all the directories from the listing.
To fix this, pass true as a second argument to the RecursiveIteratorIterator:

```
$dir = new RecursiveIteratorIterator(
        new RecursiveDirectoryIterator('/www/www.example.com/'), true);
foreach ($dir as $file) {
    print "$file\n";
}
```
email.html
images
logo.gif
php.gif
includes
auth.inc
user.inc
index.html
search.html

That's still not the most readable output, because you don't know which
files live in which folders. Prepending the path helps:

```
$dir = new RecursiveIteratorIterator(
        new RecursiveDirectoryIterator('/www/www.example.com'), true);
foreach ($dir as $file) {
    print $file->getPathname() . "\n";
}
```
/www/www.example.com/email.html
/www/www.example.com/images
/www/www.example.com/images/logo.gif
/www/www.example.com/images/php.gif
/www/www.example.com/includes
/www/www.example.com/includes/auth.inc
/www/www.example.com/includes/user.inc
/www/www.example.com/index.html
/www/www.example.com/search.html

A quick call to the getPathname( ) method solves the problem. You may notice that you can call both print $file and $file->getPathname( ). Is $file a string or an object? It's an object, but it has a __toString( ) method that returns the file's name when it's printed.

Alternatively, it would be nice to display these files using a pretty directory tree–style listing. For that, you need to implement a custom class that extends RecursiveIteratorIterator:

```
class DirectoryTreeIterator extends RecursiveIteratorIterator {

    function current( ) {
        return str_repeat('| ', $this->getDepth( )) . '|-' .
            parent::current( );
    }

}

$dir = new DirectoryTreeIterator(
        new RecursiveDirectoryIterator('/www/www.example.com/'), true);

foreach ($dir as $file) {
    print $file. "\n";
}
|-email.html
|-images
| |-logo.gif
| |-php.gif
|-includes
| |-auth.inc
| |-user.inc
|-index.html
|-search.html
```

The DirectoryTreeIterator class, instead of returning a simple object that represents the file, provides a graphical representation of the directory hierarchy.

Implementing this class requires a new method that's part of RecursiveIteratorIterator: getDepth( ). The getDepth( ) method returns a number that indicates how many levels down the current item lives. For files in the top-level directory, it returns 0; for files inside the *images* and *includes* directories, it returns 1; and so on.

With getDepth( ), it's easy to prepend a pipe and space (|) for each level beyond the first. You could use a for loop here from 0 to getDepth( ), but it's faster to use str_repeat( ). After those characters come a pipe and dash (|-) and then the filename. This produces a simple graphic directory tree.

Implementing the RecursiveIterator Interface

The RecursiveIterator interface extends the existing Iterator interface to include two additional methods: hasChildren( ) and getChildren( ). These methods are used to navigate through sublists.

If you have an existing Iterator, it's natural to extend it to include the additional methods. SPL actually comes with a RecursiveDirectoryIterator, so there's no need to add these methods to DirectoryIterator, but it's a useful exercise to see how these methods should behave.

Here's how it's done:

```
class MyRecursiveDirectoryIterator extends MyDirectoryIterator
                                    implements RecursiveIterator {

    protected function getPath( ) {
        return $this->path . DIRECTORY_SEPARATOR . $this->current( );
    }

    public function hasChildren( ) {
        return is_dir($this->getPath( ));
    }

    public function getChildren( ) {
        return new MyRecursiveDirectoryIterator($this->getPath( ));
    }
}
```

Wow! This is much shorter than the code that was needed for iterate_dir( ). Since you can inherit methods from your earlier iterator, the implementation is three one-line methods.

The first method, getPath( ), constructs a complete pathname from the original path and the current filename. It uses the $path property that was stored in the constructor for MyDirectoryIterator in Example 6-1 because I knew you'd need it now.

The other two methods required by the interface also turn out to be easy to code. A file has children if it's a directory, so hasChildren( ) only needs to check the return value of is_dir( ).

Likewise, you can create a child iterator for a directory by instantiating a new instance of MyRecursiveDirectoryIterator and using the subdirectory's path in the constructor. This is analogous to calling iterate_dir( ) inside of iterate_dir( ).

Notice how there's no need to keep track of where you've been, what files you've seen, and when a directory needs to be processed. This is all taken

---

care of by the RecursiveIteratorIterator and is another major advantage of iterators.

If you actually run this code, however, it doesn't work:

```
$dir = new DirectoryTreeIterator(
        new MyRecursiveDirectoryIterator('/www/www.example.com/'), true);
foreach ($dir as $file) {
    print "$file\n";
}
```

You end up with an amusing series of warnings, including this:

```
PHP Warning:  opendir(./././././././././././././././././././././././
.././././././././././././././././././././././././././././././././././
.././././././././././././././././././././././././././././././././././
.././././././././././././././././././././././././././././././././././
.././././././././././././././././././././././././././././././././././
.././././././././././././././././././././././././././././././././././
.././././././././././././././././././././././././././././././././././
.././././././././././././././././././.): failed to open dir: Too many open
files
```

PHP just spirals off into an endless cycle. The directory files . and .. cause an infinite loop as the same directory is opened repeatedly, again and again.

It turns out the best solution is eliminating those two files completely. This requires using one new method and redefining two more:

```
public function isDot() {
    return ($this->current() == '.' ||
            $this->current() == '..');

}

public function rewind() {
    rewinddir($this->dir);
    $this->key = 0;
    while ($this->valid = $this->readDir() and
            $this->isDot()) { }
}

public function next() {
    $this->key++;
    while ($this->valid = $this->readDir() and
            $this->isDot()) { }
}
```

The isDot() method returns true if a file is one of the two nasty directory links. The method is used in rewind() and next() to detect those files and cause the iterator to skip over them. These redefined methods no longer retrieve just a single file using readDir(), but use a while loop to keep retrieving files until they get one that isn't a dot.

Everything now works as expected:

```
$dir = new DirectoryTreeIterator(
    new MyRecursiveDirectoryIterator('/www/www.example.com/'), true);
foreach ($dir as $file) {
    print "$file\n";
}
|-email.html
|-images
| |-logo.gif
| |-php.gif
|-includes
| |-auth.inc
| |-user.inc
|-index.html
|-search.html
```

Most recursive iterators don't contain these special self-referential aliases, so they don't need to go through the complicated steps necessary in this example. Directories are a unique case.

Array and Object Property Iteration

In PHP you can iterate through all the elements in an array using foreach. Although other methods are available, this is the preferred syntax for looping though results:

```
$person = array('firstname' => 'Rasmus',
                'lastname'  => 'Lerdorf');

foreach ($person as $key => $value) {
    print "$key: $value\n";
}
firstname: Rasmus
lastname: Lerdorf
```

You can also use foreach to view an object's properties:

```
class Person {
    // hardcode values for demonstration
    public $firstname = 'Rasmus';
    public $lastname  = 'Lerdorf';
}

$person = new Person;
foreach ($person as $property => $value) {
    print "$property: $value\n";
}
firstname: Rasmus
lastname: Lerdorf
```

In PHP 5, if an object property cannot be accessed because it is set as protected or private, then it will be skipped during iteration.

For example, update Person to include a private email attribute:

```
class Person {
    // hardcode values for demonstration
    public  $firstname = 'Rasmus';
    public  $lastname  = 'Lerdorf';
    private $email     = 'rasmus@php.net';
}

$person = new Person;
foreach ($person as $property => $value) {
    print "$property: $value\n";
}
firstname: Rasmus
lastname: Lerdorf
```

The email property is not printed, because you cannot access it from outside the class, but the results are different when you do a foreach inside the class. For instance, add a method named printInfo():

```
class Person {
    // hardcode values for demonstration
    public  $firstname = 'Rasmus';
    public  $lastname  = 'Lerdorf';
    private $email     = 'rasmus@php.net';

    public function printInfo() {
        foreach ($this as $property => $value) {
            print "$property: $value\n";
        }
    }
}

$person = new Person;
$person->printInfo();
firstname: Rasmus
lastname: Lerdorf
email: rasmus@php.net
```

While the code inside printInfo() is the same as the foreach outside the class (except that you refer to the object as $this instead of $person), the first loop cannot see the private email property, because it is restricted from public access. Class methods, however, are able to view all three properties, so email is printed.

Redefining Class Iteration

By default, when you iterate over an object, PHP serves up all of the object's properties. That's great for debugging, but it isn't what you want in every situation.

For example, you've mapped all property accesses in your class though the special __get( ) and __set( ) methods. In this implementation, you're storing all the data in a protected array named $data. It's logical that when someone iterates over the class, they're served up another element of $data. However, as things stand now, not only would they see other variables, but they're *not* going to see $data, because it's protected.

Fortunately, PHP 5 gives you the ability to control which items should appear during iteration. This lets you refine the default behavior to what's appropriate for the class.

Before getting into the specifics, here's a Person class for the later examples:

```php
class Person {
    protected $data;

    public function __construct($firstname, $lastname) {
        $this->firstname = $firstname;
        $this->lastname = $lastname;
    }

    public function __get($p) {
        if (isset($this->data[$p])) {
            return $this->data[$p];
        } else {
            return false;
        }
    }

    public function __set($p, $v) {
        $this->data[$p] = $v;
    }

    public function __toString() {
        return "$this->firstname $this->lastname";
    }
}
```

The Person class has a constructor that stores the person's firstname and lastname. Since property access has been overridden by __get( ) and __set( ), $this->firstname really references $this->data['firstname'].

There's also a __toString( ) method that defines how to print the person. That means you can use a Person object in a print statement and it'll look nice:

```php
$person = new Person('Rasmus', 'Lerdorf');
print $person;
Rasmus Lerdorf
```

However, when you iterate over $person, nothing appears:

```
$person = new Person('Rasmus', 'Lerdorf');

foreach($person as $property => $value) {
    print "$property: $value\n";
}
```

Since $data is protected, the foreach omits it. You could change $data's visibility to public, but that defeats the whole purpose of using accessors.

Not surprisingly, this is the perfect opportunity for a custom iterator. This requires two steps. First, you need to implement the IteratorAggregate interface. This interface tells PHP that you're going to provide your own iterator for the class and also lets PHP know where to get it. Second, you must return an object that implements the Iterator interface containing the data for PHP to iterate over.

In essence, you're aggregating an Iterator object into your original class. If you remember from way back in Chapter 2, aggregation is when you embed one class inside another and arrange it so that when a person calls methods on the main class, they're actually handled by the embedded class.

Implementing IteratorAggregate

IteratorAggregate is a simple interface because you must add only a single method to your class: getIterator().

When you iterate over a class that implements IteratorAggregate, instead of looping through the object's properties, PHP calls getIterator() and iterates through whatever is returned by the method.

Here's how to modify Person:

```
class Person implements IteratorAggregate {

    // Everything from before, plus:

    public function getIterator() {
        // insert code to return Iterator here...
    }
}
```

Person now implements IteratorAggregate and has a getIterator() method, but there's still the question of what the method should return.

Turning Arrays and Objects into Iterators

At first glance, the solution seems trivial. Since $data is an array and PHP can iterate over arrays, $data is an iterator. Just return $data and you're done.

Unfortunately, that doesn't work. PHP requires an actual object that implements Iterator. It won't accept an array as a substitute even though it acts similarly. Therefore, you need to find a way to convert an array into an Iterator that behaves like an array.

You could solve this by writing your own Iterator, but the SPL extension provides an ArrayObject class that does exactly this for both arrays and objects:

```
$data = array('firstname' => 'Rasmus',
              'lastname' => 'Lerdorf');

foreach (new ArrayObject($data) as $key => $value) {
    print "$key: $value\n";
}
firstname: Rasmus
lastname: Lerdorf
```

From an external point of view, there's little difference between using ArrayObject and iterating over the array directly. When you pass ArrayObject an array, it allows you to loop over its elements. When you pass ArrayObject an object, it allows you to loop over the object's properties. Since that's how arrays and objects already work, the difference is subtle.

However, the ArrayObject class has the advantage of turning your variable into an Iterator. Since PHP requires that getIterator( ) return an Iterator instead of an array, this is an extraordinarily handy class to solve the problem of what to do with $data.

Armed with ArrayObject, the implementation is easy:

```
    public function getIterator( ) {
        return new ArrayObject($this->data);
    }
```

Now you can iterate over the object:

```
$person = new Person('Rasmus', 'Lerdorf');

foreach ($person as $property => $value) {
    print "$property: $value\n";
}
firstname: Rasmus
lastname: Lerdorf
```

That completes the work necessary to make Person iterable, but ArrayObject has one additional advantage worth mentioning. Although using foreach on a variable is easy, it's not particularly memory efficient, because PHP does not directly operate on the variable. Instead, it first makes a copy of the variable and loops through the duplicate.

ArrayObject optimizes array iteration because it makes fewer internal copies of the array. This speeds up code. Therefore, if speed is important in your application, make this switch:

```
$person = array('firstname' => 'Rasmus',
                'lastname' => 'Lerdorf');

// FAST
foreach ($person as $key => $value) {
    print "$key: $value\n";
}

// FASTER
foreach (new ArrayObject($person) as $key => $value) {
    print "$key: $value\n";
}
```

Writing Dynamic Iterable Objects

The iterator returned by getIterator( ) doesn't need to return data already stored in the object. You can return any iterator, even one that accesses external information.

You've already briefly seen the SQLite iterator, which returns information from a database query:

```
$db = new SQLiteDatabase($database);
foreach ($db->query($sql) as $row) {
    // operate on $row
}
```

Since the SQLite result handle is also an object that implements Iterator, you can use it in your classes in place of ArrayIterator.

This example creates an object, addressBook. Pass addressBook a Person and it returns all the information in the database about that person:

```
class addressBook implements IteratorAggregate {
    protected $person;
    protected $db;

    public function __construct(Person $person) {
        $this->person = $person;
        $this->db = new SQLiteDatabase('address-book.db');
    }

    public function getIterator( ) {
        $firstname = sqlite_escape_string($this->person->firstname);
        $lastname  = sqlite_escape_string($this->person->lastname);
        return $this->db->query("SELECT * FROM persons
                                WHERE firstname LIKE '$firstname'
                                AND lastname  LIKE '$lastname'");
```

```
        }
    }

    $person = new Person('Rasmus', 'Lerdorf');
    $ab = new addressBook($person);
    foreach($ab as $p) {
        // $p contains an array of information about $person
    }
```

When you create a new addressBook, it saves the $person in a protected property. Then, when you iterate over the object in a foreach, PHP calls getIterator( ).

Inside getIterator( ), you escape the SQL and make the query. Since the result object implements the Iterator interface, return it and you're done.

The $p variables are arrays with numerical keys. You can then operate on these fields as if you had called SQLite's sqlite_fetch_array( ) function.

For more on SQLite, see Chapter 5.

Iterator and SPL Classes and Interfaces

This chapter demonstrates many classes, abstract classes, and interfaces, yet it only begins to touch on the full nature of SPL.

Table 6-3 is a quick-reference guide to the complete collection of SPL iterators, including some not mentioned in this chapter. For more information, see the SPL section of the PHP Manual at *http://www.php.net/spl*.

Table 6-3. Iterator and SPL classes and interfaces

Name	Type	Relationship	Description
ArrayObject	Class	Implements IteratorAggregate interface	Converts arrays and objects into iterators
ArrayIterator	Class	Implements Iterator interface	Used by ArrayObject; cannot be instantiated directly
CachingIterator	Class	Implements Iterator interface	Provides "look ahead by one" capability using hasNext( )
CachingRecursive Iterator	Class	Extends CachingIterator class; implements RecursiveIterator interface	Adds caching support to recursive iterators
DirectoryIterator	Class	Implements Iterator interface	An iterator for directory files
FilterIterator	Abstract class	Implements Iterator interface	Allows filtering of other iterators using accept( ) method

Table 6-3. Iterator and SPL classes and interfaces (continued)

Name	Type	Relationship	Description
Iterator	Interface	Defines Iterator interface	Implements an iterator
Iterator Aggregate	Interface	Defines IteratorAggregate interface	Allows classes to control iteration by returning iterator from getIterator( ) method
LimitIterator	Class	Implements Iterator interface	Emulates database LIMIT clause
ParentIterator	Class	Extends FilterIterator class; implements RecursiveIterator interface	Filters out leaf items, so only parents (items with children) are processed
RecursiveDirectory Iterator	Class	Implements RecursiveIterator interface	A recursive iterator for directory files; goes through all subdirectories
RecursiveIterator	Interface	Extends Iterator interface	Implements a recursive iterator
RecursiveIterator Iterator	Class	Implements Iterator interface	An iterator for classes that implement RecursiveIterator interface
SeekableIterator	Interface	Extends Iterator interface	Adds ability to seek( ) within an iterator; used by LimitIterator class
SimpleXMLIterator	Class	Implements Iterator interface	An iterator for XML files using SimpleXML functions; only iterates over XML text nodes

CHAPTER 7

Error Handling and Debugging

Bolstering PHP's reputation of practicality, PHP 5 has two new tools for handling errors and debugging applications: *exceptions* and *backtraces*. These topics aren't sexy, but most code has more lines of error checking than actual application logic, and you likely spend more time tracking down obscure bugs than writing the original program (although you probably don't like to think about this).

Error handling is particularly important in a networked environment, where you're granting anyone with an Internet account access to your computer and retrieving data from sites you don't control. It's vital that you handle problems gracefully for users while not providing information to people who are looking to break into your system.

Exception handling allows you to trap major errors in a separate section of your code devoted to processing errors. This allows you to recover gracefully whenever a serious problem occurs. Exceptions are new to PHP, but are a long-time feature in other languages. Right now, only a few PHP extensions use exceptions, but they're slowly being phased in. However, they're available right now for any PHP code you write.

PHP 5 also eases your bug hunt with its debug_backtrace( ) function. Developers with programs that include files and have complex hierarchies can now easily determine the exact state of their script without placing lots of print statements in their code.

Before and After: Handling Errors

This section compares PHP 4's style of error handling, where you check the return values of functions, with the new PHP 5 method known as exceptions.

PHP 4: Checking Return Values

Traditional error handling as implemented in PHP 4 requires you to inter-
leave a significant amount of bug-handling code with your program logic.
This not only makes scripts hard to understand, but it's annoying to check
every return value.

For instance, Example 7-1 shows how most people use the DOM XML
extension.

Example 7-1. Failing to check for errors

```
$version = '1.0';
$element = 'address-book';

$dom = domxml_new_doc($version);
$ab = $dom->create_element($element);
$ab = $dom->append_child($ab);
```

It seems unlikely that any of these methods will fail, so most people omit
error checking. However, it's entirely possible that something could go
wrong. For instance, create_element( ) fails when the element name contains illegal characters, such as spaces or ampersands (&). Since this code
does zero error handling, there's no way to identify a problem and proceed
accordingly.

Example 7-2 is a rewritten version of Example 7-1 that handles errors.

Example 7-2. Checking return values

```
$version = '1.0';
$element = 'address-book';

if ($dom = domxml_new_doc($version)) {
    if ($ab = $dom->create_element($element)) {
        if ($ab = $dom->append_child($ab)) {
            // Successfully appended address-book element
        } else {
            // Cannot append child
        }
    } else {
        // Cannot create <address-book> element
    }
} else {
    // Cannot create new document
}
```

When a PHP 4 DOM method has an error, it returns false. This lets you
identify problems and handle them inside the else blocks.

This code is more robust, but it's 16 lines instead of 6. It's also more difficult to decipher. As a result, many of the benefits of proper error handling are outweighed by these deficits.

PHP 5: Catching Exceptions

PHP 5 provides a different way to identify and track errors. This method is called exception handling. Exceptions make it possible to handle errors in a clear and comprehensive fashion by avoiding nested if statements.

An exception is a signal that some error (or other non-normal activity) has occurred. When an exception occurs, it is "thrown" by the offending method. A thrown exception can be "caught" by a block of code known as an exception handler, which processes the exception and takes action as necessary.

Exceptions become more clear when you see them in PHP instead of English. Using PHP 5 and exceptions, Example 7-2 turns into Example 7-3.

Example 7-3. Catching exceptions

```
$version = '1.0';
$element = 'address-book';

try {
    $dom = new DOMDocument($version);
    $ab = new DOMElement($element);
    $ab = $dom->appendChild($ab);
} catch (DOMException $e) {
    print $e;
}
```

Exception handlers operate on code wrapped around a try block. (Here it's checking DOM objects.) Then, just like you set up an if/else, there's a catch block below the try.

The catch block specifies the type of exception to catch and the variable in which to store it. This example uses the special DOM exception class called DOMException, and names it $e. Inside the catch, you can access $e to find out more information about the problem. $e isn't anything magical; it's just a variable that PHP populates with an object when an exception is thrown.

The easiest way to get an overview of the exception is by printing $e. This triggers the object's __toString( ) method, which returns a formatted version of all the data stored in the object.

For instance, if $element is set to an illegal XML element name, such as &, Example 7-3 prints:

```
exception 'DOMException' with message 'Invalid Character Error'
  in /www/www.example.com/dom.php:7
Stack trace:
#0 {main}
```

The exception is a DOMException, which tells you it's from the DOM extension. Its message is Invalid Character Error, and it occurred in on line 7 of /www/www.example.com/dom.php. At the bottom is a stack trace, something that's described in more detail in "Debugging Functions," later in this chapter.

PHP dies with a fatal error when you fail to catch an exception, as in Example 7-4.

Example 7-4. Failing to catch an exception

```
$version = '1.0';
$element = '&'; // & is an ILLEGAL element name

$dom = new DOMDocument($version);
$ab = new DOMElement($element);
$ab = $dom->appendChild($ab);

PHP Fatal error:  Uncaught exception 'DOMException' with message
  'Invalid Character Error' in /www/www.example.com/dom.php:7
Stack trace:
#0 {main}
  thrown in /www/www.example.com/dom.php on line 7
```

You can control this output using a custom exception handler. See "Setting a Custom Exception Handler," later in this chapter, for more details.

The Benefits of Exceptions

Nothing demonstrates the benefits of exceptions more than the previous section. Any time you can improve upon a piece of code *and* reduce the overall number of lines, it's a great change.

Another major boon from exceptions is that they "bubble up." When an exception isn't caught in the method it is thrown, the exception moves up a level in the call stack. In other words, the method that called the method gets a chance to handle the exception. This process continues until either the exception is finally caught or you're back in the top level. For example:

```
function createAddressBook( ) {
    $version = '1.0';
    $element = 'address-book';

    $dom = new DOMDocument($version);
    $ab = new DOMElement($element);
```

```
        $ab = $dom->appendChild($ab);

        return $dom;
    }

    try {
        $ab = createAddressBook();
    } catch (DOMException $e) {
        print $e;
    }
```

Since `createAddressBook()` doesn't catch the exceptions it generates, the exceptions flow back up a level and can be caught in the `try/catch` block that wraps around the call to `createAddressBook()`.

This behavior makes exceptions particularly well-suited for large-scale applications and frameworks. Without exceptions, you're forced to check the return value of every method, even at the relatively high level of development that occurs when you're combining full-blown objects.

However, at that point in your code, checking return values is not always useful, because there's very little you can do about a problem you discover. By the time it's reached that spot in the code, it's hard to tell whether the error was triggered by some truly nasty bug deep inside the bowels of your program, or whether it's a relatively benign warning that occurred one level down. As a result, you're likely to just log the error, display an innocuous message to the user, and quit.

With exceptions, this form of error handling is trivial. Additionally, it allows you to relocate the code to handle errors someplace out of the way, so your top-level application logic is easy to read and unencumbered by error handling.

System Exceptions

In contrast to some languages, notably Python and Java, PHP 5 doesn't throw exceptions whenever there's a problem. In fact, it never throws exceptions when you're using a procedural function. Instead, exceptions are strictly reserved for objects.

Furthermore, even when you're using an object, PHP throws exceptions only in two instances:

- Errors in constructors
- "Serious" problems in *some* extensions

These are the two instances when you must place your code inside a `try/catch` or risk a fatal error.

Constructors

Whenever there's an error during object instantiation, PHP throws an exception to signal failure. It must throw an exception because a constructor always returns an object, so it cannot return `false` or another value to indicate that it couldn't properly create an object.

You've already seen one example of a constructor throwing an exception back in Example 7-3. When you pass `DOMElement` an illegal tag name, `DOMElement` throws an exception.

A non-DOM example is the SQLite extension, which issues an exception when you don't provide a database name:

```
try {
    $db = new SQLiteDatabase();
} catch (Exception $e) {
    print $e;
}

exception 'SQLiteException' with message 'SQLiteDatabase::__construct()
expects at least 1 parameter, 0 given' in /www/www.example.com/sqlite.php:2
Stack trace:
#0 {main}
```

Serious Problems

In PHP 5, extensions throw exceptions only when there's serious logic error. Other errors are still returned in the traditional manner, by returning a designated error value such as `false` or `-1`.

There's no cut-and-dry definition of "serious." It varies from extension to extension, depending on the circumstances. Some extensions, such as DOM, throw exceptions in accordance with the DOM specification, which defines those instances as follows:

> DOM operations only raise exceptions in "exceptional" circumstances, i.e., when an operation is impossible to perform (either for logical reasons, because data is lost, or because the implementation has become unstable). In general, DOM methods return specific error values in ordinary processing situations.

In contrast, other extensions, such as MySQLi and SQLite, *never* throw exceptions (except in their constructors).

Because the decision of if and when to throw exceptions is left up to the extension developer, there's no rule of thumb to determine whether a given method will or will not issue an exception. The only way to know how an extension behaves is to read its documentation in the PHP Manual (*http://www.php.net/manual/*).

The Exception Class

What you're actually catching when PHP throws an exception is either an instance of the Exception class or a class that's descended from Exception.

The methods of the Exception class provide you with easy access to the individual details of the exception, such as the message, error code, filename, and line number. Use them when the overview you get from printing an object doesn't help you find the information you need.

For example, you might want to take different action based upon the specific error code stored in the exception. Some problems may be recoverable, while others aren't.

Table 7-1 contains a list of all the exception methods and what they do.

Table 7-1. Exception methods

Method name	Description
getMessage( )	A text description of the error
getCode( )	A numeric error code
getFile( )	The filename where the error occurred
getLine( )	The line where the error occurred
getTrace( )	The array output of debug_backtrace( )
getTraceAsString( )	The string output of debug_print_backtrace( )
__toString( )	A comprehensive description of the exception

Example 7-5 calls four of the Exception class methods.

Example 7-5. Retrieving exception specifics

```
$version = '1.0';
$element = '&'; // & is an ILLEGAL element name

try {
    $dom = new DOMDocument($version);
    $ab = new DOMElement($element);
    $ab = $dom->appendChild($ab);
} catch (Exception $e) {
    error_log('Error in file ' . $e->getFile() . ' on line ' .
        $e->getLine() . ".\n" . 'Error message: "' . $e->getMessage() .
        '" and error code: ' . $e->getCode() . '.');
}

Error in file /www/www.example.com/dom.php on line 7.
Error message: "Invalid Character Error" and error code: 5.
```

The getFile( ) and getLine( ) methods return the filename and line number where the error occurred. They're what you would get if you captured the __FILE__ and __LINE__ constants at the location of the error. (Printing these constants inside the catch give you the current filename and line number inside the catch, not the name and number where the error actually took place.)

The getMessage( ) and getCode( ) methods provide a text description of the error and an error number. According to the DOM specification, trying to create an element with an illegal name must generate an invalid character error, which has an error code of 5.

The Exception class also provides access to a backtrace of the current working environment at the time of the error. Access it through getTraceAsString( ). Since the code in Example 7-5 lives in the main scope, it's not too exciting or useful:

```
#0 {main}
```

There is also getTrace( ), which returns the same information as getTraceAsString( ) but with each line as an element in an array. Backtraces and their format are the topic of the last section of this chapter.

As you've seen, DOM actually throws a DOMException instead of a regular Exception. A DOMException is a subclass of the base Exception class. It doesn't contain any additional methods or properties, but it lets you easily differentiate DOM errors from errors thrown by other extensions.

Unlike Java, PHP does not support the finally keyword. The finally block designates a region of code that's always run, regardless of whether there's an exception. It's used to close open connections and release locked files. The solution is to place as much cleanup code inside your objects' destructors and handle the remaining details (if any) inside the catch block.

User Exceptions

Exceptions aren't restricted to extensions. You can trigger your own exceptions by throwing an instance of the Exception class.

User-thrown exceptions are useful because they allow you to integrate the error handling for your own errors with exceptions thrown by PHP. Inside your methods, you may still need to check a return value; however, converting those errors into exceptions allows the developer using your classes to know he can reliably trap all errors using a try/catch block.

This section covers when it's appropriate to throw exceptions of your own, and also how to create and throw an exception. Chapter 10 contains an address book application that demonstrates, among other things, how to put these exception-handling techniques into practice.

When to Use Exceptions

There many categories of errors, and exceptions are not always an appropriate way to handle them in PHP. In general, there are three major groups:

Programming errors
> You, the programmer, have made a mistake. For instance, you passed an incorrect number of arguments to a method.

Client code errors
> Your code is okay, but there's a problem with an external resource. For instance, your code uses an XML file from a third-party web site, but that file isn't valid XML. Or, a person has tried to join your site, but has requested a username already in use.

Resource failures
> Your code is failing because of a breakdown in communication with another process. For instance, you cannot connect to a third-party web site because of network traffic. Or, your database is refusing additional connections because it is overloaded.

Unlike Java, PHP does not use exceptions internally. Therefore, many programming errors still need to be trapped in the traditional manner. You can then choose to either handle them in place or create an exception for them.

Client code errors are also highly dependent on the extension. Many extensions also do not throw exceptions or they throw them only when you use their object-oriented interface instead of their procedural interface. However, it makes sense to use exceptions when dealing with client code errors.

Most PHP programs don't try to recover from resource failures. If a web site or database doesn't respond the first time, it's usually assumed to be down. Sometimes it makes sense to retry the connection, but that can often be handled more easily without exceptions.

Exceptions are not an object-oriented version of goto. They're not for flow control; they're for handling exceptional events. In addition to any other goto evils, exceptions also have unnecessary overhead compared to alternative, and superior, methods, such as a while loop.

Throwing an Exception

Example 7-6 is part of a larger user registration system. It tries to insert a new user into the database, but throws an exception if there's already someone in the table with the same username.

Example 7-6. Inserting new users into a member database

```
// Add user to database, throw exception if duplicate entry
function addUser($db, $user) {
    $db->query("INSERT INTO users
                    VALUES ('${user[0]}', '${user[1]}');");

    // Error code 19 means INSERT violates UNIQUEness constraint
    if ($db->lastError() == 19) {
        throw new Exception("${user[0]} already in database.", 19);
    }
}

// First element is username, second is password
$user = array('rasmus', 'z.8cMpdFbNAPw');

try {
    $db = new SQLiteDatabase('address-book.db');
    addUser($db, $user);
} catch (Exception $error) {
    print "Message: ".$error->getMessage()."\n";
    print "Error Code: ".$error->getCode()."\n";
}
```

When there's a username collision, you get:

```
Message: rasmus already in database.
Error Code: 19
```

Assume the user table's first field was declared UNIQUE during table creation. Therefore, when there's already a rasmus user in the database, trying to insert a second rasmus violates this constraint. This causes SQLite's lastError() method to return 19.

While SQLite's constructor throws exceptions, the query() method does not. Therefore, you must manually trigger the exception by creating a new Exception object and passing a message and error code.

The Exception class stores the constructor's first and second parameters in getMessage() and getCode(). The first parameter, the message, is a string; the second, the error code, must be an integer. Trying to pass a non-number as the second argument causes PHP to complain with a fatal error.

Use the throw keyword to throw an Exception object. In this example, the object is instantiated and thrown in one line, but these operations can occur separately.

The exception isn't caught inside addUser(), so it bubbles up a level. However, since the call to addUser() is wrapped inside a try/catch block, it's caught and handled there. This is a perfect example of placing the dirty job of checking return values inside a function, thus freeing up the core application logic to use exceptions.

In Example 7-6, the exception handling is minimal. All it does is print out two lines of debugging information. In a full system, you should make the exception trigger a page that requests that the person select a different username. This wasn't demonstrated here, but it's a nicer way to handle problems than just dying.

Writing and Catching Custom Exceptions

There are two good reasons to define custom exception classes: to customize your processing of different errors and to embed additional information inside your exception objects.

Handling multiple exception types

Besides throwing the default Exception class, you can create and throw custom exception objects by extending Exception. For instance, Example 7-7 throws a duplicateUsernameException exception.

Example 7-7. Catching a custom exception

```
class duplicateUsernameException extends Exception { };

// Add user to database, throw exception if duplicate entry
function addUser($db, $user) {
    $db->query("INSERT INTO users
                    VALUES ('${user[0]}', '${user[1]}');");

    // Error code 19 means INSERT violates UNIQUEness constraint
    if ($db->lastError() == 19) {
        throw new duplicateUsernameException(
                "${user[0]} already in database.", 19);
    }
}

// First element is username, second is password
$user = array('rasmus', 'z.8cMpdFbNAPw');

try {
    $db = new SQLiteDatabase('address-book.db');
    addUser($db, $user);
} catch (duplicateUsernameException $error) {
    print "Message: ".$error->getMessage()."\n";
    print "Error Code: ".$error->getCode()."\n";
}
```

The methods and properties of duplicateUsernameException are identical to its parent, but by subclassing Exception you can catch this error separately and handle it accordingly. This is a good reason to subclass Exception.

To handle the different types of exceptions, define multiple catch blocks. When PHP detects a thrown exception, it works its way down the list of catches. For each block, PHP compares the exception type against the class name using an instanceof check. PHP uses the first matching block.

Therefore, you must catch a duplicateUsernameException before an Exception. Since duplicateUsernameException is a subclass of Exception, switching the order results in all exceptions being caught in the first block.

For instance, Example 7-8 continues to throw duplicateUsernameException as before, but also remembers that SQLite throws an SQLiteException from its constructor.

Example 7-8. Catching multiple exceptions

```
class duplicateUsernameException extends Exception { };

// Add user to database, throw exception if duplicate entry
function addUser($db, $user) {
    $db->query("INSERT INTO users
                    VALUES ('${user[0]}', '${user[1]}');");

    // Error code 19 means INSERT violates UNIQUEness constraint
    // Throw duplicateUsernameException
    if ($db->lastError() == 19) {
        throw new duplicateUsernameException(
                "${user[0]} already in database.", 19);
    }
}

// First element is username, second is password
$user = array('rasmus', 'z.8cMpdFbNAPw');

try {
    $db = new SQLiteDatabase('address-book.db');
    addUser($db, $user);
} catch (duplicateUsernameException $error) {
    // This function not implemented
    requestDifferentUsername($user);
} catch (SQLiteException $error) {
    print "Message: ".$error->getMessage()."\n";
    print "Error Code: ".$error->getCode()."\n";
}
```

In this example, a duplicateUsernameException error is thrown if the username is already in the database. Since that's only a minor error, call requestDifferentUsername() to recover gracefully.

A failure in the constructor is more severe. Since that's of type SQLiteException, it's trapped in a separate catch block, where you can handle it accordingly.

Without subclassing Exception, you need to place a giant switch inside catch and check the type of each error. This is ugly and doesn't scale well. Additionally, one pattern of object-oriented programming is replacing the switch statements that check an object's type with different subclassed objects.

Embedding custom exception data

Another reason to subclass Exception is to add custom methods:

```
class duplicateUsernameException extends Exception {

    private $username;

    public function __construct($username) {
        parent::__construct();
        $this->username = $username;
    }

    public function getUsername() {
        return $this->username;
    }

    public function getAlternativeNames() {
        // return an array of similar names, like "rasmus34"
    }
}
```

The getAlternativeNames() method returns an array of similar names that the application can pass on to the person trying to sign up. You can integrate this method into your code:

```
// First element is username, second is password
$user = array('rasmus', 'z.8cMpdFbNAPw');

try {
    $db = new SQLiteDatabase('address-book.db');
    addUser($db, $user);
} catch (duplicateUsernameException $error) {
    requestDifferentUsername($error);
} catch (Exception $error) {
    print "Message: ".$error->getMessage()."\n";
    print "Error Code: ".$error->getCode()."\n";
}
```

Now the requestDifferentUsername() function is passed an object it can use to discover both the original username and a list of valid alternatives.

Setting a Custom Exception Handler

PHP always dies with a fatal error whenever you fail to catch an exception. However, you can control what PHP does before it dies by creating a custom exception-handling function and registering it using set_exception_handler( ). For example:

```
function my_exception_handler($e) {
    error_log('Error in file ' . $e->getFile() . ' on line ' .
        $e->getLine() . ".\n" . 'Error message: "' . $e->getMessage() .
        '" and error code: ' . $e->getCode() . '.');
}

set_exception_handler('my_exception_handler');

$version = '1.0';
$element = '&'; // & is an ILLEGAL element name

$dom = new DOMDocument($version);
$ab = new DOMElement($element);
$ab = $dom->appendChild($ab);
```

Error in file /www/www.example.com/dom.php on line 14.
Error message: "Invalid Character Error" and error code: 5.

Because the exception isn't caught inside a catch block, the exception handler kicks in and prints the message to the error log. When the function finishes, PHP dies.

If you're writing new PHP 5 code, there's really no reason to use set_exception_handler( ), because you can just wrap the main section of your code inside a try/catch block. However, you may find it useful when converting older PHP 4 code that wasn't designed with exception handling in mind over to PHP 5.

In particular, if you're using set_error_handler( ), adding a call to set_exception_handler( ) may be a good stop-gap method. It would allow you to handle exceptions like you're already handling errors, without being forced to restructure your code.

Processing Errors with a Custom Handler

In PHP 4, you can enable a custom error handler for all errors by calling set_error_handler( ). PHP 5 lets you refine that behavior by allowing you to specify which types of errors the handler should process.

To restrict set_error_handler( ) to a subset of errors, pass it a second argument. For example:

```
set_error_handler('my_error_handler', E_NOTICE);

function my_error_handler($errno, $errstr, $errfile, $errline) {
```

```
    print "A notice occurred\n";
}

$a++;
```

A notice occurred

This example sets my_error_handler( ) as the handler for E_NOTICE errors, but lets PHP handle all other error types. Since incrementing an undefined variable triggers a notice, PHP invokes the function.

If the custom error handler returns false, then PHP also does its own set of error handling, in addition to whatever you code inside your handler. For instance:

```
set_error_handler('my_error_handler',  E_NOTICE);

function my_error_handler($errno, $errstr, $errfile, $errline) {
    print "A notice occurred\n";
    return false;
}

$a++;
```

PHP Notice: Undefined variable: a...
A notice occurred

This example is identical to the last one, except that my_error_handler( ) now returns false. As a result, you get two sets of messages: PHP's and yours.

Debugging Functions

Debugging is the bane of every programmer. When you're trying to untangle why a variable isn't set correctly inside a function—which was itself called from another function, which was included from an include file, which was wrapped inside a class—it can be maddening to track down where in the chain of events everything started to go wrong.

PHP 5 includes a set of functions that ease your pain. The debug_backtrace( ) and debug_print_backtrace( ) functions return and print, respectively, an assortment of information about the current function and every previous function in the call stack.

Integrating Debugging into Your Code

One good strategy for deploying debug_print_backtrace( ) is to define( ) a DEBUG constant whose value determines whether your code should run in

---

debugging mode. Example 7-9 is a modified version of Example 7-8 with integrated debugging scaffolding.

Example 7-9. Integrating backtrace debugging

```
// Enable debug mode;
// Can be placed in a file that's added using the
// auto_prepend_file configuration directive
define('DEBUG', true);

class duplicateUsernameException extends Exception { };

// Add user to database, throw exception if duplicate entry
function addUser($db, $user) {
    $db->query("INSERT INTO users
                    VALUES ('${user[0]}', '${user[1]}');");

    // Error code 19 means INSERT violates UNIQUEness constraint
    // Throw duplicateUsernameException
    if ($db->lastError() == 19) {
        throw new duplicateUsernameException(
                "${user[0]} already in database.", 19);
    }

    // Another error, like a malformed SQL statement
    if (DEBUG && $db->lastError()) {
        debug_print_backtrace();
    }
}
```

At the top of the script, DEBUG is defined to true. This enables debug mode. Using a constant instead of a variable prevents a script from modifying the value. Another advantage is that constants have global scope, which means you can use them inside of functions and classes without declaring them global. (Forgetting to reference the global $debug variable results in a bug in the bug-catching code, which is quadruply frustrating.)

A good place to define DEBUG is in a file that's automatically included at the top of every file using the auto_prepend_file configuration directive. This ensures that you won't forget to set a value for the constant.

Underneath the check to throw a duplicateUsernameException inside addUser( ) is:

```
if (DEBUG && $db->lastError()) {
    debug_print_backtrace();
}
```

This block causes PHP to print out debugging information and helps you locate the error.

The debug_print_backtrace( ) function is always available, but if you're using exceptions, you can also call the getTraceAsString( ) method, which returns equivalent results:

```
// Another error, like a malformed SQL statement
// Throw Exception
if ($db->lastError()) {
    $e = new Exception(
                sqlite_error_string($db->lastError()),
                $db->lastError());
        if (DEBUG) { print $e->getTraceAsString() . "\n"; }
        throw $e;
}
```

Example 7-10 works correctly when you test it, but triggers an exception for some (but not all) people trying to sign up for your site.

Example 7-10. Inserting new users incorrectly

```
// Can be placed in a file that's added using
// auto_prepend_file configuration directive
define('DEBUG', true);

class duplicateUsernameException extends Exception { };

// Add user to database, throw exception if duplicate entry
function addUser($db, $user) {
    $db->query("INSERT INTO users
                    VALUES ('${user[0]}', '${user[1]}');");

    // Error code 19 means INSERT violates UNIQUEness constraint
    // Throw duplicateUsernameException
    if ($db->lastError() == 19) {
        throw new duplicateUsernameException(
                "${user[0]} already in database.", 19);
    }

    // Another error, like a malformed SQL statement
    if (DEBUG && $db->lastError()) {
        print sqlite_error_string($db->lastError());
    }
}

$user = array($_GET['username'], $_GET['password']);

try {
    $db = new SQLiteDatabase('address-book.db');
    addUser($db, $user);
} catch (duplicateUsernameException $error) {
    requestDifferentUsername($user);
} catch (SQLiteException $error) {
    print "Message: ".$error->getMessage()."\n";
```

Example 7-10. Inserting new users incorrectly (continued)

```
    print "Error Code: ".$error->getCode()."\n";
}
```

The SQLite error message for this bug, as reported by sqlite_error_string($db->lastError()), is:

SQL logic error or missing database

The SQLite error message doesn't provide you with much to go on. You know the database exists because you see it on the filesystem. You also know it's not a permissions problem because you're accessing the database in the same manner as everyone else. Besides, it works for most people, so it's not like the code is completely broken.

Eventually, you find a case that triggers debug_print_backtrace(). Here's the output from the function:

```
#0 addUser(SQLiteDatabase Object (), Array ([0] => rasmus,[1] => sec'ret%))
called at [/www/www.example.com/sqlite.php:31]
```

The username looks okay, but maybe there's something wrong with the password. Aha! It contains a single quotation mark ('), and you're not calling sqlite_escape_string() on the input. In addition to a security vulnerability, this causes an SQL parse error because your INSERT statement terminates early.

The fix is simple. You must escape the values before passing them to SQLite, as shown in Example 7-11.

Example 7-11. Inserting new users correctly

```
// Add user to database, throw exception if duplicate entry
function addUser($db, $user) {
    // Escape input parameters
    foreach ($user as &$value) {
        $value = sqlite_escape_string($value);
    }

    $db->query("INSERT INTO users
                VALUES ('${user[0]}', '${user[1]}');");

    // Error code 19 means INSERT violates UNIQUEness constraint
    // Throw duplicateUsernameException
    if ($db->lastError() == 19) {
        throw new duplicateUsernameException(
                "${user[0]} already in database.", 19);
    }

    // Another error, like a malformed SQL statement
    if (DEBUG && $db->lastError()) {
```

Example 7-11. Inserting new users correctly (continued)

```
        debug_print_backtrace( );
    }
}
```

The foreach loop cycles through the elements of $user using a new PHP 5 feature: iteration by reference. Placing an ampersand (&) before $value makes foreach provide you with a reference to array elements. This allows you to reassign the output of sqlite_escape_string( ) to $value instead of $user[$key].

Redirecting Output to a File

Use PHP's output-buffering functions to redirect the results of debug_print_backtrace( ) to the error log or a file:

```
// Another error, like a malformed SQL statement
if (DEBUG && $db->lastError( )) {
    $ob = ob_start( );
    debug_print_backtrace( );
    error_log(ob_get_clean( ));
}
```

This creates an output buffer, $ob, and places the contents of debug_print_backtrace( ) inside it. The buffer is then flushed to the error log using ob_get_clean( ).

CHAPTER 8

Streams, Wrappers, and Filters

PHP's streams provide a file-like interface for reading and writing data. A single interface for many different data sources lets you write reusable code: a program that extracts data from a local file can just as easily extract data from a web page, and new streams data sources can immediately be used with any existing streams code. This reuse makes streams a powerful and underused feature in PHP.

Streams were a late addition to PHP 4, arriving only in PHP 4.3. As a result, they're barely covered in other PHP books, and hardly anyone uses them to their full extent. Therefore, while PHP 5 introduces some new streams features, that's not the focus of this chapter. Instead, it compares programming with and without streams and discusses the advantages streams provide over alternatives, such as cURL.

An extension that provides a streams interface to a new data source is called a *wrapper*. The streams interface consists of 14 methods, but you need only implement the methods that make sense for your data source. For example, if you wanted to provide a streams interface to a mailbox of messages, you might not support renaming or rewriting. You can write wrappers in C or in PHP.

The SimpleXML extension is written to use the streams interface for its data. This means that the same function that loads XML from a datafile (simplexml_load_file( )) also loads XML from a URL, an FTP site, and any other data source you have a wrapper for.

Sometimes, in addition to transporting data, you want to modify it. For example, you might want to encode HTML entities, strip HTML tags, or otherwise alter the text. Since these conversions are independent of the wrapper, it doesn't make sense for the wrapper to handle the job. Stripping HTML tags is something you may want to do for local files and text retrieved via HTTP, and there's no point in writing one function for each location.

PHP streams support filters to make modifications to a stream's data. Once installed, a *filter* sits between a streams wrapper and PHP code that reads from or writes to a stream. The filter intercepts the data and may modify it. This makes a filter's actions transparent to a wrapper and to user code, allowing you to associate a filter with any stream, regardless of the wrapper the stream is using.

While it makes sense only to have one wrapper per data source, you can chain multiple filters in a row. The Unix shell has a similarly powerful feature, pipelines, where you can connect a series of programs to modify data. In Unix, as in PHP streams, all a filter knows is that it must take the data provided as input, filter it according to some rules, and then provide the new data as output. It doesn't care if this information has already been filtered or if another filter or two follows it.

This chapter shows how to use streams by explaining the wrappers available with PHP 5: file, http, ftp, and php. php is a PHP-specific wrapper that handles information passed to and emitted from PHP using standard input, output, and error. There are also a few compression wrappers and SSL-enabled wrappers that are available depending upon how your version of PHP is configured.

Next, you learn how to write a wrapper of your own so you can extend PHP. The section "Creating Wrappers" shows how to build a shared memory wrapper that uses PHP's shared memory functions. Shared memory allows you to easily communicate among all PHP processes on the same web server in an efficient manner.

After wrappers come filters. Again, PHP has a few built-in filters. In particular, the string.strip_tags and convert.iconv filters are extremely useful, as they allow you to eliminate HTML tags and convert text from one character encoding to another, respectively.

However, the main power of filters comes from the ability to write your own filters using PHP. Since filters are so flexible, there's a bit of wrapping code necessary to implement even a very simple filter, but once the basic structure is in place, it's easy to modify what you have in all sorts of directions.

This chapter concludes by showing how to write custom filters, using the htmlentities( ) function as an example, and also demonstrates how to chain multiple filters together.

For a complete streams reference, see the "Streams" section of the PHP Manual at *http://www.php.net/stream*. If you're interested in implementing wrappers and filters in C, read *http://www.php.net/streams*.

Using the Streams API

This section covers reading and writing files using the streams functions. For now, the examples only use the file wrapper, which is for local files. Other wrappers, along with their different configuration options, are covered in the next section. However, due to the miracle of streams, you won't need to learn any new functions to use those new wrappers.

The syntax for specifying a stream is *scheme://target*. The *scheme* can be the name of any installed wrapper, such as file or http. The *target* varies depending upon the wrapper, but is usually a path to the file, with an optional hostname if applicable. For instance, to reference the local file */www/www.example.com/index.html*, use file:///www/www.example.com/index.html.

The best way to read the entire contents of a stream into a variable is the file_get_contents( ) function. For example:

```
// get the index page
$index = file_get_contents('file:///www/www.example.com/index.html');

// short hand syntax for above
$index = file_get_contents('/www/www.example.com/index.html');
```

These examples locate the file */www/www.example.com/index.html* on the hard drive, read its contents, and place them in the $index variable. Since the file wrapper is the default wrapper for file_get_contents( ), you can omit it for brevity.

You can make file_get_contents( ) also search your include_path. To enable this feature, pass true as the second argument:

```
$classes = file_get_contents('classes.php', true);
```

Now instead of looking only in the current directory, file_get_contents( ) also works through the include hierarchy, so its behavior is identical to include.

The file_get_contents( ) function respects read permissions and PHP's internal access restrictions, such as open_basedir. Trying to read in a restricted file causes PHP to produce a warning:

```
$forbidden = file_get_contents("/etc/shadow");
PHP Warning:  file_get_contents(/etc/shadow): failed to open stream:
    Permission denied
```

In these cases, file_get_contents( ) returns false.

While file_get_contents( ) is the most efficient way to retrieve an entire file, a large file will use up lots of memory. If you don't need to access the entire file at once, use fopen( ) instead:

```
$stream = 'file:///www/www.example.com/index.html';

$handle = fopen($stream, 'rb');
```

```
$contents = '';
while (!feof($handle)) {
    $data = fread($handle, 8192);
    print $data; // or another function to handle the data
}
fclose($handle);
```

The fopen( ) function returns a file handle, or file pointer, to the file. Passing this handle to file functions such as feof( ), fread( ), and fclose( ) makes them act upon your file.

This code, however, is far more complex because you need to worry about opening the file for read access and then looping through its contents one chunk at a time. You also need to check repeatedly if you've read the entire file. Therefore, unless you're manipulating very large files on a regular basis, it's best to always use file_get_contents( ).

When you need to do the reverse (save a variable as a file), use file_put_contents( ):

```
file_put_contents('file:///www/www.example.com/index.html', $index);
```

```
file_put_contents('/www/www.example.com/index.html', $index);
```

These two functions place the contents of $index into */www/www.example.com/index.html*.

The default behavior is to overwrite an existing file; however, you can make file_get_contents( ) append to a file by passing the FILE_APPEND constant as a third parameter:

```
file_put_contents('/var/log/http/error_log', $error, FILE_APPEND);
```

This adds the contents of $error to the end of */var/log/http/error_log*.

An alternative method of sending data is fwrite( ):

```
$stream = '/www/www.example.com/index.html';

$handle = fopen($stream, 'wb');
fwrite($handle, $index);
fclose($handle);
```

This opens the stream for writing and sends the contents of $index to the file */www/www.example.com/index.html*.

Wrapper Overview

As long as there's a wrapper that supports it, you can use streams to read from and write to any location or protocol using the same set of file manipulation functions from the previous section.

For example, here are a few streams that access nonlocal files:

- `http://www.example.com/index.html`
- `https://secure.example.com/secret.html`
- `ftp://user:password@ftp.example.com/www/www.example.com/index.html`

The first stream makes an HTTP request to *www.example.com* and retrieves the file from the Internet. The second makes a secure HTTP connection using SSL and accesses *secret.html* from *secure.example.com*. The final wrapper transfers a file using FTP, passing along a username and password in the process.

However, while streams do abstract away most implementation specifics, they can't alter the inherent nature of the protocol itself. For instance, although it's quite easy to read files using HTTP, most web servers are not set up to allow you to save files using HTTP. Likewise, when you use FTP, you need to provide a username and password or the FTP server won't be able to authenticate you as a legitimate user.

Bundled Wrappers

Before getting into the specifics of each individual wrapper, here's a brief overview of all the wrappers bundled with PHP 5, as well as the additional wrappers you can enable with certain extensions.

PHP 5 automatically provides you with four wrappers:

`file`
> Talks to the local filesystem

`http`
> Requests a file from a web server

`ftp`
> Reads and writes files from an FTP server

`php`
> Handles reading from standard in and writing to standard out and error.

Compiling in certain extensions enables four additional wrappers:

`compress.bzip2`
> Automatically (de)compresses bzipped files on the fly; requires `BZip2` support

`compress.zlib`
> Automatically (de)compresses gzipped files on the fly; requires `zlib` support

`ftps`

Securely reads and writes files from an FTP server; requires `OpenSSL`

`https`

Securely reads files from an HTTP server; requires `OpenSSL`

During the configuration process, enable `bzip2` compression support with `--with-bz2`, `zlib` compression with `--with-zlib`, and `OpenSSL` with `--with-openssl`.

The `stream_get_wrappers( )` function returns an array of available wrappers. Use this to discover which filters are available on your machine:

```
print_r(stream_get_wrappers( ));
```

which prints:

```
Array
(
    [0] => php
    [1] => file
    [2] => http
    [3] => ftp
    [4] => compress.zlib
)
```

This copy of PHP has the basic set of wrappers and the `zlib` wrapper, but not the extra SSL or `bzip2` wrappers.

Wrapper Details

The following sections show how to read from and write to different locations using PHP 5's bundled wrappers. You've already seen how to process files stored on your server's hard drive. Now you use the `http` and `ftp` wrappers to access remote files using HTTP and FTP.

The `http` and `ftp` wrappers require the `allow_url_fopen` configuration directive set to `On`. This is the default setting, but `allow_url_fopen` may be turned off on some systems because it allows crackers to more easily exploit insecurely written code.

Specifically, when `allow_url_fopen` is on, `include $file` will even include remote files. If a cracker is somehow able to set `$file` to a value of her own, she can make your web server execute any PHP code she wants just by posting it on a web site and setting `$file` to that URL.

Another wrapper you'll learn how to use is the php wrapper for standard in, out, and error. This wrapper is particularly useful for people using PHP on the command line or with web services.

The final set of wrappers are the compression wrappers. These wrappers are similar to the file wrapper, except that they let you read and write data that is compressed using gzip and bzip2.

HTTP and HTTPS

While file_get_contents( ) and file_put_contents( ) may seem to work only for local files, they're actually valid for any stream that enables them. Since PHP comes with an http stream, this means you can retrieve files using HTTP.

For example, you can fetch *index.php* from *www.example.com*:

```
$index = file_get_contents('http://www.example.com/index.php');
```

This tells PHP to use the http wrapper to retrieve the target www.example. com/index.php. The wrapper knows it should make an HTTP GET request of the web server located at *www.example.com*.

You can also pass along a username and password to be used as HTTP Basic Authentication credentials, like this:

```
$index = file_get_contents('http://rasmus:FbNAPw@www.example.com/index.php');
```

The username comes immediately after the double slashes and is separated from the password by a colon. After the password, place an @.

Modify the HTTP request by passing a stream context to file_get_ contents( ). A *stream context* is a way to tweak the default behavior associated with a wrapper. For example, the http wrapper allows you to modify the HTTP method from GET to POST or add HTTP headers such as cookies.

Here's how to add a cookie to your request using streams and file_get_ contents( ):

```
$options = array(
    'http' => array(
        'header' => "Cookie: username=rasmus\r\n"
    )
);

$context = stream_context_create($options);
$index = file_get_contents('http://www.example.com/index.php',
                           false, $context);
```

The stream_context_create( ) function takes an array of options and returns a context resource. Use the wrapper name as the array key. In this example it's http. These elements hold another array that specifies the wrapper options.

Each wrapper has its own set of options that vary depending upon what's appropriate for the wrapper. The http wrapper has a header option where you can enter data to be added to the HTTP header of your request.

The text Cookie: username=rasmus\r\n sets a cookie named username to the value rasmus. Every HTTP header needs to begin with a header name (Cookie), followed by a colon and a space, the header value, and then \r\n.

Pass the context as the third parameter to file_get_contents( ) and set the second parameter to false. The second parameter controls whether file_get_contents( ) should search the include_path, an option that makes no sense for the http wrapper.

Now when the web server on *www.example.com* processes the request, it will pass along your cookie.

Compiling PHP with the --with-openssl option enables an https wrapper. Its behavior is identical to the http wrapper, except that it uses SSL.

Table 8-1 has a list of all http and popular https context options.

Table 8-1. http and https wrapper context options

Name	Description	Default	Requires https?
allow_self_signed	Allow self-signed SSL certificates; value must be true or false	false	Yes
cafile	Path to certificate authority file used to authenticate remote peers; used when verify_peer is true		Yes
header	HTTP header, such as Cookie and Content-length		No
method	HTTP method, such as GET and POST	GET	No
proxy	Proxy server URL		No
request_fulluri	Send requests as full instead of relative URLs (necessary for some broken proxy servers); value must be true or false	false	No
verify_peer	Verify SSL certificate; value must be true or false	false	Yes
user_agent	HTTP User-agent header, overridden by header option	Value in user_agent configuration directive	No

Additional SSL context options are located at *http://www.php.net/transports*.

Since HTTP does not distinguish between getting and putting information on a protocol level, you cannot use file_put_contents( ) with the http wrapper. However, you can make an HTTP POST or PUT using http_get_ contents( ). Here's an example of an HTTP POST request:

```
$post_variables = array('usernamed' => 'rasmus');
$content = http_build_query($post_variables);
$content_length = strlen($content);

$options = array(
    'http'=>array(
        'method'  => 'POST',
        'header'  =>
            "Content-type: application/x-www-form-urlencoded\r\n" .
            "Content-length: $content_length\r\n",
        'content' => $content
    )
);

$context = stream_context_create($options);
$index = file_get_contents('http://www.example.com/index.php', false,
$context);
```

This code makes an HTTP POST request and sends along form data that sets the username variable equal to rasmus.

The new PHP 5 function http_build_query( ) then iterates through all the elements in the $post_variables array and encodes with urlencode( ) to ensure they're valid inside an HTTP request. Variables are then joined with their values using an equals sign (=) and then linked all together using ampersand (&).

This conversion is similar to what's done for an HTTP GET request. One difference between GET and POST, however, is that you must calculate your data's content length and pass that along as an HTTP header. This is done using strlen( ).

Now you have all the data necessary to create the stream context. The method is set to POST; the header is has two lines, a Content-type and a Content-length; and the content is set to $content, your encoded data. All HTTP POST forms must set a Content-type of application/x-www-form-urlencoded so the web server will know how to interpret the data.

This causes the $_POST array of *index.php* to contain your form data. Calling print_r($_POST) for this request gives you:

```
Array
(
    [username] => rasmus
)
```

There's one value, username, and it's set to rasmus.

One benefit of using streams over an extension like cURL is that you're guaranteed that the http wrapper is always available. Since cURL requires an external library, it's not enabled on all copies of PHP.

FTP and FTPS

The ftp wrapper allows you to speak to FTP servers. This wrapper behaves similarly to the http wrapper:

```
$index = file_get_contents(
    'ftp://rasmus:FbNAPw@ftp.example.com/www/www.example.com/index.html');
```

This logs into *ftp.example.com* as user rasmus and retrieves the *index.html* file in the */www/www.example.com/* directory.

If a username or password is not provided, PHP attempts to log in as user anonymous.

You can save a file to an FTP server using file_put_contents( ). This command saves $index to the server:

```
file_put_contents('ftp://rasmus:FbNAPw@ftp.example.com/www/www.example.com/
index.html', $index);
```

By default, if a file already exists on the FTP server, PHP will not overwrite it. Set the overwrite context option to change this behavior, like so:

```
$options = array(
    'ftp' => array(
        'overwrite' => true
    )
);

$context = stream_context_create($options);
file_put_contents(
    'ftp://rasmus:FbNAPw@ftp.example.com/www/www.example.com/index.html',
    $index, false, $context);
```

If the ftp overwrite option is set to true, the stream won't issue an error when there's a file at the location where you're saving the stream. Failing to do this causes file_put_contents( ) to return NULL and issue a warning:

```
PHP Warning:
file_put_contents(ftp://...@ftp.example.com/www/www.example.com/index.html):
failed to open stream: Cannot overwrite files in current mode
FTP server reports 213 3
```

As with the http wrapper, there's an ftps wrapper that is an SSL version of ftp.

PHP Input and Output

The php wrapper is particularly useful for people using PHP on the command line or with web services because it allows you to access any information sent to PHP from another program, regardless of format.

Normally, you can rely on the superglobal variables to contain all the data passed to PHP. HTTP GET and POST variables are in $_GET and $_POST, cookies are in $_COOKIES, and file uploads are in $_FILES. However, this happens only because this information is specially structured to be parsed into variables. When PHP is sent data in other formats, such as a SOAP packet that's structured as XML, the superglobal variables are not helpful at all. Similarly, when you use PHP to write a command-line tool, you communicate with the user through standard input instead of the superglobals.

The php wrapper is also handy for sending data from PHP. This wrapper makes it easy to send output to multiple locations in a consistent fashion. You can write to both standard out and standard error or control whether your data goes to the screen, a file, or both.

Standard input, output, and error

When you use PHP on the command line, it reads and writes information to and from three different locations. These places are known as standard input, standard output, and standard error.

Standard input is all the data sent to PHP, and *standard output* is the data coming from PHP. Standard input and output are typically abbreviated as stdin and stdout. These are the names used by the php filter.

This command makes the shell pass the contents of *input.txt* to the PHP script *wordwrap.php* on standard input and stores PHP's standard output in *output.txt*:

```
$ php wordwrap.php < input.txt > output.txt
```

Inside your script, however, you don't know about *input.txt* and *output.txt*. You only know that you're to process data from php://stdin and print the results to php://stdout. This allows you to create a generalized script that works in conjunction with other command-line tools.

To read from standard input, do this:

```
$stdin = file_get_contents('php://stdin');
```

To write to standard output, do this:

```
file_put_contents('php://stdout', $data);
```

This simple script rewraps text to 10 characters:

```
$stdin = file_get_contents('php://stdin');
$data = wordwrap($stdin, 10);
file_put_contents('php://stdout', $data);
```

When *input.txt* contains:

```
Hello! My name is Rasmus Lerdorf.
```

the file *output.txt* ends up as:

```
Hello! My
name is
Rasmus
Lerdorf.
```

Standard error is similar to standard output, but it's a special channel for error messages. It's often shortened as stderr, so to write to standard error, do this:

```
file_put_contents('php://stderr', $errors);
```

Standard error is used when you're storing standard output to a file and want to see warning messages on the console. Think of standard error as error_log( ) for the command line. For instance, whenever standard input is empty, Example 8-1 reports a warning using standard error.

Example 8-1. Wrapping standard input

```
$stdin = file_get_contents('php://stdin');

if (empty($stdin)) {
    file_put_contents('php://stderr', "wordwrap.php received no data.\n");
    $data = '';
} else {
    $data = wordwrap($stdin, 10);
}

file_put_contents('php://stdout', $data);
```

Now if you process *blank.txt*, a file without any data, you're given the following warning:

```
% php wordwrap.php < blank.txt > output.txt
wordwrap.php received no data.
```

You're not allowed to write to standard input, nor can you read from standard output or standard error—these streams work in only one direction. Writing to standard input won't write any bytes, which leads to an (inaccurate) warning message from PHP:

```
PHP Warning:  file_put_contents( ): Only 0 of 1 bytes written, possibly out
of free disk space.
```

Reading from standard output or error won't generate an error, but these streams never return any data, so there's really no point.

Also, PHP has its own set of output buffering functions that let you capture printed data. Writing to standard output circumvents these buffers, so be sure you really want standard output before you use this target.

To ensure you send data to the current PHP output buffer, use the output target instead. More details on output appear in the next section.

General input and output

While standard input and output are perfect for command-line tools, most people use PHP in combination with a web server to process requests. In these cases, you should use another set of streams instead.

The php://input stream contains data sent in using HTTP POST. This is identical to what's stored in the $HTTP_RAW_POST_DATA variable, but it's always available, regardless of the setting of the always_populate_raw_post_ data configuration directive. Using php://input is also more efficient than $HTTP_RAW_POST_DATA.

This filter is most commonly used for processing SOAP requests. For example, this simple SOAP server code for a Weather_Server service:

```
require 'SOAP/Server.php';

// Your Web Service class
require 'WebServices/Weather_Server.php';

$server = new SOAP_Server;
$server->addObjectMap(new Weather_Server,
                      'http://www.example.com/weather');
$server->service(file_get_contents('php://input'));
```

The complement to php://input is php://output. This stream is similar to standard output, but it respects your PHP output buffering settings. Therefore, unless you explicitly want standard out, you should use php://output as a stream alternative to print. This holds true even if you ultimately send the results to standard output. For example:

```
$ob = ob_start();                        // Start buffering of output
print '1';                               // Captured by buffer
file_put_contents('php://stdout', '2');  // Direct to standard out
file_put_contents('php://output', '3');  // Captured by buffer
ob_implicit_flush($ob);                  // Flush buffer contents
213
```

This snippet creates a PHP output buffer and then prints 1, 2, and 3. Since the output of print and file_put_contents('php://output') are captured by

the buffer, they appear *after* the number 2. This happens even though ob_
implicit_flush( ) sends data to standard out when used on the command
line, because writing directly to php://stdout bypasses the buffering scheme.

The php://output filter is also useful when you want to write a generic function that sends data to either the screen or a file:

```
function log_error($stream, $message) {
    $time = strftime('%c'); // default time reprentation
    fwrite($stream, "Error occured at time: $time\n");
    fwrite($stream, $message);
}

$screen = fopen('php://output', 'w+');
log_error($screen, "Cannot connect to database.");
fclose($screen);
```

The log_error( ) function prints the current time and logs the error. In this
case, it's sent through the standard output buffer, but you could also send
the message to a file. All you need to do is open a different stream and pass
that into log_error( ). Without php://output, you would need two separate
pieces of code to handle both cases.

Filtered input and output

There's one final php wrapper, php://filter. This isn't so much a wrapper
as a way to use filters with stream functions that don't let you attach a filter
before reading data.

Normally, you need to tell PHP that you want to filter a stream after you
open the stream but before you read from or write to it. However, some
functions—for example, file_get_contents( )—both open and read in the
file in one step. Therefore, you're unable to attach the filter to the stream.

The php://filter wrapper is a way around this problem. The exact details
of its use are explained in "Using php://filter," later in this chapter.

Compression

The compression wrappers allow you to automatically compress and
decompress files on the hard drive. The compress.zlib filter handles gzip,
and the compress.bzip2 filter handles bzip2.

To use the compress.zlib wrapper, you must configure PHP with the --with-
zlib flag, whereas compress.bzip2 needs the --with-bzip2 flag. While the primary applications of these libraries are to the zlib and bzip2 extensions, you
also automatically get the wrappers.

Use them just like the file wrapper:

```
$log = file_get_contents('compress.zlib:///var/log/access.log.gz');
```

This uncompresses */var/log/access.log.gz* and returns it to $log.

Or you can use the compress.bzip2 wrapper:

```
$log = file_get_contents('compress.zlib:///var/log/access.log.bz2');
```

Both wrappers also allow you to write files:

```
file_put_contents('compress.zlib:///pub/php/php-5.0.0.gz', $php);
```

The compression wrappers work only on local files; you cannot combine them with the http wrapper to open compressed files via HTTP.

Creating Wrappers

You can write custom wrappers in PHP. This lets you extend PHP to "speak" any protocol you want while still letting you use the standard stream functions, such as file_get_contents( ).

Stream wrappers are implemented as a class with specific methods. These methods are called by the stream-handling code when a stream using your wrapper is opened, read from, written to, and so forth.

In all, there are 17 potential methods that make up a complete wrapper, but it's rare to actually code all of these. Table 8-2 contains a list of wrapper methods and when they're evoked.

Table 8-2. Wrapper methods

Method	Function	PHP 5 only?
boolean stream_open(string path, string mode, int options, string opened_path)	fopen( )	No
void stream_close(void)	fclose( )	No
string stream_read(int count)	fread( ), fgets( )	No
int stream_write(string data)	fwrite( ), fputs( )	No
boolean stream_eof(void)	feof( )	No
int stream_tell(void)	ftell( )	No
boolean stream_seek(int offset, int whence)	fseek( )	No
boolean stream_flush(void)	fflush( )	No
array stream_stat(void)	fstat( )	No
boolean unlink(string path)	unlink( )	Yes
boolean mkdir(string path, int mode, int options)	mkdir( )	Yes

Table 8-2. Wrapper methods (continued)

Method	Function	PHP 5 only?
boolean rmdir(string path, int options)	rmdir()	Yes
boolean dir_opendir(string path, int options)	opendir()	No
string dir_readdir(void)	readdir()	No
boolean dir_rewinddir(void)	rewinddir()	No
boolean dir_closedir(void)	closedir()	No
array url_stat(string path, int flags)	stat()	No

In many cases, a method will have no meaningful concept for a wrapper, or will be impossible to implement due to technical limitations. For example, you cannot rename a file using HTTP.

Also, some higher-level functions, such as file_get_contents() and file_put_contents(), call multiple lower-level streams functions. For instance, you can't call file_get_contents() if you haven't implemented stream_open(), stream_read(), and stream_close().

If you try to call a method that's not defined by your wrapper, PHP issues a warning. Here's an example using a contrived fake wrapper that has no methods:

```
file_get_contents('fake://not/a/real/wrapper');
PHP Warning:  file_get_contents(fake://): failed to open stream:
  "fake::stream_open" call failed
```

The wrapper method specifications are like an informal interface. The big difference is that you're not required to implement all the methods.

This section shows how to implement a wrapper for PHP's shared memory functions. Shared memory is a way to store data in your server's RAM. When it's stored in RAM, you can access the information very quickly because you don't need to read from your disk drive.

Additionally, as the name suggests, this data is easily shared among different programs. This can be multiple copies of PHP running on the same machine, such as in a typical web server setup. Or, it can be other programs written in a different language.

The downside to using shared memory is that it takes up valuable RAM space, so you don't want to store very large files in shared memory. Also, the data is lost completely when the machine is rebooted. Finally, to use shared memory with Windows, you must run Windows 2000 or greater and run PHP as module. It won't work with the CGI or CLI modules.

PHP has a couple of different ways to interact with shared memory. This wrapper uses the shmop extension because it's most similar to the standard file interface and thus requires the least work to fit it to the stream's interface.

The shmop extension is included in PHP, but it's not enabled by default. To turn it on, add the --enable-shmop flag when compiling PHP.

Opening and Closing

A wrapper is a class with particular methods. Register a class as a wrapper using stream_wrapper_register( ). This call registers the shmop protocol with the ShmopWrapper class:

```
stream_wrapper_register('shmop', 'ShmopWrapper');
```

The first argument is the name of the protocol and the second is the class name. If stream_wrapper_register( ) cannot register the class, it returns false.

It's vital to implement stream_open( ) and stream_close( ) because you can't work with streams without them—even file_get_contents( ) implicitly calls stream_open( ) and stream_close( )

The stream_open( ) method tries to open the file (or, in this example, the shared memory segment). If it's successful, it returns true; it returns false if there's an error. The stream_close( ) method closes the file.

Example 8-2 shows how you implement stream_open( ) and stream_close( ) for ShmopWrapper.

Example 8-2. ShmopWrapper: stream_open() and stream_close()

```
class ShmopWrapper {
    private $id;
    private $position;
    private $length;

    public function stream_open($path, $mode = "c", $options, &$opened_path) {
        // hardcode some values for now
        $project = 'p';   // project PHP
        $perms   = 0600;  // user read and write only
        $size    = 16384;

        list($scheme, $target) = explode('://', $path);

        // convert path to key
        if (-1 === ($key = ftok($target, $project))) {
            if ($options & STREAM_REPORT_ERRORS) {
                trigger_error("Cannot convert path to shmop key.",
                    E_USER_WARNING);
```

Example 8-2. ShmopWrapper: stream_open() and stream_close() (continued)

```
            }
            return false;
    }

    // mode fix ups for file_(get|put)_contents()
    if ($mode == 'rb') {
        $mode = 'c';
    } elseif ($mode == 'wb') {
        $mode = 'w';
    }

    // illegal mode
    if (strlen($mode) != 1 || stripos("acwn", $mode) === false) {
        if ($options & STREAM_REPORT_ERRORS) {
            trigger_error("Illegal mode. Must be one of: a, c, w, n.",
                          E_USER_WARNING);
        }
        return false;
    }

    if (! $this->id = shmop_open($key, $mode, $perms, $size)) {
        if ($options & STREAM_REPORT_ERRORS) {
            trigger_error("Cannot open shmop segment.", E_USER_WARNING);
        }
        return false;
    }

    $this->position = 0;
    $this->length = shmop_size($this->id);
    return true;
    }

    public function stream_close() {
        shmop_close($this->id);
    }
}
```

The stream_open( ) method takes four parameters: $path, $mode, $options, and &$opened_path.

The $path variable is the complete path passed to fopen( ), including the protocol—for example, shmop://www/www.example.com/index.html. The $mode specifies how the stream is to be opened. This is one of four potential values:

a

Access: open an existing segment for read-only access.

c

Create: create a new segment, or open an existing segment for read and write access.

w

Write: open an existing segment for read and write access, but do not create a new segment.

n

New: create a new segment, but fail if the segment already exists.

The third parameter is either or both of these two options:

STREAM_USE_PATH

Search the include_path when passed a relative path. If the file is found in the include_path and opened, set the fourth parameter, &$opened_path, to its full pathname.

STREAM_REPORT_ERRORS

Report errors using trigger_error( ).

The stream_open( ) function in Example 8-2 first breaks apart the $path into the $scheme and the $target. The $scheme should always be shmop, and the $target should be a full pathname to a file.

This pathname is then converted to a shmop key using ftok( ). The ftok( ) function converts a filename and a project identifier into a unique key for shmop_open( ). This key distinguishes one shared memory segment from the others. The project identifier must be a one-letter code. For now, the project identifier is always p, for PHP.

When ftok( ) fails, it returns -1. When this occurs, stream_open( ) issues an error if the STREAM_REPORT_ERRORS constant is set in $options. This condition is checked by logically ANDing the two values together. The method then returns false and exits.

The next step is checking that the mode is a single digit long and contains one of the four acceptable modes: a, c, n, or w. If this fails, a similar series of error handlers kicks in.

You're finally ready to open the shared memory segment by calling shmop_open( ). This function takes four parameters. You've already seen the $key and the $mode, but it also uses the $perms and $size arguments.

The $perms parameter is the set of file permissions to use when creating the segment, and the $size parameter is the size of the segment to create in bytes. Like the project identifier, these two values are currently fixed, but later on these will be editable using stream context options.

When everything goes okay, the shared memory identifier is stored in the id property and the method returns true. If this fails, it returns false.

Thankfully, the stream_close( ) function is less complex. It releases the connection using shmop_close( ) and doesn't return anything.

Reading and Writing

Now that you can open and close the stream, the next step is to enable reading and writing. Example 8-3 shows this.

Example 8-3. ShmopWrapper: stream_read( ) and stream_write( )

```
public function stream_read($count) {
    // don't read beyond the end of the file
    $count = min($count, $this->length - $this->position);

    $data = shmop_read($this->id, $this->position, $count);
    $this->position += strlen($data);
    return $data;
}

public function stream_write($data) {
    $bytes_written = shmop_write($this->id, $data, $this->position);
    $this->position += $bytes_written;
    return $bytes_written;
}
```

When you call fread( ) and fwrite( ), the streams-handling code invokes your wrapper's stream_read( ) and stream_write( ) methods.

The fread( ) method takes one parameter, $count. This is the number of bytes to read from the stream; however, you're responsible for checking that this number isn't greater than the remaining bytes left in the stream. When $count is too big, the call to min( ) resets it to $this->length - $this->position, which is the maximum number of remaining bytes.

You now read the data from the stream with shmop_read( ). This function takes the shared memory handle, the position in the segment to read from, and the number of bytes to return. It returns the data stored in that portion of the segment.

When you read data, you must update your position in the stream by the size of your read. This way, you can read chunks of data from the stream and eventually reach the end. If you don't adjust the position, you just read the same segment again and again.

To account for the read, increment $this->position by the string length of the data. Once that's done, return the data.

Writing to shared memory is a similar process, but instead of taking the number of bytes to read and returning data, it takes data and returns the number of bytes written. It also updates the position property.

You're almost done, but there are still three necessary methods remaining—stream_tell( ), stream_eof( ), and stream_seek( )—which are contained in

---

Example 8-4. They help the stream know where it is, see if it's at the end of the file, and navigate through the file.

Example 8-4. ShmopWrapper: stream_tell(), stream_eof(), stream_seek()

```
public function stream_tell( ) {
    return $this->position;
}

public function stream_eof( ) {
    return $this->position >= $this->length;
}

public function stream_seek($offset, $whence) {
    switch($whence) {
    case SEEK_SET:
        if ($offset >= 0 && $offset < $this->length) {
            $this->position = $offset;
            return true;
        } else {
            return false;
        }
        break;

    case SEEK_CUR:
        if ($offset >= 0 &&
            $this->$position + $offset < $this->length) {
            $this->position += $offset;
            return true;
        } else {
            return false;
        }
        break;

    case SEEK_END:
        if ($this->length + $offset >= 0) {
            $this->position = $this->length + $offset;
            return true;
        } else {
            return false;
        }
        break;

    default:
        return false;
    }
}
```

Because you're already tracking your position, the first method, stream_tell( ), is essentially an accessor for the $position property.

The stream_eof( ) method reports when you're at the end of the segment. This occurs when the current position is greater than or equal to the size of the shared memory segment. The position should never exceed the $length, but it's better to be safe than sorry.

The last method is the most complex because it's really handling three different jobs. While the primary goal of stream_seek() is moving to a new location in the stream, you can specify that position in three different ways: SEEK_SET, SEEK_CUR, and SEEK_END. Here's how they're related:

SEEK_SET
Move $offset spaces from the *beginning* of the stream.

SEEK_CUR
Move $offset spaces from the *current* position of the stream.

SEEK_END
Move $offset spaces from the *end* of the stream. This value should be negative, so you move back into the stream instead of past the end.

The stream_seek() method uses a switch statement because the three types are handled similarly. After the request passes some out-of-bounds checking, to prevent moving past the beginning or end of the segment, the position is updated and the method returns true. Bad seek requests generate a return value of false.

Using ShmopWrapper

Now that you've implemented the basics necessary to get the wrapper up and running, use it:

```
stream_register_wrapper("shmop", "ShmopStream")
    or die("Failed to register shmop wrapper");

$file = __FILE__; // pass current file to key generator
file_put_contents("shmop://$file", 'Rasmus Lerdorf');
print file_get_contents("shmop://$file");
Rasmus Lerdorf
```

This example saves the string Rasmus Lerdorf to a shared memory segment and then retrieves it and prints it out. It uses the special __FILE__ constant as the pathname because it ensures the path will always be valid.

Since this value (Rasmus Lerdorf) is stored in shared memory, it's available on subsequent requests:

```
stream_register_wrapper("shmop", "ShmopWrapper")
    or die("Failed to register shmop wrapper");

$file = __FILE__; // pass current file to key generator
print file_get_contents("shmop://$file");
Rasmus Lerdorf
```

This code wrote nothing to the segment: the value persisted from the previous example.

The shmop wrapper also works with the lower-level streams manipulation functions:

```
stream_register_wrapper("shmop", "ShmopWrapper")
    or die("Failed to register shmop wrapper");

$file = __FILE__; // pass current file to key generator

$shmop = fopen("shmop://$file", 'c') or die("Can't open segment.");
fwrite($shmop, 'Zeev Suraski');
rewind($shmop);
print fread($shmop, 20);
fclose($shmop);
Zeev Suraskirf
```

Surprise! The old value of Rasmus Lerdorf was still stored in the segment, so calling fwrite( ) with Zeev Suraski only overwrote the first 12 letters. This left the last two—rf—in the segment. That's why you got the nonsense value of Zeev Suraskirf when you printed out the first 20 characters.

Deleting

A new feature in PHP 5 is the ability to delete files using streams. In PHP 4, you can only read and write data, not delete it, so it was impossible to clean up existing resources.

True to PHP's Unix roots, the method to delete an item is called unlink( ), as shown in Example 8-5.

Example 8-5. ShmopWrapper: unlink()

```
public function unlink($path) {
    if ($this->stream_open($path, 'w', 0, $opened_path) &&
        shmop_delete($this->id) &&
        $this->stream_close()) {
        return true;
    }

    return false;
}
```

The unlink( ) method from Example 8-5 takes a path to delete, such as shmop:///www/www.example.com/index.php. However, the shmop_delete( ) function needs a shared memory resource.

To circumvent this problem, unlink( ) calls stream_open( ) to convert the path to a segment. Now the id property holds the segment resource, which is passed to shmop_delete( ). Finally, to clean up, the segment is closed.

Adding this method to your class lets you remove segments:

```
stream_register_wrapper("shmop", "ShmopWrapper")
    or die("Failed to register shmop wrapper");

$file = __FILE__; // pass current file to key generator

unlink("shmop://$file");
$shmop = fopen("shmop://$file", 'c') or die("Can't open segment.");
fwrite($shmop, 'Zeev Suraski');
rewind($shmop);
print fread($shmop, 20);
fclose($shmop);
Zeev Suraski
```

Everything works okay now because the segment was cleared out before you wrote Zeev Suraski.

Adding Context Options

There's still one problem with the wrapper. Back in stream_open( ), you hardcoded values for the project name, the segment permissions, and the segment size. There isn't a good way to specify alternative values using the regular *wrapper://target* syntax.

That's why streams implements stream contexts. You can use a context to modify the three fixed values. First, here's how to pass context values to the wrapper:

```
$options = array(
    'shmop' => array(
        'size' => 32768
    )
);

$context = stream_context_create($options);
file_put_contents("shmop://$file", $data, false, $context)
    or die("Can't open segment.");
```

As with the http wrapper, place your options in a multidimensional array. The first array has a key of shmop; the second array can have keys of project, perms, and size. This example sets the size option to 32768 but leaves the other two options untouched.

After converting the array to a context with stream_context_create( ), pass it to file_put_contents( ) as the third parameter.

Here's a revised start of stream_open( ) from Example 8-2 that processes the context options:

```
public function stream_open($path, $mode = "c", $options, &$opened_path) {
        $contexts = stream_context_get_options($this->context);
```

```
$context = $contexts['shmop'];

$project = empty($context['project']) ? 'p'   : $context['project'];
$perms   = empty($context['perms'])   ? 0600  : $context['perms'];
$size    = empty($context['size'])    ? 16384 : $context['size'];

// rest of method follows...
}
```

When a person passes a context, the wrapper object automatically stores it in the $context property. Convert this context resource back into an array using stream_context_get_options( ). The shmop options, if any, are stored in the shmop key of the array.

Once these options are stored in $context, you need to check whether each option is set. If it is, use its values; otherwise, use the default value. This is done using the ? : ternary operator.

The most important part of adding context options is documentation. There's no standard naming convention, because options vary from wrapper to wrapper. So, without documentation, nobody will know what options they can use. There's no documentation standard for wrappers, but Php-Documentor (*http://pear.php.net/package/PhpDocumentor*) is a good choice.

Other Methods

This shmop wrapper implements eight different wrapper methods:

- stream_open( )
- stream_close( )
- stream_read( )
- stream_write( )
- stream_tell( )
- stream_eof( )
- stream_seek( )
- unlink( )

However, that's less than half of the total number of available methods. You can also implement:

- stream_flush( )
- stream_stat( )
- mkdir( )
- rmdir( )
- dir_opendir( )

- dir_readdir
- dir_rewinddir( )
- dir_closedir
- url_stat( )

Most of these methods operate on directories, but a few, such as stream_flush( ), work on files.

For more information on the other wrapper methods, consult Table 8-2 or read the documentation for stream_wrapper_register( ) in the PHP Manual at *http://www.php.net/stream-wrapper-register*.

Filtering Streams

Use filters to modify the contents of a stream. They allow you to pre- and postprocess data without altering the original. Stream filters are like output buffer handlers only better, because they're more flexible and efficient.

Unlike the output buffer handler, which is best suited for information that's either being printed out or stored in a variable, you can use a filter wherever you can use a stream. This makes it possible to filter, for example, data going to a file. With an output buffer you'd need to store the entire dataset in a buffer, capture it to a variable, and then send it to the file.

You can filter input data as well as output data. PHP's output buffering only works on output data. A filter lets you automatically encode all HTML entities from a user's input, for example.

PHP comes with a few built-in filters, but you can also create your own. The built-in filters are:

string.rot13
    Performs rot13 encoding

string.toupper
    Turns all characters to uppercase

string.tolower
    Turns all characters to lowercase

string.strip_tags
    Eliminates HTML tags

convert.iconv.*
    Alters the character set using iconv

Use stream_get_filters( ) to determine which filters are available. It works just like stream_get_wrappers( ).

Filters observe an unofficial namespace convention. For instance, string filters begin with `string.` and conversion filters begin with `convert.`.

To use a filter with a stream, you must associate the two using `stream_filter_prepend( )` or `stream_filter_append( )`. Since you can place multiple filters upon a single stream, the first function adds the new filter to the front of the list, whereas the second function adds it to the end. If your stream uses only a single filter, there's no difference between the two functions.

Stripping HTML Tags

One of the built-in filters is `string.strip_tags`. This filter removes HTML tags from the data. For example:

```
$html = 'I am <b>bold</b>. I am <i>italic</i>.';

$fp = fopen("php://output", "r");
stream_filter_prepend($fp, "string.strip_tags");
fwrite($fp, $html);
fclose($fp);
```

prints:

I am bold. I am italic.

This code opens a stream and then prepends the `string.strip_tags` filter to the filter chain. When the string $html is sent to the stream using `fwrite( )`, the filter intercepts the stream and removes the HTML tags.

Converting Character Sets

Another useful filter is `convert.iconv.*`. This allows you to convert text from one character set to another.

As of PHP 5, the iconv library is enabled by default, but it's not required to run PHP, so it's possible (but unlikely) that your copy of PHP won't have this filter.

For example, you have text stored in UTF-8 and want to convert it to ISO-8859-1 (aka Latin 1):

```
$fp = fopen("data.UTF-8.xml", "r");
stream_filter_prepend($fp, "convert.iconv.UTF-8/ISO-8859-1");
$converted = '';
while (!feof($fp)) {
    $converted .= fread($fp, 1000);
}
fclose($fp);
```

This opens *data.UTF-8.xml*, a UTF-8–encoded XML file. The filter convert.iconv.UTF-8/ISO-8859-1 takes this UTF-8 data and converts it to ISO-8859-1.

convert.iconv.* is a special "wildcard" filter that matches any filter name that begins with convert.iconv.. Specify the source and destination encodings after the period and separate them with a slash (/). As long as iconv supports those encodings, the filter will work and there's no need to explicitly write filters for every single combination of encoding translations.

You cannot get PHP to provide you with complete list of available encodings. Instead, use the command-line iconv tool with the -l flag:

```
% iconv -l
```

This prints a long list of encodings, probably beginning with:

```
ANSI_X3.4-1968 ANSI_X3.4-1986 ASCII
UTF-8
ISO-10646-UCS-2 UCS-2 CSUNICODE
```

To determine if a system supports a particular encoding, check the return value of iconv( ):

```
if (!iconv('ASCII', 'UTF-8', '')) {
    // Oops! iconv doesn't support this encoding
}
```

The function will return false when it cannot convert from one character set to another.

iconv supports two special modifiers for the destination encoding: //TRANSLIT and //IGNORE. The first option tells iconv that whenever it cannot exactly duplicate a character in the destination encoding, it should try to approximate it using a series of other characters. The other option makes iconv silently ignore any unconvertible characters.

For example, the file *geb-UTF-8.txt* holds the text Gödel, Escher, Bach. A straight conversion to ASCII produces an error:

```
$fp = fopen("geb.UTF-8.txt", "r");
stream_filter_prepend($fp, "convert.iconv.UTF-8/ASCII");
$converted = '';
while (!feof($fp)) {
    $converted .= fread($fp, 1000);
}
fclose($fp);
PHP Warning:  fread( ): iconv stream filter ("UTF-8"=>"ASCII"): unknown error
```

Enabling the //IGNORE feature allows the conversion to occur:

```
$fp = fopen("geb.UTF-8.txt", "r");
stream_filter_prepend($fp, "convert.iconv.UTF-8/ASCII//IGNORE");
$converted = '';
while (!feof($fp)) {
```

```
    $converted .= fread($fp, 1000);
}
fclose($fp);
```

However, the output isn't nice, because the ö is missing:

Gdel, Escher, Bach

The best solution is to use //TRANSLIT:

```
$fp = fopen("geb.UTF-8.txt", "r");
stream_filter_prepend($fp, "convert.iconv.UTF-8/ASCII//TRANSLIT");
$converted = '';
while (!feof($fp)) {
    $converted .= fread($fp, 1000);
}
fclose($fp);
```

This produces a better-looking string:

G"odel, Escher, Bach

However, be careful when you use //TRANSLIT, as it can increase the number of characters. For example, the single character ö becomes two characters: "o.

Using php://filter

Since it doesn't expose a file pointer such as fopen( ), the file_put_contents( ) function doesn't give you the opportunity to attach a filter using stream_filter_append( ). The solution is to use the php://filter target.

This weird target exists solely for the purpose of allowing you to integrate filters with functions such as file_put_contents( ). It lets you specify both filters and another target, like so:

```
$html = 'I am <b>bold</b>. I am <i>italic</i>.';

// Stripping HTML tags on data sent to php://output
file_put_contents(
    'php://filter/write=string.strip_tags/resource=php://output', $html);
```
I am bold. I am italic.

This code does the same thing as the longer version here:

```
// The long version
$fp = fopen("php://output", "r");
stream_filter_prepend($fp, "string.strip_tags");
fwrite($fp, $html);
fclose($fp);
```

Because filter isn't an actual target, you have to pass the true destination using the string /resource=. For example, use /resource=php://output to send information to the current output buffer.

You can also insert multiple filters into the stream. Filters can process data being read, written, or both. (Some streams are unidirectional, but others are bidirectional.) To designate a filter for reading, add /read=; for writing, add /write=; and, for both directions, add /=. For example, /write=string. strip_tags strips HTML tags from any data being written.

Chain multiple filters with the pipe character (|). Filters are applied in the order present. So, /write=string.strip_tags|string.string.toupper first strips tags and then uppercases letters.

Creating Filters

PHP 5 comes with very few stream filters, but it introduces the ability to write your own filters in PHP, effectively giving you unlimited possibilities. PHP 4 requires all filters to be implemented in C.

The filter interface is much less complex than the wrapper interface. It has only three different methods, and it's common to implement only a single method, filter( ). Table 8-3 contains an overview of the API.

Table 8-3. Filter methods

Method	Description
int filter(resource in, resource out, int &consumed, bool closing)	Called during data filtering; may be called multiple times per stream
void onCreate(void)	Called during filter instantiation
void onClose(void)	Called during filter destruction

The filter( ) method is where all the action takes place. Inside this method, you're required to process the incoming data, filter it when you can, and then alert the filter of your progress.

This section shows how to implement two different filters: one that encodes special characters (such as & and <) to their HTML entities equivalents, and one the does the reverse, by transforming HTML entities back into characters.

Converting to HTML Entities

Example 8-6 shows a filter that encodes HTML entities using the htmlentities( ) function.

Example 8-6. Encoding HTML entities with a filter

```
class htmlentitiesFilter extends php_user_filter {

    function filter($in, $out, &$consumed, $closing) {
        while ($bucket = stream_bucket_make_writeable($in)) {
            $bucket->data = htmlentities($bucket->data);
            $consumed += $bucket->datalen;
            stream_bucket_append($out, $bucket);
        }
        return PSFS_PASS_ON;
    }
}
```

This class looks complicated because there are many new functions and objects, but it's actually quite boring and simple.

Filters written in PHP are implemented as objects. There's a predefined base class, php_user_filter, which is automatically available for you to use; it does not need to be included. All filters must extend this class and implement the filter( ) method.

The filter( ) method is where the actual data conversion takes place. This method takes four parameters: $in, $out, &$consumed, and $closing. The first two parameters are the input and output bucket resources. These resources hold stream data.

The third parameter, &$consumed, is set to the amount of data in the stream already processed, or "eaten up," by the filter. This parameter must always be passed as a reference. The final argument is $closing. It's set to true when filter( ) is called for the last time, so you can be sure to flush any remaining data if necessary.

Your primary goal inside filter( ) is to take data from the input bucket, convert it, and then add it to the output bucket. However, you can't just operate on the bucket resources directly; instead, you need to call a few helper functions to convert the data from a resource to an object that is modifiable in PHP.

The stream_bucket_make_writable( ) function retrieves a portion of the data from the input bucket and converts it to a PHP bucket object. This object has two properties: data and datalen. The data property is a string holding the bucket's data, whereas datalen is its length.

Since this filter wants to modify all the input data to escape HTML entities, pass $bucket->data to htmlentities( ) and assign the return value back to $bucket->data. This alters the data inside the bucket object.

Your next step is to let the filter know you've processed some data. Do this by incrementing the value of $consumed by the length of the data you've filtered. Since in this case you've filtered the entire data property, you can just add the value of $bucket->datalen.

The last step is to take the bucket object and add it as output. The stream_bucket_append( ) function takes a bucket resource and appends a bucket object to it. Therefore, to add the converted bucket object back to the stream, call stream_bucket_append($out, $bucket).

This entire process takes place inside a while loop because the stream passes data to you in chunks instead of sending the entire dataset at once. When there's no more data, stream_bucket_make_writable( ) returns false and the loop terminates.

Once the loop is completed, you must return one of three constants: PSFS_PASS_ON, PSFS_FEED_ME, or PSFS_ERR_FATAL. When everything goes as planned, return PSFS_PASS_ON. When everything's okay but your filter cannot yet return any data because it needs additional data to complete the filtering process, return PSFS_FEED_ME. Whenever there's an unrecoverable error, return PSFS_ERR_FATAL.

Register the class as a filter with stream_filter_register( ):

```
stream_filter_register('convert.htmlentities', 'htmlentitiesFilter')
    or die('Failed to register filter');

$html = 'I am <b>bold</b>. I am <i>italic</i>.';

$fp = fopen('php://output', 'r');
stream_filter_prepend($fp, 'convert.htmlentities');
fwrite($fp, $html);
fclose($fp);
```

This prints:

```
I am &lt;b&gt;bold&lt;/b&gt;. I am &lt;i&gt;italic&lt;/i&gt;.
```

Converting from HTML Entities

The inverse operation, decoding HTML entities, requires special handling. Because HTML entities are multiple characters, they may span buckets. For example, one bucket could end with &a and the next one could begin with mp;.

When you don't have a good algorithm for identifying partial sequences, store the entire dataset into a property and wait until the $closing parameter is true, as in Example 8-7.

Example 8-7. Decoding HTML entities with a filter

```
class dehtmlentitiesFilter extends php_user_filter {

    function onCreate( ) {
        $this->data = '';
        return true;
    }

    function filter($in, $out, &$consumed, $closing) {
        while ($bucket = stream_bucket_make_writeable($in)) {
            $this->data .= $bucket->data;
            $this->bucket = $bucket;
            $consumed = 0;
        }

        if ($closing) {
            $consumed += strlen($this->data);

            // decode named entities
            $this->data = html_entity_decode($this->data);

            $this->bucket->data = $this->data;
            $this->bucket->datalen = strlen($this->data);
            stream_bucket_append($out, $this->bucket);

            return PSFS_PASS_ON;
        }

        return PSFS_FEED_ME;
    }
}
```

Unlike the filter in Example 8-6, Example 8-7 uses the onCreate( ) method to initialize a property. This method is run the first time the filter is invoked. There's also an onClose( ) method that's called when the filter finishes, but neither of the two example filters uses it.

Instead of reading in buckets and converting data as it arrives, filter( ) stores all the data locally and executes the conversion only at the end. This way you're assured that you're never caught mid-entity.

Inside the while, append each bucket's data to the $data property. You also store the bucket in the $bucket property; otherwise, PHP destroys the bucket when the loop terminates. Finally, since none of the data is consumed right now, always set $consumed to 0.

After processing all the buckets, check to see if the stream is closing. If it's true, you know all the data has arrived, so you can begin the conversion.

First, update $consumed to the length of the data. Then, decode the HTML entities with html_entity_decode( ), storing the results in $this->data.

With the mapping complete, it's time to update the bucket. Its data property gets the converted data, and its datalen property is set to the data's length. This is not the same as $consumed. It will be shorter because you're converting & back into &, for example.

Now append the bucket to the output and return PSFS_PASS_ON. However, when $closing is false, omit the conversions and return PSFS_FEED_ME to let the stream know that your filter needs additional data to process.

Use this filter like the HTML entity encoding filter:

```
stream_filter_register("convert.dehtmlentities", "dehtmlentitiesFilter")
    or die("Failed to register filter");

$ascii = 'I am &lt;b&gt;bold&lt;/b&gt;. I am &lt;i&gt;italic&lt;/i&gt;.';
$fp = fopen("php://output", "r");
stream_filter_prepend($fp, "convert.dehtmlentities");
fwrite($fp, $html);
fclose($fp);
I am <b>bold</b>. I am <i>italic</i>.
```

Other Extensions

This chapter covers three new parts of PHP 5: the SOAP and Tidy extensions and the Reflection classes.

SOAP is an XML-based protocol for exchanging information over the Internet that you can use to build or utilize web services. The SOAP extension provides you with an easy way to both query SOAP servers and implement a SOAP server of your own.

The Tidy extension tackles the problem of invalid HTML. It converts malformed web pages into fully valid HTML and XHTML. Tidy also lets you optimize your web pages by removing unnecessary characters. This translates into faster download times and lower bandwidth bills, a double advantage. Finally, Tidy helps you out when you're in the unfortunate position of parsing HTML to extract data, such as when you're screen-scraping.

With the Reflection classes, you can programmatically extract information about classes, functions, methods, and properties. This allows you to produce automated class documentation, write a PHP debugger, and other tasks that require object introspection.

SOAP

Web services allow you to exchange information over HTTP using XML. When you want to find out the weather forecast for New York City, the current stock price of IBM, or the best-selling DVD according to Amazon.com, you can write a short script to gather that data in a format you can easily manipulate. From a developer's perspective, it's as if you're calling a local function that returns a value.

A major advantage of web services is ubiquity across platforms and languages. A PHP script running on Linux can talk to an IIS server on a

Windows box using ASP without any communication problems. When the server switches over to Solaris, Apache, and JSP, everything transitions without a glitch.

SOAP is a popular web services format. It's a W3C standard for passing messages across the network and calling functions on remote computers. SOAP provides developers with many options; however, this flexibility comes at a price. SOAP is quite complex, and the full specification is large and growing.

As a result, PHP 4's SOAP support is only fair. While there are a few SOAP packages, the most mature ones are written in PHP instead of C. Therefore, they are slow, and you have to download and install them yourself.

With PHP 5, there's finally a usable SOAP extension written in C. Additionally, it's bundled with PHP 5, so you can enable SOAP support by adding --enable-soap to your PHP configure line. The only external library you need is libxml2, which is the same requirement for any of PHP 5's XML extensions.

Right now, this extension implements most, but not all, of SOAP 1.2. This is a significant improvement over previous C extension, and Zend's Dmitry Stogov is actively working on filling in the remaining pieces. Complete details on SOAP are available on the W3 web site at *http://www.w3.org/2000/xp/Group/* and in *Programming Web Services with SOAP*, by James Snell, Doug Tidwell, and Pavel Kulchenko (O'Reilly).

This section shows how to create a SOAP client and a SOAP server. The SOAP client demonstrates how to query a server to find out the current temperature. Then, the section "Processing Requests with a SOAP Server" shows how to replicate a similar interface using PHP. Along the way, you also see how to handle SOAP faults, either with exceptions or with traditional error-handling code.

WSDL

Before getting into the details of SOAP, it's necessary to first discuss *WSDL*. WSDL (Web Services Description Language) is an XML vocabulary that lets the implementor create a file that defines what methods and arguments his web service supports. This file is then placed on the Web for others to read.

Since WSDL is written in XML, it's not particularly friendly for humans, but it's great for machines. When you point the SOAP extension at a WSDL file, the extension automatically creates an object for the web service, and you can manipulate this object as you would a PHP class.

The object even knows what parameters each method takes and each parameter's type. This is important because, unlike PHP, SOAP is a strictly typed language. You cannot provide a string 1 when SOAP wants an integer 1. WSDL allows the SOAP extension to coerce PHP variables into the appropriate types without any action on your part.

Unfortunately, the SOAP extension cannot generate WSDL for your own web service servers. This makes it difficult, although not impossible, for people to talk to your web services, because they need to go through more steps to make a client request. Hopefully, this feature will be added in the near future. This is addressed in more detail in "Processing Requests with a SOAP Server."

For more on WSDL, see *http://www.w3.org/TR/wsdl*, or read Chapter 6 of Ethan Cerami's *Web Services Essentials*, available at *http://www.oreilly.com/ catalog/webservess/chapter/ch06.html*.

Requesting Information with a SOAP Client

The most common task when using a web service is querying a server for information. Before you can do this, of course, you need to know the location of a web service to query and what parameters the method takes.

One place to go is XMethods (*http://www.xmethods.net*), a site that provides a few useful web services and also contains a giant directory of publicly available web services. The examples in this section query XMethods's Temperature service, which lets you discover the current temperature for a Zip Code.

WSDL requests

Whenever possible, you want to know the location of the server's WSDL file. This makes it much easier to make SOAP requests. Example 9-1 shows how to make a query using WSDL.

Example 9-1. SOAP client using WSDL

```
$wsdl_url =
    'http://www.xmethods.net/sd/2001/TemperatureService.wsdl';

$client = new SoapClient($wsdl_url);

$temp = $client->getTemp('10001'); // New York, NY
print $temp;
68
```

From XMethods's web site, you know that the WSDL file for this service is at *http://www.xmethods.net/sd/2001/TemperatureService.wsdl*.

You now instantiate a new SoapClient object by passing $wsdl_url, the location of the WSDL file, to the constructor. This returns a client object, $client, that you use to make SOAP requests.

The constructor creates a SOAP client, but you still need to make the actual query itself. The method to find the temperature is called getTemp( ). It takes one argument, the Zip Code. Pass your Zip Code, in this case 10001, directly to the method.

When you call $client->getTemp(10001), the SOAP extension converts the PHP string 10001 to a SOAP message written in XML and sends an HTTP request to XMethods's server. After XMethods receives and processes your query, it replies with a SOAP message of its own. The SOAP extension listens for this response and parses the XML into a PHP object, which is then returned by the method and stored in $temp.

The $temp variable now holds the current temperature, in Fahrenheit. Right now it's 68 degrees in New York City.

Non-WSDL requests

It's harder to query web services that don't provide a WSDL file. Example 9-2 shows how to query the identical service without WSDL.

Example 9-2. SOAP client without WSDL

```
$opts = array('location' =>
              'http://services.xmethods.net:80/soap/servlet/rpcrouter',
              'uri'       => 'urn:xmethods-Temperature');
$client = new SoapClient(NULL, $opts);

$temp = $client->__call('getTemp', array('10001'));

print $temp;
68
```

In Example 9-2, since you're not using WSDL, pass NULL as the first argument to SoapClient. This tells the SOAP extension that you're passing the details about the web service in the second parameter.

This information is stored as array. At a minimum, you must provide two entries: the URL where the SOAP server is located and the namespace URI that identifies the service.

The server's URL is the location element; here, the server is at *http://services.xmethods.net:80/soap/servlet/rpcrouter*. The server's namespace is set using the uri element. This is urn:xmethods-Temperature.

Now you have a SOAP client, but with a non-WSDL–based client, you can't directly invoke SOAP methods on the $client object. Instead, you reference the __call( ) method, passing the method name as your first argument and an array of parameters as the second.

Since the SOAP client no longer knows how many parameters to expect, you must bundle your parameters to __call( ) inside of an array. Therefore, your Zip Code is now passed as array('10001') instead of '10001'.

This code is more complex than the WSDL solution, and it even takes advantage of some default SOAP settings assumed by SoapClient.

Multiple parameter queries

The XMethods getTemp( ) method takes one only parameter, the Zip Code. This allows you to pass it directly to the method because there's no potential confusion about which value belongs to which parameter.

Some web service methods take multiple parameters. For these methods, you can either remember the argument order or pass the arguments in an array. The parameter names and values are the array element keys and values, respectively.

Example 9-3 demonstrates what you would do if the getTemp( ) method allowed you to specify a Zip Code and temperature scale.

Example 9-3. SOAP client with multiple parameters

```
$wsdl_url =
    'http://www.example.com/TemperatureService.wsdl';

$client = new SoapClient($wsdl_url);

$params = array(
    'Zipcode' => 10001, // New York, NY
    'scale'   => 'C'    // Celsius
);
$temp = $client->getTemp($params);
20
```

The Zipcode parameter is the five-digit Zip Code, and scale is either F or C, for Fahrenheit and Celsius, respectively.

This code won't actually work, because XMethods doesn't support multiple conversion scales. However, the later section "Processing Requests with a SOAP Server" demonstrates how to implement this example as a SOAP web service.

Catching SOAP Faults

When a SOAP server generates an error, it returns a SOAP fault. This can be a mistake on your part, such as calling a method that doesn't exist or passing the incorrect number (or type) of parameters, or it can be a server error. For instance, the service lacks temperature information for a particular Zip Code, but for reasons external to your SOAP request.

The SOAP extension transforms SOAP faults into PHP exceptions, as shown in Example 9-4.

Example 9-4. Detecting SOAP faults with exceptions

```
try {
    $wsdl_url =
        'http://www.example.com/TemperatureService.wsdl';

    $client = new SoapClient($wsdl_url);

    $temp = $client->getTemp('New York'); // This should be a Zip Code
    print $temp;
} (SOAPFault $exception) {
    print $exception;
}
SoapFault exception: [SOAP-ENV:Server] Zip Code New York is unknown.
  in /www/www.example.com/soap.php:8
Stack trace:
#0 /www/www.example.com/soap.php(8): SoapClient->getTemp('getTemp', Array)
#1 {main}
```

Since the server requires a Zip Code but Example 9-4 passed New York, the server returned a SOAP fault. Printing the exception gives you, among other debugging information, the error Zip Code New York is unknown..

If you dislike exceptions, you can make SOAP return faults instead by setting the exceptions configuration setting to 0. This is done in Example 9-5.

Example 9-5. Detecting SOAP faults without exceptions

```
$wsdl_url =
    'http://www.example.com/TemperatureService.wsdl';

// Disable exceptions
$opts = array('exceptions' => 0);
$client = new SoapClient($wsdl_url, $opts);

$temp = $client->getTemp('New York'); // This should be a Zip Code
if (is_soap_fault($temp)) {
    print $exception;
} else {
    print $temp;
}
SoapFault exception: [SOAP-ENV:Server] Zip Code New York is unknown.
  in /www/www.example.com/soap.php:8
#0 {main}
```

To alter the default settings for a SoapClient object, pass in an array as the second argument to the constructor. This is the same array that you use to specify information about non-WSDL servers.

When exceptions are disabled, $temp contains either the valid response or a SOAP fault. Check is_soap_fault( ) to discover if there's an error.

Caching WSDL

The largest problem with WSDL is that before you can make the actual request, the SOAP extension needs to fetch the WSDL file over the Internet and parse the document to create the proxy object. This effectively doubles the time required to make the query.

The SOAP extension solves this by implementing a caching system. When a local WSDL file exists, the extension uses the local copy instead of making another request.

The caching system is controlled by three configuration directives:

soap.wsdl_cache_enabled
    Whether to enable the WSDL cache

soap.wsdl_cache_dir
    Where to store the WSDL files

soap.wsdl_cache_ttl
    How long to keep the WSDL files

By default, all WSDL files are cached in the */tmp* directory for 86000 seconds, or one day.

Adjust the soap.wsdl_cache_ttl value to a higher number if you know the WSDL file is unlikely to change (for instance, you're in control of the SOAP server or you know you'll receive advance notice of any modifications). Turn off soap.wsdl_cache_enabled when you're developing a web service and you know you're going to be modifying a WSDL file on a frequent basis.

Processing Requests with a SOAP Server

To process SOAP requests, you must first create a class to contain the methods you will allow people to query using SOAP. Then, create a SOAPServer instance to handle the job of handing off the SOAP requests to your class's methods.

Implementing getTemp( ) in PHP

Example 9-6 is a replication of the XMethods temperature SOAP server in PHP using the SOAP extension.

Example 9-6. Implementing a SOAP server

```
class TemperatureService {
    private $temps = array('10001' => 68);

    public function getTemp($Zipcode) {
        if (isset($this->temps[$Zipcode])) {
            return $this->temps[$Zipcode];
        } else {
            throw new SoapFault('Server', "Zip Code $Zipcode is unknown.");
        }
    }
}

$server = new SoapServer(NULL,
                        array('uri' => 'http://www.example.org/temp'));
$server->setClass('TemperatureService');
$server->handle();
```

In Example 9-6, the TemperatureService class contains getTemp( ), the one SOAP method supported by your web service.

The getTemp( ) method takes a Zip Code and returns the current temperature. Since you don't have access to actual temperature data, getTemp( ) checks the private $temp property. That property holds a fixed array that maps Zip Codes to the "current" temperature.

When the Zip Code isn't in the array, the SOAP server issues a SoapFault. This fault is thrown using PHP's exception-handling mechanism, and the SOAP extension will automatically convert the exception into the correct XML to signal an error in SOAP.

Once your class is complete, there are three commands to create, configure, and start the SOAP server. The first step is to instantiate a new instance of SoapServer. The first parameter is a WSDL file that describes the server. Since you don't have one, pass NULL instead, and add the information using the second parameter.

The second argument takes an array of items. In this example, there's only a uri element (which is set to http://www.example.com/temp). Each SOAP server is uniquely identified by a namespace of your own choosing, and this one lives in http://www.example.com/temp.

Now you bind the object to the server by calling setClass( ). This tells the SOAP server to call the methods of the TemperatureService class when processing requests.

The last step is to make your PHP script grab the incoming SOAP request and give it to the SOAP server for processing. This is done with a call to handle( ).

This is not complicated. However, there's one problem: since the SOAP extension can't (yet) generate WSDL for a PHP class, it's not easy for people to query your SOAP server. They can't just read in the WSDL and call a method. Instead, they need to use the non-WSDL query technique.

Example 9-7 shows what you need to do instead to query your web service.

Example 9-7. Querying your SOAP server

```
try {
    $opts = array('location' => 'http://www.example.org/temp.php',
                  'uri'      => 'http://www.example.org/temp');
    $client = new SoapClient(NULL, $opts);
    $temp = $client->__call('getTemp', array('10001'));
    print $temp;
} catch (SOAPFault $e) {
    print $e;
}
```

This is similar to Example 9-2, but there's a different location and uri. The location is http://www.example.org/temp.php, or whatever URL you choose to place your script. The uri namespace needs to match the uri element you passed to SoapServer, so it's http://www.example.org/temp.

One short-term solution to the lack of WSDL generation capabilities is to use the PEAR SOAP classes as the backend to your SOAP server. PEAR::SOAP can autogenerate WSDL, so that solves the problem. However, PEAR::SOAP is slower than the SOAP extension because it is written in PHP instead of C.

If you need the speed of the SOAP extension, you can first hook up your class to PEAR::SOAP, have it generate your WSDL, and then hook up your class to the SOAP extension. This isn't as complex as it sounds, but it's not explained here, because hopefully this workaround won't be necessary for very long.

For more on PEAR::SOAP, including how to make it create a WSDL file for your server, see *Essential PHP Tools* by David Sklar (Apress).

Optional parameters

You can modify getTemp( ) to support an optional temperature scale parameter that controls whether the temperature is reported in Fahrenheit or Celsius, as shown in Example 9-8.

Example 9-8. Extending your SOAP server

```
class WeatherSOAP {
    private $temps = array(10001 => 68);
```

Example 9-8. Extending your SOAP server (continued)

```
    function getTemp($Zipcode, $scale = 'F') {
      if (isset($this->temps[$Zipcode])) {
          if ($scale == 'F') {
             return $this->temps[$Zipcode];
          } elseif ($scale == 'C') {
             // Convert from F to C
             return ($this->temps[$Zipcode] - 32) / 9 * 5;
          } else {
             throw new SoapFault('Server', "Invalid temperature scale.");
          }
      } else {
          throw new SoapFault('Server', "Zip Code $Zipcode is unknown.");
      }
    }
  }
}
```

In Example 9-8, when $scale is set to C, the server converts the temperature to Celsius before it's returned.

To trigger the conversion, add another element to the argument array, as in Example 9-9.

Example 9-9. Finding the temperature in Celsius

```
try {
    $opts = array('location' => 'http://www.example.org/temp.php',
                  'uri'      => 'http://www.example.org/temp');
    $client = new SoapClient(NULL, $opts);
    $words = $client->__call('getTemp',
                             array('10001', 'C'),
                             array('uri' => 'http://www.example.org/temp'));
} catch (SOAPFault $e) {
    print $e;
}
```

When your server uses WSDL, you can define your method parameters in any order using an array, like this:

```
$params = array('scale' => 'C', 'Zipcode' => '10001')
```

However, when you're not using WSDL, as in this case, you *must* define them in the order that the method expects. WSDL lets the server rearrange the parameters into the correct order, something the server cannot do otherwise.

Tidy

The Tidy extension "cleans up" messy HTML and XML files into valid and pretty-looking documents. This feature is particularly useful when you're serving lots of externally generated content.

For example, you want to allow visitors to enter HTML-enabled messages, but you don't want them to be able to create an invalid page. Manually checking each post is quite laborious, but with Tidy you can automate this process.

Alternatively, Tidy can be used to reformat documents, either to reduce their file size or to make them easily understandable by humans. The first option saves you bandwidth, making your pages arrive more quickly and reducing your overall hosting costs. The second option simplifies your debugging process, as you're not tracking down stray closing tags.

The Tidy extension is bundled with PHP, but not enabled, because it requires you to install the Tidy library. Download the Tidy library from *http://tidy.sourceforge.net/* and add `--with-tidy=DIR` to turn on Tidy support in PHP.

Basics

Interacting with Tidy is a simple three step process. You parse the file, then clean its contents, and finally print or save the repaired file.

Use `tidy_parse_file( )` to read in a file for tidying:

```
$tidy = tidy_parse_file('index.html');
```

When your data is in a string, use `tidy_parse_string( )` instead:

```
// This string is missing a closing </i> tag
$tidy = tidy_parse_string('I am <b>bold and I am <i>bold and italic</b>');
```

Transform the document using the `tidy_clean_repair( )` command:

```
$tidy = tidy_parse_string('I am <b>bold and I am <i>bold and italic</b>');
tidy_clean_repair($tidy);
```

The `tidy_clean_repair( )` function takes a Tidy resource. It returns `true` if everything went okay, and `false` on an error. It *does not* return the tidied document. Use `tidy_get_output( )` to retrieve the altered file:

```
$tidy = tidy_parse_string('I am <b>bold and I am <i>bold and italic</b>');
tidy_clean_repair($tidy);
print tidy_get_output($tidy);
```

This prints:

```
<!DOCTYPE html PUBLIC "-//W3C//DTD HTML 3.2//EN">
<html>
<head>
<title></title>
</head>
<body>
I am <b>bold and I am <i>bold and italic</i></b>
</body>
</html>
```

Tidy has not only repaired the missing </i> tag, but also turned the string into a valid HTML 3.2 file.

Configuring Tidy

You can configure Tidy in innumerable ways. These options can be set at parse time in an array or in a configuration file.

For example, to make Tidy return only the body of a cleaned document:

```
$options = array('show-body-only' => true);
$tidy = tidy_parse_string('I am <b>bold and I am <i>bold and italic</b>');
tidy_clean_repair($tidy);
print tidy_get_output($tidy);
I am <b>bold and I am <i>bold and italic</i></b>
```

This is useful when you're cleaning document fragments, such as message board posts or HTML that is placed inside a template.

Alternatively, you can place this information in a file and pass the filename:

```
show-body-only: true
logical-emphasis: true
```

In the configuration file, place each individual option on a new line, and separate options with a colon (:). Then, provide Tidy with its location:

```
$tidy = tidy_parse_string('I am <b>bold and I am <i>bold and italic</b>',
                          'tidy.cnf');
tidy_clean_repair($tidy);
print tidy_get_output($tidy);
I am <strong>bold and I am <em>bold and italic</em></strong>
```

In addition to fixing the HTML, turning on logical-emphasis has switched your b and i tags to their logical equivalents.

Table 9-1 contains commonly used Tidy settings. A complete list of available options is at *http://tidy.sourceforge.net/docs/quickref.html*.

Table 9-1. Important Tidy configuration options

Name	Description	Values	Default
clean	Should Tidy convert font tags to CSS?	Boolean	no
hide-endtags	Omit ending tags?	Boolean	no
indent	Indent block-level tags?	yes, no, auto	no
indent-spaces	Number of spaces per indent	Integer	2
markup	Create a "Pretty Print" version of the file?	Boolean	yes
output-xml	Output XML instead of HTML?	Boolean	no
output-xhtml	Output XHTML instead of HTML?	Boolean	no
show-body-only	Only return document body	Boolean	no

Table 9-1. Important Tidy configuration options (continued)

Name	Description	Values	Default
wrap	Length of line wrap	Integer	66
wrap-attributes	Wrap attribute values?	Boolean	no
wrap-php	Wrap PHP code?	Boolean	no

Optimize Files

Tidy provides options that can reduce your file size by stripping away extra whitespace and comments and by converting verbose <font> tags into CSS.

Here is a sample configuration for Tidy that aggressively strips away as many unneeded characters as possible:

```
$options = array(
    'clean' => true,
    'drop-proprietary-attributes' => true,
    'drop-empty-paras' => true,
    'hide-comments' => true,
    'hide-endtags' => true,
    'join-classes' => true,
    'join-styles' => true,
    'wrap' => 0,
);

$tidy = tidy_parse_file('http://www.example.org/', $options);
tidy_clean_repair($tidy);
print $tidy;
```

The overall effect of these options is to eliminate HTML that the browser doesn't use when rendering the page and to combine duplicated styles into one unified style. Each setting is detailed in Table 9-2.

Remember that even a small improvement in page size is multiplied by every single page your server delivers. The combined reduction in bandwidth may translate to serious cost savings on a high-traffic site.

Table 9-2. Optimizing Tidy configuration options

Name	Description	Values	Default
clean	Convert presentational tags, such as <center>, with style rules?	Boolean	no
drop-proprietary-attributes	Eliminate proprietary attributes added by programs such as Microsoft Office?	Boolean	no
drop-font-tags	Eliminate <font> tags when used with the clean option?	Boolean	no
drop-empty-paras	Eliminate empty <p> tags?	Boolean	yes

Table 9-2. Optimizing Tidy configuration options (continued)

Name	Description	Values	Default
hide-comments	Remove HTML comments?	Boolean	no
hide-endtags	Remove closing tags when possible according to the Document Type?	Boolean	no
join-classes	Merge related classes together?	Boolean	no
join-styles	Merge related styles together?	Boolean	yes
wrap	Width for line wrapping (a value of 0 disables wrapping).	Integer	68

Object-Oriented Interface

Tidy also has an object-oriented interface:

```
$tidy = new Tidy('I am <b>bold and I am <i>bold and italic</b>');
$tidy->cleanRepair();
print $this->getOutput();
```

Like other extensions with dual procedural and OO interfaces, Tidy's methods use studlyCaps instead of underscores. Additionally, you don't pass a Tidy resource to the methods, because the resource is stored in the object.

Reflection

The Reflection classes allow you to retrieve detailed data about classes. Although you don't need to use them in most web applications, they're invaluable when you're writing a program such as a class documenter, unit tester, or debugger. These applications all require generic class-manipulation routines.

PHP 4 lets you discover information about classes using a series of functions. There's get_class_methods() to get an array of class methods and get_class_vars() for an array of properties. These functions aren't integrated, so you cannot find out all the information about a class at once.

The functions are also very simplistic. They don't contain any of the new information that you can set in PHP 5. For example, there's no way to distinguish between private, protected, and public methods and properties.

That's where the Reflection classes come in. They help you extract from a class or method any piece of data you need.

Getting an Overview with Reflection::export

To understand how the Reflection classes work, Example 9-10 contains an example Person class that uses many of PHP 5's OO features.

Example 9-10. Person class

```
class Person {
    public $name;
    protected $spouse;
    private $password;

    public function __construct($name) {
        $this->name = $name
    }

    public function getName() {
        return $name;
    }

    protected function setSpouse(Person $spouse) {
        if (!isset($this->spouse)) {
            $this->spouse = $spouse;
        }
    }

    private function setPassword($password) {
        $this->password = $password;
    }
}
```

For a quick overview of the class, call Reflection::export():

```
Reflection::export(new ReflectionClass('Person'));
Class [ <user> class Person ] {
  @@ /www/reflection.php 3-25

  - Constants [0] {
  }

  - Static properties [0] {
  }

  - Static methods [0] {
  }

  - Properties [3] {
  Property [ <default> public $name ]
  Property [ <default> protected $spouse ]
  Property [ <default> private $password ]
  }

  - Methods [4] {
  Method [ <user> <ctor> public method __construct ] {
    @@ /www/reflection.php 8 - 10

    - Parameters [1] {
      Parameter #0 [ $name ]
    }
```

```
      }

      Method [ <user> public method getName ] {
        @@ /www/reflection.php 12 - 14
      }

      Method [ <user> protected method setSpouse ] {
        @@ /www/reflection.php 16 - 20

        - Parameters [1] {
          Parameter #0 [ Person or NULL $spouse ]
        }
      }

      Method [ <user> private method setPassword ] {
        @@ /www/reflection.php 22 - 24

        - Parameters [1] {
          Parameter #0 [ $password ]
        }
      }
    }
  }
```

The Reflection::export() static method takes an instance of the
ReflectionClass class and returns a copious amount of information. As you
can see, it details the number of constants, static properties, static methods,
properties, and methods in the class. Each item is broken down into component parts. For instance, all the entries contain visibility identifiers (private,
protected, or public), and methods have a list of their parameters underneath their definition.

Reflection::export() not only reports the file where everything is defined,
but even gives the line numbers! This lets you extract code from a file and
place it in your documentation.

Inspecting Classes, Methods, and Properties

Reflection::export() is a handy way to see everything about a class at once,
but it's not a very useful method of extracting specific pieces of information.

That's where the individual Reflection classes come in. There's a Reflection
class for every major entity in PHP: classes, functions, methods, parameters,
properties, and even extensions. Instances of these classes have methods
that you can query to determine whether a class is abstract, a method is
final, or a property is private. For example:

```
$class = new ReflectionClass('Person');
if ($class->isAbstract()) {
    // Person is abstract
```

```
    }

    $method = new ReflectionMethod('Person', 'getName');
    if ($method->isFinal()) {
        // Person::getName() is final
    }

    $property = new ReflectionProperty('Person', 'name');
    if ($property->isPrivate()) {
        // Person::name is private
    }
```

To inspect a class, create a new `ReflectionClass`, passing the class name to the constructor. You can query the returned object using any of the methods listed in the next section in Table 9-3.

The `ReflectionMethod` and `ReflectionProperty` classes operate similarly, except that they take two arguments. The first argument is still the class name, and the second is the method or property name. Table 9-5 has a list of all the `ReflectionMethod` methods, and Table 9-6 covers `ReflectionProperty`.

While it's somewhat useful to check specific methods or properties, the utility of the Reflection classes shines through when they're used in conjunction with each other. For instance, you want to create API documentation for your classes. However, you only want to document `public` methods because private and protected methods are reserved for internal use. Example 9-11 shows how to do this, using the `Person` class in Example 9-10 as a base.

Example 9-11. Printing public methods
```
$class = new ReflectionClass('Person');
foreach ($class->getMethods() as $method) {
    if ($method->isPublic()) {
        print $method->getName() . "()\n";
    }
}
__construct()
getName()
```

The `getMethods()` method in Example 9-11 returns an array containing all the methods in the class. The elements of the array are `ReflectionMethod()` objects.

A `ReflectionMethod` object can be intraspected similarly to a `ReflectionClass`. Therefore, you can call `isPublic()` to discover whether a method is declared `public`. If it is, the example uses `getName()` to retrieve its name and prints it out.

You can use another class, `ReflectionParameter`, to add further detail to your documentation, as in Example 9-12.

Example 9-12. Printing public methods with parameters

```
$class = new ReflectionClass('Person');
foreach ($class->getMethods() as $method) {
    if ($method->isPublic()) {
        print $method->getName() . '(';
        $params = '';
        foreach($method->getParameters() as $parameter) {
            $params .= '$' . $parameter->getName() . ', ';
        }
        print substr($params, 0, -2) . ")\n";
    }
}
```

Now you can also list method parameters:

```
__construct($name)
getName()
```

The `ReflectionParameter` methods appear in Table 9-7.

Reflection Class Methods

This section provides a complete listing of every method in all six of the Reflection classes. Each entry in Tables 9-3 through 9-8 details what parameters a method takes and what types of values it returns.

There are just over 100 methods in total, but the number of unique methods is almost half of that. As you can see, there's a lot of duplication. For example, classes, methods, and properties can all be declared `public`; therefore, the `ReflectionClass`, `ReflectionMethod`, and `ReflectionProperty` classes all have an `isPublic()` method.

The method names are largely self-explanatory, but here's a quick overview that explains the naming and behavior patterns.

All of the methods beginning with `get` retrieve values or objects. For instance, `getName()` returns the object's name.

Some `get` methods return an array of objects, such as `getMethods()`, which returns an array of `ReflectionMethods`. These methods are marked with square array brackets ([ ]), like `ReflectionMethod[ ]`.

If a method begins with `is`, it returns a boolean value: either `true` or `false`.

One method different from the rest is `invoke()`. This method is similar to `call_user_func()`, as it lets you pass arguments to a method or function. For example:

```
function add($i, $j) {
    return $i + $j;
}
```

```
$math = new ReflectionFunction('add');
print $math->invoke(1, 2);
3
```

While it makes little sense to create a ReflectionFunction just to call invoke( ), it's handy when you're using the Reflection classes to automate the processing of class methods. One example program is a unit testing application that takes an object and runs all methods beginning with the word test.

Table 9-3. ReflectionClass methods

Name	Returns
ReflectionClass::__construct(mixed argument) throws ReflectionException	ReflectionClass
ReflectionClass::__toString( )	string
ReflectionClass::export(mixed argument, [, bool return]) throws ReflectionException	mixed
ReflectionClass::getConstant(string name)	mixed
ReflectionClass::getConstants( )	array
ReflectionClass::getConstructor( )	ReflectionMethod
ReflectionClass ReflectionProperty:: getDeclaringClass( )	ReflectionClass
ReflectionClass::getDefaultProperties( )	array
ReflectionClass::getDocComment( )	string
ReflectionClass::getEndLine( )	int
ReflectionClass::getExtension( )	ReflectionExtension or NULL
ReflectionClass::getExtensionName( )	string or false
ReflectionClass::getFileName( )	string
ReflectionClass::getInterfaces( )	ReflectionClass[ ]
ReflectionClass::getMethod(string name)	ReflectionMethod
ReflectionClass::getMethods( )	ReflectionMethod[ ]
ReflectionClass::getModifiers( )	int
ReflectionClass::getName( )	string
ReflectionClass::getParentClass( )	ReflectionClass
ReflectionClass::getProperties( )	ReflectionProperty[ ]
ReflectionClass::getProperty(string name)	ReflectionProperty
ReflectionClass::getStartLine( )	int
ReflectionClass::getStaticProperties( )	array
ReflectionClass::implementsInterface(string or ReflectionClass interface_name)	boolean
ReflectionClass::isAbstract( )	boolean
ReflectionClass::isFinal( )	boolean

Table 9-3. ReflectionClass methods (continued)

Name	Returns
ReflectionClass::isInstance(object)	boolean
ReflectionClass::isInstantiable( )	boolean
ReflectionClass::isInterface( )	boolean
ReflectionClass::isInternal( )	boolean
ReflectionClass::isIterateable( )	boolean
ReflectionClass::isSubclassOf(string or ReflectionClass class)	boolean
ReflectionClass::isUserDefined( )	boolean
ReflectionClass::newInstance(mixed args)	object

Table 9-4. ReflectionFunction methods

Name	Returns
ReflectionFunction::__construct(string name)	ReflectionFunction
ReflectionFunction::__toString( )	string
ReflectionFunction::export(string name, [, bool return]) throws Reflection_Exception	mixed
ReflectionFunction::getDocComment( )	string
ReflectionFunction::getEndLine( )	int
ReflectionFunction::getFileName( )	string
ReflectionFunction::getName( )	string
ReflectionFunction::getParameters( )	Reflection_Parameter[ ]
ReflectionFunction::getStartLine( )	int
ReflectionFunction::getStaticVariables( )	array
ReflectionFunction::invoke(mixed args)	mixed
ReflectionFunction::isInternal( )	bool
ReflectionFunction::isUserDefined( )	bool
ReflectionFunction::returnsReference( )	bool

Table 9-5. ReflectionMethod methods

Name	Returns
ReflectionMethod::__construct(mixed class, string name)	ReflectionMethod
ReflectionMethod::__toString( )	string
ReflectionMethod::export(mixed class, string name, [, bool return]) throws Reflection_Exception	mixed
ReflectionMethod::getDeclaringClass( )	Reflection_Class

Table 9-5. ReflectionMethod methods (continued)

Name	Returns
ReflectionMethod::getDocComment( )	string
ReflectionMethod::getEndLine( )	int
ReflectionMethod::getFileName( )	string
ReflectionMethod::getModifiers( )	int
ReflectionMethod::getName( )	string
ReflectionMethod::getParameters( )	Reflection_Parameter[ ]
ReflectionMethod::getStartLine( )	int
ReflectionMethod::getStaticVariables( )	array
ReflectionMethod::invoke(mixed object, mixed args)	mixed
ReflectionMethod::isAbstract( )	boolean
ReflectionMethod::isConstructor( )	boolean
ReflectionMethod::isDestructor( )	boolean
ReflectionMethod::isFinal( )	boolean
ReflectionMethod::isInternal( )	boolean
ReflectionMethod::isPrivate( )	boolean
ReflectionMethod::isProtected( )	boolean
ReflectionMethod::isPublic( )	boolean
ReflectionMethod::isStatic( )	boolean
ReflectionMethod::isUserDefined( )	boolean
ReflectionMethod::returnsReference( )	boolean

Table 9-6. ReflectionProperty methods

Name	Returns
ReflectionProperty::__construct(mixed class, string name)	ReflectionProperty
ReflectionProperty::__toString( )	string
ReflectionProperty::export(mixed class, string name, [, bool return]) throws Reflection_Exception	mixed
ReflectionProperty::getDeclaringClass( )	Reflection_Class
ReflectionProperty::getModifiers( )	int
ReflectionProperty::getName( )	string
ReflectionProperty::getValue(object object)	mixed
ReflectionProperty::isDefault( )	boolean
ReflectionProperty::isPrivate( )	boolean
ReflectionProperty::isProtected( )	boolean
ReflectionProperty::isPublic( )	boolean

Table 9-6. ReflectionProperty methods (continued)

Name	Returns
ReflectionProperty::isStatic( )	boolean
ReflectionProperty::setValue(object object, mixed value)	void

Table 9-7. ReflectionParameter methods

Name	Returns
ReflectionParameter::__construct(mixed function, mixed parameter)	ReflectionParameter
ReflectionParameter::__toString( )	string
ReflectionParameter::allowsNull( )	boolean
ReflectionParameter::export(mixed function, mixed parameter, [, bool return]) throws Reflection_Exception	mixed
ReflectionParameter::getClass( )	string
ReflectionParameter::getName( )	string
ReflectionParameter::isPassedByReference( )	boolean

Table 9-8. ReflectionExtension methods

Name	Returns
ReflectionExtension::__construct(string name)	ReflectionExtension
ReflectionExtension::__toString( )	string
ReflectionExtension::export(string name, [, bool return]) throws Reflection_Exception	mixed
ReflectionExtension::getClasses( )	Reflection_Class[ ]
ReflectionExtension::getClassNames( )	array
ReflectionExtension::getConstants( )	array
ReflectionExtension::getFunctions( )	Reflection_Function[ ]
ReflectionExtension::getINIEntries( )	array
ReflectionExtension::getName( )	string
ReflectionExtension::getVersion( )	string

CHAPTER 10

PHP 5 in Action

Previous chapters demonstrate individual pieces of PHP 5, but this chapter is different. Instead of presenting new material, it combines together multiple features of PHP 5 into a unified program.

Specifically, I present a simple address book application that allows you to add new people and search for existing people. This application is designed to:

- Demonstrate a wide range of new PHP 5 features
- Work completely, even though it's limited in scope
- Be accessible both over the web and from the command line
- Separate application and presentation logic

Records are limited to first name, last name, and email address, and are stored in an SQLite database. A record can be turned into a Person object, and multiple Persons are stored in an addressBook object.

Since the application needs to work from both the Web and from the command line, you need an easy way to convert records into both HTML and plain text. To facilitate this task, every object is capable of using DOM to create an XML representation of its contents. You then use SimpleXML to manipulate these XML documents into formatted output.

The first section in this chapter covers the database schema, so you know how the records are stored. Parts two and three cover the Person and addressBook classes. These sections use many of PHP 5's new object-oriented features, including property overloading, visibility, class type hints, and custom object iterators using the IteratorAggregate interface. The classes also create, append, and import DOM documents and elements.

Now that you've defined how the data is represented, both in the underlying storage mechanism (the database) and within your program (the Person and `addressBook` classes), the next step is to translate the objects into user-visible content.

The fourth section shows how you create a set of templates, one for HTML and another for plain text. To ensure consistency, you use an abstract class to define the template interface for the page header, body, and footer. Within the templates, process the XML with SimpleXML.

Finally, you're ready to put together the actual application. However, since you've already created all the component parts, the assembly process is short. The biggest difficulty is converting input from both the Web and the command line into a similar format. One piece that is considerably simplified, however, is error handling through the use of exceptions.

Defining Your Database Schema

The first version of the address book contains only a person's first name, last name, and email address. However, you want to leave open the option of adding additional fields at a later time.

You also know that the data is accessed for reading, as you look up existing records. Writes will be relatively infrequent, but will definitely occur.

Based on those criteria, SQLite is a good choice as a database. Your dataset isn't gigantic, nor do you need advanced features such as replication. SQLite also retrieves data very quickly, so it's perfect for pulling records out of the database.

The next step is writing a database schema and creating a new database, as shown in Example 10-1.

Example 10-1. Database schema for address book

```
$sql = <<< _SQL_
CREATE TABLE people (
            id INTEGER PRIMARY KEY,
        firstname TEXT,
         lastname TEXT,
            email TEXT);
CREATE INDEX people_firstname_index ON people(firstname);
CREATE INDEX people_lastname_index  ON people(lastname);
CREATE INDEX people_email_index     ON people(email);
_SQL_;

$db = new SQLiteDatabase('addressBook.db');
$db->query($sql);
```

Example 10-1 creates a new database file called *addressBook.db* and adds a people table with four fields: id, firstname, lastname, and email.

The `id` field is an integer and the primary key. The other three fields are simply defined as TEXT. Since you need to search against the text fields, you create indexes for all `firstname`, `lastname`, and `email` fields using the CREATE INDEX command.

See Chapter 4 for more on SQLite, and see "Indexes" in that chapter for more on indexes specifically.

The Person Class

The next step is creating `Person`, an object representation of the data. This class encapsulates the address book entry's information into an object you can manipulate. You need to be able to create a new object, get and set information, cycle through all the fields, and convert the object to XML.

Constructor

The class begins with its constructor, as shown in Example 10-2.

Example 10-2. Person::__construct()

```
class Person implements IteratorAggregate {
    private $data;

    public function __construct($person = NULL) {
        $this->data = array('firstname' => '',
                            'lastname'  => '',
                            'email'     => '',
                            'id'        => 0);

        if (is_array($person)) {
            foreach ($person as $field => $value) {
                $this->$field = $value;
            }
        }
    }
}
```

Example 10-2 initializes the `$data` property as an array of four elements: `firstname`, `lastname`, `email`, and `id`. The first three hold information about a person, and the last one is the record's unique database key.

When nothing's passed into the constructor, you're left with an empty `Person` object, which can then be defined. However, you can optionally pass an array of data that contains information about a person.

When this happens, the constructor loops through the array and converts each element into an object property. As you'll see, this class actually overloads property access with __get( ) and __set( ), so the information is really going inside `$data`.

You've probably noticed that none of the properties are set by name. For example, there's no call to $this->firstname. Instead, the code references $this->$field.

It's somewhat unusual to refer to a property name with a variable; however, this allows you to avoid hardcoding property names inside the foreach. In general, you want to write generic code like this, as it reduces headaches when you modify your code.

The foreach converts an array with any combination of keys into properties. Assume, for instance, that $person is array('firstname' => 'Rasmus'). Then inside the loop, $field is firstname and $value is Rasmus. Therefore, $this->$field = $value translates to $this->firstname = 'Rasmus'.

When $person holds additional elements, the foreach automatically takes care of every field in turn without any action on your part. Don't worry if someone tries to pass in additional array elements, such as address. These are filtered out inside of __set( ).

Encapsulating Property Access with __get( ) and __set( )

Public properties break encapsulation, so Person implements the property overload methods of __get( ) and __set( ). The methods in Example 10-3 actually retrieve and store data from the protected $data property.

Example 10-3. Person::__set() and Person::__get()

```
public function __set($property, $value) {
    if (isset($this->data[$property])) {
        $this->data[$property] = $value;
    }
}

public function __get($property) {
    if (isset($this->data[$property])) {
        return $this->data[$property];
    } else {
        return false;
    }
}
```

The __set( ) method doesn't add all properties to $data. It first uses isset( ) to check that $property already exists within the array. This will return true only for the elements assigned in the constructor. If $property fails this test, the method discards $value. This check prevents you from adding arbitrary data to the object, so you can be sure of the class's properties.

The __get( ) method behaves in a similar fashion. If the property isset( ), the method returns the property's value. If it's not set, the method returns false.

See "__get() and __set()" in Chapter 2 for more on property overloading.

Enabling Custom Object Iteration with getIterator( )

Since you're overloading property access, the object is no longer iterable using PHP's default iteration behavior. There's only one class property, $data, and its visibility is restricted from public view.

The fix is to implement the IteratorAggregate interface and to write a getIterator( ) method, as shown in Example 10-4.

Example 10-4. Person::getIterator()

```
public function getIterator( ) {
    return new ArrayObject($this->data);
}
```

This method must return an iterator. Instead of creating a custom iterator, it's better to use SPL's ArrayObject. This object takes an array, such as $this->data, and converts it into an iterator object that acts just like an array.

Chapter 6 covers iteration in detail. In particular, see "Array and Object Property Iteration" and "Redefining Class Iteration."

Converting a Person Object to an XML Document Using DOM

Your final method is toDOM( ), shown in Example 10-5. This method converts Person into a DOM object for use with the XML functions.

Example 10-5. Person::toDOM()

```
public function toDOM( ) {
    $xml = new DOMDocument('1.0', 'UTF-8');
    $xml->formatOutput = true; // indent elements

    $person = $xml->appendChild(new DOMElement('person'));

    foreach ($this as $key => $value) {
        $person->appendChild(new DOMElement($key, $value));
    }

    return $xml;
}
```

The goal of Example 10-5 is to create a DOM object and populate it with child elements for each piece of data stored in the object.

Your first step is instantiating a new DOMDocument. Set the XML version to 1.0 and the encoding to UTF-8. The second line indents the output with spaces. This makes the XML easier to read for humans.

Now you create the DOM elements. The root element is a new person. Next, a foreach loop creates elements for each of the current object's properties.

It's important to loop through $this instead of $this->data. Right now, you happen to store your data inside the $data property, but that could change. If you do loop through $this->data and then change this, you would have to update all your methods. Looping through $this invokes getIterator( ), so as long as you update getIterator( ), it's a seamless change every place else.

The code uses a feature of the DOMElement constructor. When a second parameter is passed, the object creates a text node containing $value and places it as a child of the new DOM element.

See "Before and After: Creating New XML Documents" in Chapter 5 for more details on creating DOM objects.

Creating and Manipulating a Person Object

Example 10-6 shows the Person class in action.

Example 10-6. Creating a new Person

```
$rasmus = new Person;
$rasmus->firstname = 'Rasmus';
$rasmus->lastname  = 'Lerdorf';
$rasmus->email     = 'rasmus@php.net';

foreach($rasmus as $property => $value) {
    print "$value\n";
}

print $rasmus->toDOM( )->saveXML( );
```

Example 10-6 creates a new Person, assigns values to the object, and then iterates through it. It also prints the object's DOM representation. This is the result:

```
firstname: Rasmus
lastname: Lerdorf
email: rasmus@php.net
id: 0

<?xml version="1.0" encoding="UTF-8"?>
```

```
<person>
  <firstname>Rasmus</firstname>
  <lastname>Lerdorf</lastname>
  <email>rasmus@php.net</email>
  <id>0</id>
</person>
```

The properties all hold their assigned values; however, since `id` wasn't changed, it's still at the default value of 0.

Alternatively, you can pass an array to the constructor:

```
$info = array('firstname' => 'Zeev',
              'lastname'  => 'Suraski',
              'email'     => 'zeev@php.net');

$zeev = new Person($info);

print $zeev->toDOM( )->saveXML( );

<?xml version="1.0" encoding="UTF-8"?>
<person>
  <firstname>Zeev</firstname>
  <lastname>Suraski</lastname>
  <email>zeev@php.net</email>
  <id>0</id>
</person>
```

Passing an array is functionally equivalent to setting properties one by one, but it's more concise.

The addressBook Class

Now that you have a `Person`, it's time to turn to the address book. Just like a physical address book, an `addressBook` object holds a collection of information about people.

The `addressBook` class gives you two actions: you can either add a new record or search existing records. That's it. Updating and deleting records is left for Version 2.0. However, as always, you want to design the class so that it's easy to add these methods.

Like `Person`, `addressBook` has a `toDOM( )` method, which exports an entire collection of people to XML as a group.

Constructor

Besides instantiating the object, `addressBook`'s constructor connects to the database, as shown in Example 10-7.

Example 10-7. addressBook::__construct()

```
class addressBook implements IteratorAggregate {

    protected $data;
    protected $db;

    public function __construct() {
        $this->data = array();
        $this->db = new SQLiteDatabase('addressBook.db');
    }
```

The constructor opens the SQLite database *addressBook.db* that was created earlier in "Defining Your Database Schema." The result handle is stored in the $db property.

Adding a Person to an addressBook

An empty address book isn't very interesting, so Example 10-8 implements the addPerson() method. This method takes a Person object, converts it into an SQL query, and inserts it into the database.

Example 10-8. addressBook::addPerson()

```
    public function addPerson(Person $person) {
        $data = array();
        foreach ($person as $fields => $value) {
            $data[$fields] = "'" . sqlite_escape_string($value) . "'";
        }
        $data['id'] = 'NULL';

        $sql = 'INSERT INTO people '.
                       '(' . join(',', array_keys( $data)) . ')' .
                'VALUES (' . join(',', array_values($data)) . ');';

        if ($this->db->query($sql)) {
            $rowid = $this->db->lastInsertRowid();
            $person->id = $rowid;
            return $rowid;
        } else {
            throw new SQLiteException(
                        sqlite_error_string($this->db->lastError()),
                                            $this->db->lastError());
        }
    }
}
```

Since addPerson() will work only on a Person object, the argument is type hinted to require a Person.

This method's main job is converting the Person object into an SQL statement. Like Person::__construct( ), the goal is to have little or no Person-specific details inside of addPerson( ).

You want to be able to update Person to include, for example, a cell phone number field, without modifying addressBook. This reduces the coupling between the classes, which is a major design goal of object-oriented programming. A class should be able to modified without affecting the behavior of any of the other classes.

The top half of the method iterates through the fields returned by $person's iterator. It creates an array whose keys are the object's properties. The array's values are escaped SQLite strings, wrapped inside single quotation marks.

To ensure that SQLite generates the correct row ID, you explicitly set the id element to NULL. This prevents someone from assigning their own id and disturbing the auto-increment sequence.

The general syntax for an SQL INSERT statement is INSERT INTO *table* (*field1, field2, ..., fieldN*) VALUES (*value1, value2, ..., valueN*). So, you need a way to put all the field names into one comma-separated list and all the values into another.

Fortunately, the $data array's keys are the field names and the array's values are the escaped SQL values. Therefore, you can extract the desired portion of the array with array_keys( ) or array_values( ).

Those arrays are then join( )ed together with commas (,) to create the proper SQL statement. This algorithm works regardless of the name or number of fields in the database.

If the query succeeds, the new primary key is assigned to $rowid from SQLite's lastInsertRowid( ) method. The method also updates $person to contain the correct value instead of 0. This code takes advantage of PHP 5's pass-by-reference feature for objects. Without it, the change in $person would exist only in the local copy within the method. The method returns $rowid on a successful query or throws an SQLiteException on an error.

Because DOM already throws exceptions, it's cleaner for you to manually throw SQLiteExceptions of your own. This allows you to process all errors, from DOM and from SQLite, in a consistent manner.

Since the SQLite extension isn't throwing the error, you need to populate the exception's message and code fields yourself. SQLite's lastError( ) method returns an integer error code that describes of the problem. You can convert that number into an English description with `sqlite_error_string( )`. These are the two pieces of data you need to pass when you create the `SQLiteException`.

Example 10-9 inserts a new `Person` into a clean `addressBook`.

Example 10-9. Adding a Person into an addressBook

```
$rasmus = new Person;
$rasmus->firstname = 'Rasmus';
$rasmus->lastname  = 'Lerdorf';
$rasmus->email     = 'rasmus@php.net';

try {
    $ab = new addressBook;
    $ab->addPerson($rasmus);
    print $rasmus->toDOM( )->saveXML( );
} catch (Exception $e) {
    // Error!
}
```

The results look like:

```
<?xml version="1.0" encoding="UTF-8"?>
<person>
  <firstname>Rasmus</firstname>
  <lastname>Lerdorf</lastname>
  <email>rasmus@php.net</email>
  <id>1</id>
</person>
```

As you can see, the id element is 1 instead of the default value of 0.

When there's an SQLite error, such as when the people table does not exist, the addPerson( ) method throws an exception and print `$rasmus->toDOM( )->saveXML( );` is never called. Instead, control immediately jumps to the catch block for error processing. For now, the examples are only trapping the error, not processing it. Later on, once you assemble the full application, you'll add in more complete error handling.

Searching for People Within an addressBook

It's boring just to enter people into an address book. The real fun comes when you retrieve them using search( ), as shown in Example 10-10.

Example 10-10. addressBook::search( )

```
public function search(Person $person) {
    $where = array( );
    foreach ($person as $field => $value) {
        if (!empty($value)) {
            $where[ ] = "$field = '" . sqlite_escape_string($value) . "'";
```

Example 10-10. addressBook::search( ) (continued)

```
        }
    }

    $sql = 'SELECT * FROM people';
    if (count($where)) {
        $sql .= ' WHERE ' . join(' AND ', $where);
    }

    if ($people = $this->db->query($sql)) {
        foreach ($people as $person) {
            $this->data[] = new Person($person);
        }

        return $people->numRows();
    } else {
        throw new SQLiteException(
                    sqlite_error_string($this->db->lastError()),
                                      $this->db->lastError());
    }
}
```

The method works similarly to addPerson( ), using a foreach loop to build up an SQL statement. However, unlike an INSERT, a SELECT doesn't require a parallel set of records joined by commas. Instead, fields and values are separated with an equals sign (=).

To keep searches loose, the WHERE clause doesn't include any empty( ) valued fields. This allows you to find all the people with a firstname of Rasmus by keeping the other fields as blanks.

Since an empty WHERE clause is illegal, WHERE is appended to $sql only if $where has at least one element. These elements are then ANDed together using join( ).

The query results are retrieved using the SQLite iterator that fetches rows as associative arrays. Inside the loop, pass the result array to Person. This creates a new Person object with all the correct details that are stored in the $data property.

Finally, the method returns the total number of found rows, using the numRows( ) method of the SQLite result object. When no rows are found, this is equal to 0.

Example 10-11 shows one search that finds records and another that fails.

Example 10-11. Searching an addressBook

```
$ab = new addressBook;

$rasmus = new Person;
```

Example 10-11. Searching an addressBook (continued)

```
$rasmus->firstname = 'Rasmus';
print 'Rasmus: ' . $ab->search($rasmus) . "\n";

$zeev = new Person;
$zeev->firstname = 'Zeev';
print 'Zeev: ' . $ab->search($zeev) . "\n";
```

Rasmus: 1
Zeev: 0

Since you've already inserted Rasmus into the address book back in Example 10-9, the first search returns 1. However, Zeev is not to be found.

The search( ) method is quite basic. It doesn't allow you to find all people named Rasmus or Zeev in a single query, for instance. However, you can run two search( )es against the same address book to create a composite search result.

Converting an addressBook Object to an XML Document Using DOM

It's not very interesting merely to see the number of matches for your search. What you really want is access to the information about each person. Like Person, this is accomplished using a combination of iterators and XML, as shown in Example 10-12.

Example 10-12. addressBook::getIterator()

```
public function getIterator() {
    return new ArrayObject($this->data);
}
```

As in Example 10-4, getIterator( ) returns the object's $data property.

Example 10-13 contains the code for the addressBook::toDOM( ) method.

Example 10-13. addressBook::toDOM()

```
public function toDOM() {
    $xml = new DOMDocument('1.0', 'UTF-8');
    $xml->formatOutput = true; // indent elements
    $ab = $xml->appendChild(new DOMElement('addressBook'));

    foreach ($this as $person) {
        $p = $person->toDOM();
        $p = $xml->importNode($p->documentElement, true);
        $ab->appendChild($p);
    }
```

Example 10-13. addressBook::toDOM( ) (continued)

```
        return $xml;
    }
```

The toDOM( ) method here acts similarly, but not identically, to the toDOM( ) method in Person. Its first half is the same, but the second is different.

This method also creates a new DOMDocument and uses the same set of XML versions and document encodings. It creates a root element, too, but this time it's called addressBook instead of person.

Inside the foreach, there's no need to iterate through $person like you did inside Person::toDOM( ). Instead, you can just ask $person to convert itself into a DOM object using its own toDOM( ) method.

However, it's illegal to directly append parts of one DOMDocument to another. You must first convert the object using DOM's importNode( ) method. The first parameter is the part of the document you want, and the second indicates whether you want to make a deep or shallow copy. The call in this example grabs everything from the root node down and does a deep copy. The imported nodes are then appended to the address book to create a master XML document that contains all the matching People.

With toDOM( ), you can view the results of your searches in Example 10-14.

Example 10-14. Converting search results to XML

```
$zeev = new Person;
$zeev->firstname = 'Zeev';
$zeev->lastname = 'Suraski';
$zeev->email = 'zeev@php.net';

$ab = new addressBook;
$ab->addPerson($zeev);

$ab->search(new Person);
print $ab->toDOM( )->saveXML( );

<?xml version="1.0" encoding="UTF-8"?>
<addressBook>
  <person>
    <firstname>Rasmus</firstname>
    <lastname>Lerdorf</lastname>
    <email>rasmus@php.net</email>
    <id>1</id>
  </person>
  <person>
    <firstname>Zeev</firstname>
    <lastname>Suraski</lastname>
    <email>zeev@php.net</email>
```

Example 10-14. Converting search results to XML (continued)

```
    <id>2</id>
  </person>
</addressBook>
```

Perfect! Here's an XML document containing all the people in the address book. Additionally, since neither search( ), getIterator( ), nor toDOM( ) hardcode any details about Person, they're not affected when you modify the Person class.

The Template Class

Since the application needs to produce multiple output formats, you need a way to control the display. For example, the HTML output starts with <html>, but you certainly don't want that to appear on the command line.

Good programming style says that it's bad form to mix programming and display logic. This leads to messy code because everything becomes intertwined. Additionally, since you already know you need a minimum of two different types of output, doing everything inline not only makes it harder to add additional output styles, but it's also more difficult to maintain your existing styles.

Therefore, you should create template objects. Each object should have the same set of display methods, such as getHeader( ) and getFooter( ). However, they'll return different content—for example, HTML or plain text.

This is the perfect place to use an abstract base class. The abstract class specifies the exact names and prototypes for all your methods. Then, you create one class for each format and make sure that each of those classes extends the base.

The Template class in Example 10-15 has four methods.

Example 10-15. Template abstract class

```
abstract class Template {
    abstract public function getHeader( );
    abstract public function getBody(DOMDocument $dom);
    abstract public function getFooter( );

    public function printAll(addressBook $ab) {
        print $this->getHeader( );
        print $this->getBody($ab->toDOM( ));
        print $this->getFooter( );
    }
}
```

Two methods—getHeader( ) and getFooter( )—take no parameters. They display the page header and footer, respectively.

In between them is getBody( ). It requires a DOMDocument, which should contain an XML address book full of the information that you want to print.

The last and only nonabstract method, printAll( ), is a convenience method that calls the other three methods and prints them out.

Creating an HTML Template

The HTML class is mostly static HTML, but the getBody( ) method is generated dynamically, as shown in Example 10-16.

Example 10-16. htmlTemplate class

```
class htmlTemplate extends Template {
    public function getHeader( ) {
        $action = $_SERVER['PHP_SELF'];

        $header = <<< _HEADER_
<!DOCTYPE HTML PUBLIC "-//W3C//DTD HTML 4.01//EN"
        "http://www.w3.org/TR/html4/strict.dtd">
<html>
<head>
        <title>Address Book</title>
</head>
<body>
<form action="$action" method="POST">
<select type="select" name="mode">
    <option value="add">Add</option>
    <option value="search" selected="selected">Search for</option>
</select>

<label for="firstname">First Name</label>
<input type="text" name="firstname" id="firstname" size="8">

<label for="lastname">Last Name</label>
<input type="text" name="lastname"  id="lastname" size="14">

<label for="email">Email</label>
<input type="text" name="email" id="email" size="14">

<input type="submit" value="Do it!">
</form>
_HEADER_;

        return $header;
    }
```

Example 10-16. htmlTemplate class (continued)

```php
    public function getBody(DOMDocument $dom) {
        $body = "<table>\n";

        $people = simplexml_import_dom($dom);
        foreach ($people as $person) {
            $body .= "<tr>\n<td>" . $person->firstname . ' ' .
                        $person->lastname . "</td>\n<td>" .
                        $person->email . "</td></tr>\n";
        }

        $body .= "</table>\n";

        return $body;
    }

    public function getFooter() {
        $footer = "</body>\n</html>\n";
        return $footer;
    }
}
```

While getHeader( ) is mostly static HTML, it contains an HTML form that allows you to both insert new people into and search the address book. The form's action is set to $_SERVER['PHP_SELF'], so your script also processes the form. The input elements are named the same as the properties of your Person class. This allows you to instantiate a Person object from the form without needing to munge the input data.

The getBody( ) method in Example 10-16 takes a DOM object, but that doesn't mean it needs to parse the XML with DOM. SimpleXML is the perfect way to handle this basic type of XML document.

The simplexml_import_dom( ) function converts an object from DOM to SimpleXML. Now it's no problem to create an HTML table: you iterate though the SimpleXML object using foreach, turning every $person into another HTML table row. See "SimpleXML" in Chapter 5 for more on this extension.

Creating a Plain-Text Template

The text template, shown in Example 10-17, is less complex than the HTML version because its header and footer are empty.

Example 10-17. textTemplate class

```php
class textTemplate extends Template {
    private $nameLength;
    private $emailLength;
```

Example 10-17. textTemplate class (continued)

```php
    public function __construct($nameLength = 30, $emailLength = 30) {
        $this->nameLength  = (int) $nameLength;
        $this->emailLength = (int) $emailLength;
    }

    public function getHeader() {
        return;
    }

    public function getBody(DOMDocument $dom) {
        // 7 is the size of the column divider
        // spacers: "| ", " | ", and " |"
        $lineLength = $this->nameLength + $this->emailLength + 7;

        $text = str_repeat('-', $lineLength) . "\n";

        $people = simplexml_import_dom($dom);
        foreach ($people as $person) {
            $name = $person->firstname . ' ' . $person->lastname;
            $text .= sprintf("| %{$this->nameLength}s
                              | %-{$this->emailLength}s |\n",
                             $name, $person->email);
        }

        $text .= str_repeat('-', $lineLength) . "\n";

        return $text;
    }

    public function getFooter() {
        return;
    }
}
```

This class has a constructor with two optional arguments, $nameLength and $emailLength. These parameters control the length of the printed name and email columns, respectively. They both default to 30, but you can adjust them if your data is particularly long or short.

Again, the getBody( ) method is the most interesting of the three methods. Since there's no way to automatically place data into a table from the command line, the method uses str_repeat( ) and sprintf( ) to recreate a table. The calls to str_repeat( ) create the top and bottom table borders.

Inside the foreach, sprintf( ) formats the individual lines. The string that reads | %{$this->nameLength}s | %-{$this->emailLength}s |\n has two special codes. The first, %{$this->nameLength}s, turns the input into a $this->nameLength character-wide, right-aligned, space-padded string. The second,

%-{$this->emailLength}s, does something similar, but aligns the data on the left side instead of the right.

Displaying Multiple Output Formats with a Template

Now that you've defined your templates, the next step is printing out address books. This is done in Example 10-18.

Example 10-18. Printing addressBook results using templates

```
try {
    // Create address book and find all people
    $ab = new addressBook;
    $ab->search(new Person);

    // Create HTML template
    $template = new htmlTemplate();

    // Convert address book XML and print results
    $template->printAll($ab);
} catch (Exception $e) {
    // Error
}
```

Figure 10-1 shows the rendered output.

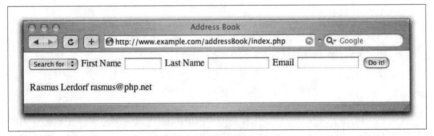

Figure 10-1. HTML version of the address book

Alternatively, setting $template to a new textTemplate produces:

Assembling the Application

Finally, you can integrate the classes and templates into a complete application. This section creates a dual web and command-line program that shares the same set of code but abstracts out the details, such as processing the different sources of input data.

Creating the Web Version

The web version gets its input from a form embedded in the HTML template's header, as shown in Example 10-19.

Example 10-19. Web-enabled address book application

```
// Configure format-specific details
$input = $_POST;
$template = new htmlTemplate;

// Set mode
if (isset($input['mode'])) {
    $mode = $input['mode'];
} else {
    $mode = false;
}

try {
    // Create address book
    $ab = new addressBook;
    // Load data into Person
    $person = new Person($input);

    // Add person, if necessary
    if ($mode == 'add') {
        $ab->addPerson($person);
    }

    // Return results
    $ab->search($person);

    // Print page
    $template->printAll($ab);
} catch (Exception $e) {
    $ob = ob_start();
    print $e;
    error_log(ob_get_clean());
}
```

At the top of Example 10-19, you set a few configuration variables. Since this is the web version, the $input comes from $_POST and the $template is an htmlTemplate. Later, you will set $input and $template to different values in the command-line version.

The $mode variable, which controls whether you should add a new person, is assigned using the mode element of the input source.

Once everything is set up, create the addressBook and Person objects. Use the $input array to configure Person.

Now, if the $mode is set to add, call addPerson( ) to insert the person into the database. This converts Person into SQL and makes a new entry.

The next step is populating the address book with results. If you're doing a search, $ab contains all the matching records. If you're inserting a record, $ab contains the new record.

The last action is the call to print out your template methods using the handy printAll( ) method instead of making individual calls.

All that assumes, of course, that everything goes smoothly and you encounter no exceptions. Many of the underlying methods throw exceptions, some because the extension does so automatically and some because you're actually throwing them yourself.

However, here's where the benefit of exceptions shines through. You don't need to worry which methods do or don't throw exceptions, nor do you need to care if the exception is actually thrown by a second method called by a first one. Everything propagates up to this location and is caught by your catch block. You've effectively replaced the necessity to check the return value of every function and method in your application with five lines:

```
} catch (Exception $e) {
    $ob = ob_start( );
    print $e;
    error_log(ob_get_clean( ));
}
```

As described in Chapter 7, you can print an exception to get a full set of debugging messages. By wrapping the print call within a output buffer, you can redirect these lines from the screen to the error log.

For example, when the SQLite can't find the person database table, you get:

```
[Thu Jul 22 10:30:14 2004] [error] exception 'SQLiteException' with message
 'SQL logic error or missing database' in
 /www/www.example.com/addressBook/index.php:48
Stack trace:
#0 /www/www.example.com/addressBook/index.php(48): addressBook->
search(Object(Person))
#1 {main}
```

Sure, you still need to check occasional return values at the component level, i.e., inside individual methods. However, those checks are all encapsulated within your objects, so they occur at a lower level. When you assemble a program by combining multiple objects together, which is a higher level of programming, you only need to handle exceptions.

One thing your code doesn't do is print out any error message to a person using the address book. This is discussed later on in this chapter, in "Wrap-Up and Future Directions."

Creating the Command-Line Version

The largest difference between the command-line version and the web version is that you need to parse command-line options yourself. The easiest way to do this is with PEAR's Console_Getopt class, as shown in Example 10-20.

Example 10-20. Command-line–enabled address book application

```
require_once('Console/Getopt.php');

$opts = new Console_Getopt;
// Accept these four optional command line flags.
$longopts = array('mode=', 'firstname=', 'lastname=', 'email=');
$parsed = $opts->getopt($argv, NULL, $longopts);

// Strip leading "--" from flag name
// Convert from getopt( ) array return format to one like $_POST
foreach ($parsed[0] as $opt) {
    $key = substr($opt[0], 2);
    $input[$key] = $opt[1];
}

$template = new textTemplate;
```

Console_Getopt parses $argv and breaks it apart into option pairs. You specify any or all of four possible options: --mode, --firstname, --lastname, and --email.

Since getopt( ) doesn't return an array that's formatted like $_REQUEST, you need to rework the array it returns. This requires you to strip the leading -- from the option name and reorganize how the information is stored.

After fixing $input, set the $template to new textTemplate.

And now you're done. There's nothing left to modify in the program. This command runs the command-line version of the address book program, *ab.php*, and searches for people with a first name of Rasmus:

```
$ php ab.php --firstname=Rasmus
```

```
----------------------------------------------------------------------
|              Rasmus Lerdorf | rasmus@php.net                       |
----------------------------------------------------------------------
```

Passing --firstname=Rasmus on the command line is equivalent to setting the form element firstname to Rasmus.

Creating a Unified Program

The final step is unifying the two versions into a single program. This requires you to differentiate between the command-line and web versions of PHP.

The function php_sapi_name( ) checks which version of PHP you're running and returns its name. When you're running under the command-line version, it returns cli. The unified application code shown in Example 10-21.

Example 10-21. Unified address book application

```
// Configure format-specific details
if (php_sapi_name( ) == 'cli') {
    require_once('Console/Getopt.php');

    $opts = new Console_Getopt;
    $longopts  = array('mode=', 'firstname=', 'lastname=', 'email=');
    $parsed = $opts->getopt($argv, NULL, $longopts);

    foreach($parsed[0] as $opt) {
        $key = substr($opt[0], 2);
        $input[$key] = $opt[1];
    }

    $template = new textTemplate;
} else {
    $input = $_REQUEST;
    $template = new htmlTemplate;
}

// Set mode
if (isset($input['mode'])) {
    $mode = $input['mode'];
} else {
    $mode = false;
}

try {
    // Create address book
    $ab = new addressBook;
    // Load data into Person
    $person = new Person($input);

    if ($mode == 'add') {
        $ab->addPerson($person);
    }

    // Return results
    $ab->search($person);
```

Example 10-21. Unified address book application (continued)

```
    $template->printAll($ab);
} catch (Exception $e) {
    $ob = ob_start();
    print $e;
    error_log(ob_get_clean());
}
```

Now the program will parse $argv and print text when it's run from the command line, but also produce HTML when executed under a web server.

Wrap-Up and Future Directions

Although you can write a similar address book application in PHP 4, this version is better encapsulated, doesn't need to worry about passing objects as references, has simplified error handling, and makes it easy to use XML.

In PHP 4, there's no concept of visibility, so all object properties and methods are public. However, in PHP 5, you're able to effectively wall off public properties as protected data, yet still allow people easy access using __get( ) and __set( ).

By making __set( ) accept only the properties defined in the object constructor, you're able to limit exactly which properties are and aren't valid. This allows you to iterate through properties, creating SQL statements and DOM objects, without worrying that you'll encounter some unexpected data.

Additionally, the application takes advantage of PHP 5's automatic pass-by-reference behavior for objects. After you insert a new Person into the database, you can update its id property within the addPerson( ) method and have this change affect the original object.

The program also uses exceptions to simplify error handling. DOM automatically throws exceptions for any errors mentioned in the DOM specification. SQLite also throws exceptions from its constructor. By manually throwing a few additional SQLiteExceptions, you consolidate all the error handling into a single try/catch block.

Finally, the interoperability of the new PHP XML extensions allows you to easily create documents with DOM, yet access them for printing using SimpleXML. Furthermore, it's no problem to substitute XSLT for SimpleXML within your templates, or to search an addressBook object using XPath.

However, the address book application created in this chapter is just a start, providing a solid foundation for future enhancements. For instance, it would be nice to allow people to edit and delete entries from the address book, or to enlarge the number of fields from beyond first name, last name, and email address.

Also, as mentioned earlier, this application doesn't print a friendly error message when an exception is thrown. One solution is to modify Template to provide a getErrorMessage( ) method, which displays format-appropriate text.

Another nifty feature would be enabling this application as a web service, using either SOAP or REST. You read about SOAP in Chapter 9. REST is a different approach to web services, where you make requests using HTTP methods such as GET and POST, and the method type tells the server what action it should take. For example, GET tells the server you want to retrieve existing data, whereas POST means you want to update existing data. The server then replies with the results in an XML document that you can process.

Since the application already uses XML internally, it should be a simple extension to create an xmlTemplate. For more on REST, see the REST Wiki at *http://internet.conveyor.com/RESTwiki/*.

Finally, you can add the ability to read and write other address book formats. John E. Simpson has an article on XML.com that discusses many different XML address book schemas, such as vCard. It's available at *http://www.xml.com/pub/a/2004/03/31/qa.html*.

Introduction to XML

XML is the most popular way to store data and exchange information over the Internet. Since so many languages can read and write XML files, use XML when you want to share data among different applications and platforms. One of XML's greatest features is its ubiquity.

XML also benefits from being easy to learn. Since XML looks like HTML, web developers are familiar with its tag-based syntax. However, XML is not HTML. HTML has a fixed set of elements: `<a>`, `<img>`, `<h1>`, etc. With XML, you have the flexibility to use whatever element names best represent your data.

When choosing how to represent data, developers seem to fall into one of two camps. Some people think of XML as a record format, similar to comma-separated files. But instead of separating entries with newlines and fields with commas, XML provides richer classification options.

Other developers view XML as a document specification format. The online PHP Manual (*http://www.php.net/manual*) is produced from XML files. The PHP Documentation Team's documents use tags such as `<function>`, `<parameter>`, and `<example>`. This allows them to release the manual in multiple formats, including two versions of HTML, Windows CHM help files, and PDF.

Comparing HTML and XML

HTML and XML are siblings: they are both children of Standard Generalized Markup Language (SGML). Therefore, an XML document looks somewhat like an HTML page. Example A-1 is an XML document that represents a basic address book.

Example A-1. Simple address book

```
<address-book>
    <person id="1">
        <!--Rasmus Lerdorf-->
        <firstname>Rasmus</firstname>
        <lastname>Lerdorf</lastname>
        <city>Sunnyvale</city>
        <state>CA</state>
        <email>rasmus@php.net</email>
    </person>

    <person id="2">
        <!--Zeev Suraski-->
        <firstname>Zeev</firstname>
        <lastname>Suraski</lastname>
        <city>Tel Aviv</city>
        <state/>
        <email>zeev@php.net</email>
    </person>
</address-book>
```

Similarities

Even though Example A-1 is XML, it looks similar to HTML. There are opening and closing elements, and these elements can contain text, other elements, or both. Elements can also have attributes, such as `id="1"` for the person element.

XML also uses the same syntax as HTML for comments (`<!--Rasmus Lerdorf-->`) and entities (`&lt;`). Like HTML, XML has similar restrictions on ampersands, greater- and less-than signs, and quotation marks.

Differences

There are a few differences between HTML and XML. First, an XML element must have both an opening and closing tag. To represent an element without text (also known as an *empty element*), place a closing slash at the end of the tag: `<img src="php.png" />`. You can also have completely blank elements. For instance, since Zeev Suraski lives in Israel, he doesn't have a U.S. state, so that element is completely empty: `<state/>`.

Attributes must have either double or single quotes around their values. You cannot have `<person id=1>`.

Elements are also case-sensitive. `<email>` and `<EMAIL>` are *not* identical. To circumvent this restriction, some XML processors have a case-folding setting. When case folding is enabled, all elements and attributes are converted to the same case before processing.

XML also has a few features that HTML doesn't, including XML declarations, processing instructions, and CDATA sections.

XML declarations

An *XML declaration* specifies the XML version and document encoding settings for the file. For instance:

```
<?xml version="1.0" encoding="UTF-8" ?>
```

This example tells the XML processor that the file is an XML Version 1.0 file and its contents are encoded using UTF-8, a form of Unicode.

An XML declaration appears only at the start of an XML file and is optional. The default values are those used in the example: Version 1.0 of XML and UTF-8 Unicode encoding.

Internally, libxml2 stores all content as UTF-8. While libxml2 has native support for only a few encodings, it can optionally hook into your system's iconv library to expand the number of encodings it can use. Since encoding support varies widely from system to system, see *http://www.xmlsoft.org/encoding.html* for more information on how libxml2 handles this issue.

Processing instructions

The XML declaration is a specific example of a more general feature known as *processing instructions* (PIs for short). When you want to pass information to your XML processor, use a PI. For example:

```
<title><?pdf font="Gill Sans" ?>Upgrading to PHP 5</title>
```

This informs a pdf formatting script to set the font to Gill Sans.

PIs have this standard syntax:

```
<?target data ... ?>
```

The XML declaration shown earlier has a target of xml, and its data is version="1.0" encoding="UTF-8".

It is uncommon to find an XML document that uses a PI whose target doesn't begin with xml.

Character Data sections

One difficulty with using HTML and XML is that you're always forced to call htmlentities() on your data. XML has a way to indicate that your text should be treated as literal text: a block called a *CDATA*, short for Character Data. It's written like this:

```
<![CDATA[<img src="logo.png" alt="A & P">]]>
```

You don't need to encode < and & inside a CDATA block, and it cannot contain the sequence]]>. The awkward syntax comes from XML's ancestor, SGML.

Well-Formed XML

For an XML document to be considered valid, it must satisfy the following restrictions:

- The document must have only one top-level element. This element is called the *root element*.
- Every element must have both a start and an end tag.
- All attributes must have values, and those values must be quoted.
- Elements must not overlap. You cannot use <a><b></a></b>, because the ending </a> tag comes before </b>.
- You must convert &, <, and > to their entity equivalents. You can use htmlentities( ) to solve this.

When a document meets these rules, it's valid, or *well-formed*, XML.

Schemas

When you validate HTML, your file is checked not only to see if it's well-formed, but also that your markup corresponds to the specification. While your application parses XML instead of HTML, it also expects data in a certain format. When it gets anything else, it can't work correctly.

Therefore, it's beneficial to create a data specification, or *schema*, that outlines the layout of the XML document your program requires. This allows you to check the input XML file against a specification to see if the XML is not only well-formed, but also valid.

There are three different schema formats: DTDs, XML Schema, and RelaxNG.

DTD
: DTDs, short for Document Type Definitions, are the old way to write a schema. They come from SGML and have a more limited syntax than other formats. They're not written in XML, so they can be difficult to read. Try to avoid DTDs when you can.

XML Schema
: XML Schema is the W3-approved document specification format. XML Schemas are written in XML, so your XML parser can also validate the

schema. For more on XML Schema, see Eric van der Vlist's *XML Schema* (O'Reilly) or read the specification at *http://www.w3.org/XML/Schema*.

RelaxNG
An alternative to XML Schemas is RelaxNG, written by the OASIS group. Its home page is at *http://www.relaxng.org/*.

PHP 5 can validate documents against all three formats.

Transformations

One of XML's great advantages is that you can easily manipulate an XML document into another format. It could be HTML, PDF, or even another XML document. For instance, you could create an RSS feed for the articles in your XML-based CMS.

XSLT, short for Extensible Stylesheet Language Transformations, is a W3C-defined language for modifying XML documents. With XSLT, you can create templates (written, of course, in XML) that act as a series of instructions for how an XML document provided as input should end up as output.

If you're unfamiliar with XSLT, check out *XSLT*, by Doug Tidwell, or Sal Mangano's *XSLT Cookbook* (both published by O'Reilly). *XSLT* assumes no knowledge of XSLT, while *XSLT Cookbook* is more useful for programmers who want a grab bag of recipes to solve commonly encountered XSLT tasks, such as renaming attributes and elements. The complete specification is located at *http://www.w3.org/TR/xslt*.

XML Namespaces

XML Namespaces let you place a set of XML elements inside a separate "area" to avoid tag name clashes. This is an important feature because it allows XML documents to be extended and combined. Unfortunately, using XML namespaces is tricky. For something that initially seems very straightforward, there's a surprising amount of explanation required.

Why Use Namespaces?

Using XML Namespaces, developers can work together to define a common set of markup for different sets of data, such as RSS items, meta-information about pages on the Internet, or books. When programmers everywhere represent related information using the same set of elements in the same namespace, then everyone can create powerful applications based on a large set of shared data.

That's the theory, anyway.

On a more practical side, avoiding tag name clashes is still an issue because it's useful to modify XML documents. Clashes aren't a problem when everyone is working with a fixed set of elements. However, you can run into trouble if you allow others to extend a document by adding their own elements.

For example, you may decide to use `<title>` to refer to the title of a web page, but your friend used `<title>` as the title of a person, such as Mister or Doctor. With XML Namespaces, you can keep `<html:title>` distinct from `<person:title>`.

Some languages have a similar concept, where functions and objects belonging to a package can be namespaced together. PHP does not support namespaces, which is why you may see PHP function and class names prefixed with a unique string. For example, the `PEAR::DB` MySQL module is named `DB_mysql`. The leading `DB_` means that this class will not conflict with a class named simply `mysql`.

Another example of namespaces is the domain name system: `columbia.com` is the Columbia Sportswear company, while `columbia.edu` is Columbia University. Both hosts are `columbia`, but one lives in the `.com` namespace and the other lives in `.edu`.

Syntax

In XML, a namespace name is a string that looks like a URL—for example, `http://www.example.org/namespace/`. This URL doesn't have to resolve to an actual web page that contains information about the namespace, but it can. A namespace is not a URL, but a string that is formatted the same way as a URL.

This URL-based naming scheme is just a way for people to easily create unique namespaces. Therefore, it's best only to create namespaces that point to a URL that you control. If everyone does this, there won't be any namespace conflicts. Technically, you can create a namespace that points at a location you don't own or use in any way, such as `http://www.yahoo.com`. This is not invalid, but it is confusing.

Unlike domain names, there's no official registration process required before you can use a new XML namespace. All you need to do is define the namespace inside an XML document. That "creates" the namespace. To do this, add an `xmlns` attribute to an XML element. For instance:

```
<tag xmlns:example="http://www.example.com/namespace/">
```

When an attribute name begins with the string `xmlns`, you're defining a namespace. The namespace's name is the value of that attribute. In this case, it's `http://www.example.com/namespace/`.

Namespace Prefixes

Since URLs are unwieldy, a namespace prefix is used as a substitute for the URL when referring to elements in a namespace (in an XML document or an XPath query, for example). This prefix comes after `xmlns` and a `:`. The prefix name in the previous example is `example`. Therefore, `xmlns:example="http://www.example.com/namespace/"` not only creates a namespace, but assigns the token `example` as a shorthand name for the namespace.

Namespace prefixes can contain letters, numbers, periods, underscores, and hyphens. They must begin with a letter or underscore, and they can't begin with the string `xml`. That sequence is reserved by XML for XML-related prefixes, such as `xmlns`.

When you create a namespace using `xmlns`, the element in which you place the attribute and any elements or attributes that live below it in your XML document are eligible to live in the namespace. However, these elements aren't placed there automatically. To actually place an element or attribute in the namespace, put the namespace prefix and a colon in front of the element name. For example, to put the element `title` inside of the `http://www.example.com/namespace/` namespace, use an opening tag of `<example:title>`.

The entire string `example:title` is called a *qualified name*, since you're explicitly mentioning which element you want. The element or attribute name without the prefix and colon, in this case `title`, is called the *local name*.

Note that while the `xmlns:example` syntax implies that `xmlns` is a namespace prefix, this is actually false. The XML specification forbids using any name or prefix that begins with `xml`, except as detailed in various XML and XML-related specifications. In this case, `xmlns` is merely a sign that the name following the colon (`:`) is a namespace prefix, not an indication that `xmlns` is itself a prefix.

Examples

Example A-2 updates the address book from Example A-1 and places all the elements inside the `http://www.example.com/address-book/` namespace.

Example A-2. Simple address book in a namespace

```
<ab:address-book xmlns:ab="http://www.example.com/address-book/">
    <ab:person id="1">
        <ab:firstname>Rasmus</ab:firstname>
        <ab:lastname>Lerdorf</ab:lastname>
        <ab:city>Sunnyvale</ab:city>
        <ab:state>CA</ab:state>
        <ab:email>rasmus@php.net</ab:email>
    </ab:person>

    <!-- more entries here -->

</ab:address-book>
```

If two XML documents map the same namespace to different prefixes, the elements still live inside the *same* namespace. The URL string defines a namespace, not the prefix. Also, two namespaces are equivalent only if they are identical, including their case. Even if two URLs resolve to the same location, they're different namespaces.

Therefore, this document is considered identical to Example A-2:

```
<bigbird:address-book xmlns:bigbird="http://www.example.com/address-book/">
    <bigbird:person id="1">
        <bigbird:firstname>Rasmus</bigbird:firstname>
        <bigbird:lastname>Lerdorf</bigbird:lastname>
        <bigbird:city>Sunnyvale</bigbird:city>
        <bigbird:state>CA</bigbird:state>
        <bigbird:email>rasmus@php.net</bigbird:email>
    </bigbird:person>

    <!-- more entries here -->

</bigbird:address-book>
```

The ab prefix has been changed to bigbird, but the namespace is still http:// www.example.com/address-book/. Therefore, an XML parser would treat these documents as if they were the same.

Default Namespaces

As you can see, prepending a namespace prefix not only becomes tedious, it clutters up your document. Therefore, XML lets you specify a default namespace. Wherever a default namespace is applied, nonprefixed elements and attributes automatically live inside the default namespace.

A default namespace definition is similar to that of other namespaces, but you omit the colon and prefix name:

```
xmlns="http://www.example.com/namespace/"
```

This means there's yet another way to rewrite the example:

```
<address-book xmlns="http://www.example.com/address-book/">
    <person id="1">
        <firstname>Rasmus</firstname>
        <lastname>Lerdorf</lastname>
        <city>Sunnyvale</city>
        <state>CA</state>
        <email>rasmus@php.net</email>
    </person>

    <!-- more entries here -->

</address-book>
```

It is not uncommon to find a document that uses multiple namespaces. One is declared the default namespace, and the others are given prefixes.

For more on XML Namespaces, read Chapter 4 of *XML in a Nutshell* by Elliotte Rusty Harold and W. Scott Means (O'Reilly) or see the W3 specification at *http://www.w3.org/TR/REC-xml-names/*

XPath

XPath is a W3C standard (*http://www.w3.org/TR/xpath*) for locating portions of an XML document that match a set of criteria. Use XPath to find the names of all the people in your XML address book who live in New York, all URLs for articles written on PHP in a Meerkat RSS feed, or the most recent entry into your XML-based content management system.

Think of XPath as SQL for XML documents. You can do all kinds of advanced queries using XPath, such as finding items with a certain parent, attribute, or location in the tree. XPath uses the same syntax as XSLT, so you might be familiar with parts of it, even if you're not an XPath expert.

There are two parts to an XPath query: the portion of the XML document you wish to retrieve and the restrictions you want to place upon your query. This is analogous to SQL SELECT and WHERE clauses.

For example, you can search the XML address book in Example A-1 for all the email addresses:

```
/address-book/person/email
```

Levels in an XML document are separated by a /, similar to the separators for folders in a directory path. When the query begins with a slash, it tells XPath to start looking at the top-level element. Therefore, /address-book/ person/email means gather all the email elements under a person element under an address-book element.

This is like a SQL SELECT without a WHERE. However, if you're planning a trip to Manhattan and just want to find all your friends who live in New York, NY, use this:

```
/address-book/person[city = "New York" and state = "NY"]/email
```

The text inside square brackets refines the XPath query. [city = "New York" and state = "NY"] restricts the search to entries where the city element under person is New York *and* the state is NY.

To check attributes instead of elements, prepend an @:

```
/address-book/person[@id = "1"]
```

This finds all persons with an id attribute of 1.

A good book on XPath is John E. Simpson's *XPath and XPointer* (O'Reilly). John's article "Top Ten Tips to Using XPath and XPointer" is posted on XML.com at *http://www.xml.com/pub/a/2002/08/14/xpath_tips.html*. Additionally, Chapter 9 of *XML in a Nutshell* covers XPath and is available online at *http://www.oreilly.com/catalog/xmlnut2/chapter/ch09.pdf*.

Additional New Features and Minor Changes

This appendix covers the changes made in PHP 5 that aren't documented elsewhere in the book. Some sections discuss new features, such as the command-line processing options. Other sections contain slight modifications of existing features, such as what happens when you incorrectly treat a string as an array, or how strrpos( ) handles its needle. These fixes will trip you up if you're relying on PHP 4 behavior.

Passing Optional Parameters by Reference

You can now pass optional parameters by reference. For example:

```
function updateAddress(&$address = 'NULL') {

}
```

In PHP 4, you could declare a parameter as either optional or pass-by-reference, but not both. PHP 5 removes this limitation.

New E_STRICT Error Setting

PHP 5's new E_STRICT error setting issues a warning when you use deprecated features. Specifically, it complains when you:

- Create objects without a class definition
- Use a constructor named after the class instead of __construct( )
- Use var instead of public
- Use is_a( ) instead of instanceof
- Copy an object instead of making a reference (requires zend.ze1_ compatibility_mode to be On)

- Statically invoke a nonstatic method
- Refine the prototype of an inherited method other than __construct( )
- Return a nonvariable by reference
- Assign the object returned by new by reference

All of these features work in PHP 5, but you should slowly modify your code to stop using them. Here are a few examples:

- This code automagically creates $person as an object without a class definition:

```
$person->name = 'Rasmus Lerdorf';
PHP Strict Standards:  Creating default object from empty value
```

- This Person class uses var instead of public (or, even better, private). It also defines two constructors:

```
class Person {
    var $name;

    function __construct($name) {
        $this->name = $name;
    }

    function Person($name) {
        $this->name = $name;
    }
}
PHP Strict Standards:  var: Deprecated. Please use the public/private/
protected modifiers
PHP Strict Standards:  Redefining already defined constructor for class
Person
```

E_STRICT is not enabled by default, nor is it part of E_ALL. To enable it, set your error_reporting configuration directive to E_ALL | E_STRICT. Setting E_STRICT within a PHP script using error_reporting( ) causes PHP to miss some errors because it has already parsed the file.

Treating Strings as Arrays Causes Errors

PHP 5 complains louder than PHP 4 when you treat a string as an array.

Accessing a multidimensional array element causes a fatal error in PHP 5:

```
$string = 'string';
print $string[0][0];
PHP Fatal error:  Cannot use string offset as an array
```

You can still access an individual character in a string using array notation, but as of PHP 4, this is deprecated in favor of curly braces ({ }):

```
$string = 'string';

// valid, but deprecated
for ($i = 0; $i < strlen($string); $i++) {
    print $string[$i];
}

// valid, and preferred
for ($i = 0; $i < strlen($string); $i++) {
    print $string{$i};
}
string
string
```

Passing strings to array_merge( ) and other array functions generates a warning in PHP 5:

```
$string = "string";
$array = array_merge($string, $string);
PHP Warning:  array_merge( ): Argument #1 is not an array
PHP Warning:  array_merge( ): Argument #2 is not an array
```

This does not generate any messages in PHP 4.

CLI Now Allows Individual Line Processing

The PHP 5 command-line version now allows individual line processing, similar to Perl and awk.

Use these flags on the command line to alter PHP's behavior:

-B

Run this code *before* processing the file. This is similar to auto_prepend_file.

-R

Run this code *on each line* of the file.

-E

Run this code at the *end* of processing the file. This is similar to auto_append_file.

The contents of the current line are available in $argn. This simple example prints each line of *example.txt*:

```
$ php -R 'print "$argn\n" ;' < example.txt
1
2
3
4
5
```

The current line number is stored in $argi. The first line of the file is line 1 (not 0). So, to print out select lines of a file, do this:

```
$ php -B '$start = 2; $stop = 4;' -R 'if ($argi >= $start &&
  $argi <= $stop) print "$argn\n";' < example.txt
2
3
4
```

Modifying standard input disrupts the flow. For instance:

```
$ php -R 'print fgets(STDIN);' < example.txt
2
4
```

Using the -R flag causes PHP to read in one line from standard input. Therefore, when you call fgets( ), you read in a *second* line. This results in "missing" lines because both PHP and you are processing the file.

CLI Always Provides argv and argc

The $argv and $argc variables are always available in the command-line version of PHP 5. This happens even if the register_argc_argv configuration setting is set to Off.

The $_SERVER superglobal variable also contains entries for $_SERVER['argv'] and $_SERVER['argc'] if your variables_order configuration directive contains an S to enable this variable.

Oracle (oci8) Extension Functions Renamed

The Oracle extension's function names are now consistent with the rest of PHP. For instance, ocibindbyname( ) is now oci_bind_by_name( ), and ocinewcursor( ) is now oci_new_cursor( ). See Table B-1 for a complete list of old and new function names.

 The old names are preserved for backward compatibility, but should be considered deprecated.

Table B-1. Renamed oci functions

PHP 4	PHP 5
ocibindbyname( )	oci_bind_by_name( )
ocicancel( )	oci_cancel( )

Table B-1. Renamed oci functions (continued)

PHP 4	PHP 5
ocicollappend( )	oci_collection_append( )
ocicollassignelem( )	oci_collection_element_assign( )
ocicollgetelem( )	oci_collection_element_get( )
ocicollmax( )	oci_collection_max( )
ocicollsize( )	oci_collection_size( )
ocicolltrim( )	oci_collection_trim( )
ocicolumnisnull( )	oci_field_is_null( )
ocicolumnname( )	oci_field_name( )
ocicolumnprecision( )	oci_field_precision( )
ocicolumnscale( )	oci_field_scale( )
ocicolumnsize( )	oci_field_size( )
ocicolumntype( )	oci_field_type( )
ocicolumntyperaw( )	oci_field_type_raw( )
ocicommit( )	oci_commit( )
ocidefinebyname( )	oci_define_by_name( )
ocierror( )	oci_error( )
ociexecute( )	oci_execute( )
ocifetch( )	oci_fetch( )
ocifetchstatement( )	oci_fetch_all( )
ocifreecollection( )	oci_free_collection( )
ocifreecursor( )	oci_free_cursor( )
ocifreedesc( )	oci_free_descriptor( )
ocifreestatement( )	oci_free_statement( )
ociinternaldebug( )	oci_internal_debug( )
ociloadlob( )	oci_lob_load( )
ocilogoff( )	oci_close( )
ocilogon( )	oci_connect( )
ocinewcollection( )	oci_new_collection( )
ocinewcursor( )	oci_new_cursor( )
ocinewdescriptor( )	oci_new_descriptor( )
ocinlogon( )	oci_new_connect( )
ocinumcols( )	oci_num_fields( )
ociparse( )	oci_parse( )
ocipasswordchange( )	oci_password_change( )
ociplogon( )	oci_pconnect( )

Table B-1. Renamed oci functions (continued)

PHP 4	PHP 5
ociresult( )	oci_result( )
ocirollback( )	oci_rollback( )
ocirowcount( )	oci_num_rows( )
ocisavelob( )	oci_lob_save( )
ocisavelobfile( )	oci_lob_import( )
ociserverversion( )	oci_server_version( )
ocisetprefetch( )	oci_set_prefetch( )
ocistatementtype( )	oci_statement_type( )
ociwritelobtofile( )	oci_lob_export( )

New Configuration Directives

Besides zend.ze1_compatibility_mode, PHP 5 has some new configuration directives:

mail.force_extra_parameters

> Extra parameters to always pass to the sendmail program, such as -oi and -t. This setting overrides the options provided as the fifth argument of mail( ). It defaults to the empty string.

register_long_arrays

> Whether to register the deprecated input arrays, such as $HTTP_POST_VARS and $HTTP_GET_VARS, in addition to $_POST and $_GET. This should be enabled only for legacy code. This is set to On in *php.ini-dist* and to Off in *php.ini-recommended*.

session.hash_function

> Sets the hash function used by the session module. A value of 0 means use MD5, a 128-bit algorithm, and a value of 1 means use SHA-1, a 160-bit algorithm. It defaults to 0.

session.hash_bits_per_character

> Sets the number of bits stored per character. Possible values are 4, 5, and 6; the default value is 4.

Updated COM Extension

The COM extension has undergone a rewrite to fix bugs and to take advantage of the new features in PHP 5. For example, COM errors now trigger exceptions. Additionally, the new extension supports .NET assemblies. This extension is available only on Windows.

For more information, see *http://www.php.net/com* and *http://www.zend.com/ php5/articles/php5-dotnet.php*.

Apache 2 Correctly Sets PATH_TRANSLATED

According to the CGI specification, PATH_TRANSLATED should be set only when PATH_INFO has a value.

The PHP Apache 1.x module always sets PATH_TRANSLATED, regardless of PATH_INFO. The Apache 2.x module correctly obeys the specification.

To get the actual path to the script, use SCRIPT_FILENAME instead.

strrpos( ) Uses the Entire Needle

In PHP 4, strpos( ) uses an entire string as a needle, whereas strrpos( ) limits the needle to a single character. If you pass strrpos( ) a string of more than one character, it silently uses only the first character.

In PHP 5, strrpos( ) and strripos( ) now behave identically to strpos( ), in that they find strings instead of just the first character.

Windows 95 Support Dropped

PHP 5 does not support Windows 95. You must use a more recent version, such as Windows XP or Windows 2000, if you want to run PHP 5 under Windows.

old_function Eliminated

PHP/FI had a quirky function declaration syntax:

```
function sum $a, $b (
    return($a + $b);
);
```

This was changed in PHP 3, but you could continue to use the old form in PHP 3 and PHP 4 if you declared your function as an old_function:

```
old_function sum $a, $b (
    return($a + $b);
);
```

Alas, after six years, this backward compatibility feature is now gone. Another nostalgic remnant of PHP/FI has passed away.

Installing PHP 5 Alongside PHP 4

A major difficulty in migrating from PHP 4 to PHP 5 is testing code under PHP 5 without giving up PHP 4. You cannot install both Apache modules on the same web server, but it's possible to install one as a CGI. This allows you to experiment with PHP 5 and debug your applications without giving up PHP 4 in the process.

The CGI version of PHP is less efficient than the module version and has a few limitations, such as the inability to hook into Apache's HTTP Basic Authentication mechanism. Nevertheless, this is a good way to start out using PHP 5. When you're just testing scripts, performance is less of a problem. When most of your code is PHP 5–ready, you can then install the module version of PHP 5 for final testing and benchmarking and run PHP 4 as a CGI.

This appendix is more technical than other parts of the book. It assumes you're comfortable installing PHP from source code and have root access on your machine. It also assumes you're using PHP with the Apache web server. If you're running a different server, you must translate these instructions accordingly.

General PHP 5 Configuration

Since you're already using PHP, this section does not repeat the full set of PHP installation and configuration instructions. If you get stuck, information for many web servers and operating systems is available at *http:// www.php.net/install*.

Instead of detailed instructions, this section provides a brief recap of the install process and a list of the new PHP 5 configuration options. In particular, there have been lots of changes in the MySQL extension and in all the XML extensions.

Basics

The latest version of PHP is always available from *http://www.php.net/downloads.php*. Unix installation basics are unchanged:

1. `$ gunzip php-5.x.x.tar.gz`
2. `$ tar xvf php-5.x.x.tar`
3. `$ cd php-5.x.x`
4. `$ ./configure`
5. `$ make`
6. `# make install`
7. `# apachectl restart`

The `./configure` command will require additional parameters depending on your setup. These are discussed in more detail in the individual sections that follow.

You will probably need to run the `make install` and `apachectl restart` commands as the root user or superuser.

Windows users have two choices: they can use either the prebuilt binaries or the new Windows build system. If you don't want to customize PHP yourself, be sure to read the later section "Windows" for Windows-specific information.

People who are interested in building PHP on Windows should read the *README.WIN32-BUILD-SYSTEM* file in the top level of the PHP directory.

Configuration Options

PHP 5 has many new (or modified) extensions. In order to enable them properly, you must use some new configuration options. They break down into three main groups: XML, databases, and others.

XML

Since PHP 5 uses libxml2, many of the PHP 4 configuration options have switched. Table C-1 lists the differences.

Table C-1. XML extension configuration options

Feature	PHP 4	PHP 5
libxml2	N/A	--disable-libxml --with-libxml-dir=*DIR*
DOM	--with-dom=[*DIR*] --with-dom-xslt=[*DIR*] --with-dom-exslt=[*DIR*]	--disable-dom

Table C-1. XML extension configuration options (continued)

Feature	PHP 4	PHP 5
SimpleXML	N/A	`--disable-simplexml`
SOAP	N/A	`--enable-soap`
XSLT	`--enable-xslt` `--with-xslt-sablot=<DIR>`	`--with-xsl=DIR`
XML	`--disable-xml` `--with-expat-dir=<DIR>`	`--disable-xml` `--with-libexpat-dir=DIR` (deprecated)

The largest difference is that PHP 5 really wants you to have a copy of `libxml2` on your system. If PHP cannot find it, specify its path using `--with-libxml-dir=DIR`.

Other XML extensions, including DOM and SimpleXML, are now enabled by default and will reuse the `libxml2` path, so it only needs to be set once for the entire configuration process.

The SAX XML extension now also uses `libxml2`, but you can use the old expat libraries if you insist. However, you must install them yourself: they are no longer bundled with PHP.

XSLT has switched from Sablotron to `libxslt`, so you may need to install `libxslt` to continue using XSLT.

Databases

The biggest disruption in PHP 5 is the unbundling of the MySQL client libraries. Therefore, you must download and install them yourself. Additionally, there's a new `mysqli` extension, which you should use for MySQL 4.1 and above.

A list of new database options appears in Table C-2.

Table C-2. Database extension configuration options

Feature	PHP 4	PHP 5
MySQL	`--with-mysql[=DIR]`	`--with-mysql=DIR`
MySQLi	N/A	`--with-mysqli=FILE`
SQLite	N/A	`--without-sqlite` `--enable-sqlite-utf8`

Since the MySQL libraries aren't included with PHP, you must pass a path to `--with-mysql` to specify their location. For MySQLi, you now specify the location of the *mysql_config* file instead of the installation directory. MySQL extracts your setup information from this file.

Remember, MySQLi works only with MySQL 4.1.2 and above. If you're using *both* the `mysql` and `mysqli` extensions, configure them against the same version of MySQL to minimize problems.

SQLite is now bundled and is automatically enabled.

Other options

PHP 5 also bundles a few completely new extensions and removes some obsolete and experimental ones. Table C-3 contains a rundown of the major changes.

Table C-3. Other configuration options

Feature	PHP 4	PHP 5
Overload	`--disable-overload`	N/A
SPL	N/A	`--disable-spl`
Tidy	N/A	`--with-tidy=DIR`

Since overloading is now a built-in feature, there's no need to enable this as an extension. SPL is bundled and enabled by default. It requires no additional libraries. Tidy is bundled, but not enabled by default. You need to install Tidy to use the extension.

Module and CGI

Installing PHP 5 as a CGI is a quick way to get up and running without sacrificing PHP 4. This section describes two techniques for making PHP 5 parse your code, instead of PHP 4.

Remember that the CGI version of PHP has a few limitations compared to the Apache module version. It cannot hook into HTTP Basic Authentication, nor can you read and write internal Apache values using functions such as apache_note( ).

One option is to enable PHP 5 on a directory-by-directory basis. This lets the PHP 4 module handle scripts by default, but lets you slowly release PHP 5 code when it's ready.

The second alternative is to enable PHP 5 for all files but on another port. By default, Apache listens for requests on port 80, so normal requests are still handled as usual. However, whenever a request is made to your site on port 8080, Apache now hands the script off to PHP 5. With this setup, you can easily get a complete overview of your PHP 5 compatibility without sacrificing PHP 4 support.

This process breaks down into two main parts: configuring PHP 5 and configuring Apache. The PHP 5 configuration is identical for either Apache setup, so you can easily switch between the two.

Configuring PHP 5 as a CGI

Installing PHP 5 as a CGI requires four additional steps beyond your normal configuration:

1. Remove --with-apxs.
2. Add --enable-force-cgi-redirect.
3. Add --prefix=/usr/local/php5.
4. Customize *php.ini*.

PHP defaults to a CGI installation, but it won't build it when you specify a web server module. Therefore, it's important to remove the call to --with-apxs (or whatever your specific web server is). Also, for security reasons, you should always add --enable-force-cgi-redirect when building PHP as a CGI. This prevents people from directly accessing your PHP CGI.

When adding PHP 5 to your system, it's important not to overwrite the PHP 4 files and configuration data. The two must coexist because you're not ready to eliminate PHP 4. Use the --prefix configuration option to force PHP to install PHP 5 in a separate directory hierarchy. The example in this section uses */usr/local/php5*, but any directory will work. Remember this location because you need to use it to let Apache know the location of the PHP CGI. After adding this to your PHP configuration, make and install PHP as normal.

The final step is customizing your *php.ini* file. First, copy *php.ini-recommended* to */usr/local/php5/lib/php.ini*. PHP 5 has new configuration options, so you should use this file as your base. Then, migrate over any changes you've made to your PHP 4 *php.ini* file to the PHP 5 version.

Directories

The first step to enabling PHP 5 on a directory-by-directory basis is creating a mapping between a location on your web server and the PHP CGI. To do this, add the following commands to your Apache *httpd.conf* file:

```
ScriptAlias /php5 /usr/local/php5/bin
<Directory /usr/local/php5/bin/>
    Options +ExecCGI +FollowSymLinks
    AllowOverride None
</Directory>
```

The ScriptAlias line links the web server's /php5 directory and /usr/local/php5/bin on your machine. (If you've installed PHP 5 someplace else, alter this line accordingly.) Now, whenever you access a file from http://www.example.com/php5, Apache executes the file stored in /usr/local/php5/bin instead.

With this redirection established, the next step is to force Apache to route files ending with a particular extension to the PHP CGI. You want to limit this, however, to specific directories. This can be done in one of two ways: placing the information inside a <Directory> section in httpd.conf or adding it to a .htaccess file.

Here's how to do this inside httpd.conf for all files inside the directory /www/www.example.com/php5-folder:

```
<Directory /www/www.example.com/php5-folder>
    AddHandler php-cgi-script .php
    Action php-cgi-script /php5/php
    Options +ExecCGI
</Directory>
```

The AddHandler directive says that any file ending in .php should be considered a php-cgi-script. The term php-cgi-script isn't a special name, but merely a unique way to identify the files to be parsed by PHP 5. You can place additional extensions on this line, like so:

```
AddHandler php-cgi-script .php .html
```

Now files ending in .php or .html will be parsed.

The second line adds an Action directive. This directive tell Apache that all php-cgi-scripts should be handled by the file located at /php5/php. Since you've previously said that all files in /php5 go to /usr/local/php5/bin, this command effectively passes the script to /usr/local/php5/bin/php. By a happy coincidence, this is the location where PHP 5 installed the CGI.

Last, since you're running PHP 5 as a CGI script, you need to add +ExecCGI to your Apache Options to make the script execute.

An alternative approach is to place the middle three lines inside a .htaccess file. This is a special file read by Apache where you can modify a limited set of Apache (and PHP) settings. There's no need to wrap them inside a <Directory> section, because Apache automatically assumes the current location.

Using .htaccess allows you to modify settings without restarting Apache; however, it requires you to enable the AllowOverride option. This can slow down Apache because it now must check for and parse these files on every request.

Ports

Another way to provide simultaneous PHP 4 and PHP 5 support is to run PHP 4 on one port and PHP 5 on the other. This is best used for internal debugging on development and staging servers, to allow programmers to easily check the status of a program under PHP 5.

The first step is to add a Listen directive to *httpd.conf*:

```
Listen 80
Listen 8080
```

By default, Apache (like all web servers) listens on port 80. These lines tell Apache to also listen on port 8080. Again, there's nothing particular about the number 8080, except that it's greater than 1024 and doesn't conflict with another program. (Port numbers lower than 1024 are reserved for official use.) Many people choose 8080 because it's a doubling of the official HTTP port.

Now you need to set up the CGI on port 8080. This is done using an Apache virtual host:

```
<VirtualHost _default_:8080>
    ScriptAlias /php5 /usr/local/php5/bin
    <Directory /usr/local/php5/bin/>
        Options +ExecCGI +FollowSymLinks
        AllowOverride None
    </Directory>

    AddHandler php-cgi-script .php
    Action php-cgi-script /php5/php
    Options +ExecCGI
</VirtualHost>
```

These commands are identical to the ones in the previous section, except that they're applied to all files, not just ones in a particular directory or directories.

This <VirtualHost> section matches all requests handled by Apache running on 8080 that aren't already processed by a different virtual host. When you're running multiple virtual hosts, you should substitute the hostname for _default_.

Also, if you're using multiple virtual hosts, you need to copy options, such as DocumentRoot, from the PHP 4 virtual host to the PHP 5 host. For example:

```
<VirtualHost www.example.com:80>
    # Virtual Host Specific Options
    DocumentRoot /www/www.example.com
```

```
    # Load PHP 4 Apache Module
    LoadModule php4_module /usr/lib/apache/1.3/libphp4.so
</VirtualHost>

<VirtualHost www.example.com:8080>
    # Repeated Configuration Options
    DocumentRoot /www/www.example.com

    # Add PHP 5 CGI Script
    ScriptAlias /php5 /usr/local/php5/bin
    <Directory /usr/local/php5/bin/>
        Options +ExecCGI +FollowSymLinks
        AllowOverride None
    </Directory>

    AddHandler php-cgi-script .php
    Action php-cgi-script /php5/php
</VirtualHost>
```

When you go to any page under *http://www.example.com/*, you still see the PHP 4 version. However, *http://www.example.com:8080/* now delivers a PHP 5 version.

Windows

If you're running Windows, it's not easy to compile PHP, and you're probably already using PHP 4 as a CGI. Here's how to integrate a precompiled version of PHP 5 into an existing Apache setup:

1. Download and install a precompiled Windows zip package.
2. Configure your web server to handle PHP 5.
3. Set an alternative *php.ini* location.

If you're using another web server, you will need to modify the configuration directions.

The first step is downloading and unzipping PHP 5. You can download Windows zip packages from *http://www.php.net/downloads.php*. (Be sure to grab the "zip" package instead of the installer.)

After you unzip the package, move it to a directory that is similar to your existing PHP 4 installation. On many systems, PHP 4 is at *C:/PHP/*, so these instructions place PHP 5 in *C:/PHP5/*.

Copy *php.ini-recommended* to *php.ini* and keep it in *C:/PHP5/*. Your pre-existing *php.ini* file is already located in someplace like *C:/WINNT/*, but you're not ready to overwrite it yet. Make whatever server-specific customizations you need to the new *php.ini* file.

Now you need to modify your web server configuration file to handle PHP 5. If you're running PHP 4 as a CGI, you should already have these three lines:

```
ScriptAlias /php/ "C:/PHP/"
Action application/x-httpd-php /php/php.exe
AddType application/x-httpd-php .php
```

This makes the file located at */php/php.exe* under the document root execute files ending in *.php*. The ScriptAlias directive links this location to *C:/PHP/php.exe* on your filesystem.

Supplement this with one additional line to create another ScriptAlias, this time for PHP 5:

```
ScriptAlias /php5/ "C:/PHP5/"
```

This entry lets you hand off PHP files to the PHP 5 CGI. If you've placed PHP 5 in a different location, change *C:/PHP5/* accordingly.

Now you're all set to override Apache to make PHP 5 process the files instead of PHP 4. Like the earlier examples in "Module and CGI," you can do this on either a directory-specific level or a virtual-host level. For example, for a directory:

```
<Directory "C:/Program Files/Apache Group/Apache/htdocs/php5-folder">
    Action application/x-httpd-php /php5/php-cgi.exe
    SetEnv PHPRC "C:/PHP5/"
</Directory>
```

The Action directive tells Apache to map PHP files to */php5/php-cgi.exe*. The directory name, */php5/*, is the new ScriptAlias location, and *php-cgi.exe* is the new name for the PHP 5 CGI binary. The unadorned *php.exe* is now used by the command-line version of PHP.

There's still the job of making PHP 5 use the correct *php.ini* file. PHP checks a variety of locations by default, which is bad because that's where your PHP 4 *php.ini* is stored. Because you used a prebuilt package, you couldn't alter this path during the configuration process.

Fortunately, you can still control where PHP searches for its *php.ini* file. When you set the PHPRC environment variable, PHP looks inside that directory for a *php.ini* file. Earlier, you created a configuration file in *C:/PHP5/*, so that's where you point PHPRC. You cannot specify a filename for PHPRC, only a directory.

This setup works with all the other configuration examples listed earlier in this appendix. You simply need to place the two lines just shown inside whatever Apache directive or *httpd.conf* file you want.

Index

Symbols

& (ampersand)
  preceding entities in XML, 284
  preceding variable to pass by
    reference, 16
-> (arrow), invoking method, 11
@ (at sign)
  in HTTP request, 209
  preceding attributes in XPath, 292
: (colon)
  in Tidy configuration file, 248
  preceding namespace prefix, 289
<!-- -->, comments in XML, 284
$ (dollar sign), preceding property
    name, 20
@@ (double at signs), preceding
    MySQL-specific variables, 75
:: (double colons)
  referencing static methods, 28
  referencing static properties, 29
" (double quotes)
  around attributes in XML, 284
  automatically inserted for string
    parameters, 58
  escaping in queries, 56, 94
// (double slashes), in HTTP
    request, 209
<? ?>, processing instructions in
    XML, 285
? (question mark), substituting for query
    variables, 58

' (single quotes)
  around attributes in XML, 284
  automatically inserted for string
    parameters, 58
  escaping in queries, 56, 94
/ (slash)
  empty element in XML, 284
  separating levels in XML, 291
=== (strict equality operator), 156

A

abstract classes, 32
abstract keyword, 32
abstract methods, 32
accept( ) method, FilterIterator
    class, 167
accessors, 10
  __get( ) and __set( ), 37–40
  properties as alternative to, 14
  public, 20
address book application example, 6,
    259, 281
  addressBook class, 265–272
  assembling application for, 276–281
  command-line version, 279
  creating with DOM, 143–147
  database schema for, 260
  filtering results of, 169
  future enhancement
    possibilities, 281
  Person class, 261–265

We'd like to hear your suggestions for improving our indexes. Send email to *index@oreilly.com*.

about SOAP, 238
about web security, xv
about WSDL, 239
about XML, xv
about XML namespaces, 291
about XPath, 292
about XSLT, 287
boolean stream_open( ) method, for
    wrappers, 217

C

CachingIterator class, 182
CachingRecursiveIterator class, 182
cafile option, https wrapper, 210
__call( ) method, 37, 40–42, 241
call_user_func_array( ) method, 42
capitalization of class names, 19
case-sensitivity
    class names, 19
    XML elements, 284
catch block, 186
CDATA (Character Data), 285
    sections, creating, 146
    sections, node type for, 123
Cerami, Ethan (Web Services
    Essentials), 239
CGI version of PHP, 300, 303–307
chaining filters, 204, 232
chaining iterators, 166–169
Character Data (see CDATA)
character sets, converting, 229–231
child class, 29
child_nodes( ) method, 122
childNodes property, 122
class keyword, 18
classes, 10
    abstract, 32
    base, 29
    child, 29
    creating instances of, 10, 13
    defining, 11, 18–25
    defining before creating instances
        of, 26
    extending with inheritance, 29–30
    final, 35
    hierarchies of, 31–32
    iterating, 177–182, 263
    parent, 29
    properties of, 19
    super, 29
    (see also specific classes or objects)

client code errors, 192
__clone( ) method, 37, 45–46
clone operator, 17
cloning objects, 17, 45–46
closedir( ) function, 158
code examples
    conventions used in, xv
    permission to use, when
        required, xvi
    (see also address book application
        example)
colon (:)
    in Tidy configuration file, 248
    preceding namespace prefix, 289
colons, double (::)
    referencing static methods, 28
    referencing static properties, 29
COM extension, changes to, 298
command-line version of PHP
    $argc variable for, 296
    $argi variable for, 296
    $argn variable for, 295
    $argv variable for, 296
    individual line processing, 295
Comment node type, 123
comment nodes, DOM, 146
comments about this book, xvii
comments, XML, 284
COMMIT keyword
    MySQL, 72
    SQLite, 104
compatibility mode for cloning
    objects, 17
compress.bzip2 wrapper, 207, 217
compression wrappers, 216
compress.zlib wrapper, 207, 216
configuration directives
    $argc and $argv variables, 296
    automatically prepended file, 199
    caching WSDL, 243
    cloning objects instead of using a
        reference, 17
    error settings, 294
    ftp wrapper, 208
    HTTP POST data, 215
    http wrapper, 208, 210
    https wrapper, 210
    MySQL, 51
    new for PHP 5, 298
    (see also PHP 5, configuring)
Console_Getopt package, 279

mysql extension (*continued*)
    functions modified in mysqli
        extension, 89
    functions replaced in mysqli
        extension, 90
    multiple queries, 77
    using with MySQL 4.1, 84
    (see also MySQL)
MySQL Reference Manual (Widenius;
        Axmark), xv
mysql_change_user() function, 89
mysql_close() function, 89
mysql_config file, 49
mysql_connect() function, 51, 89
mysql_convert_table_format script, 87
mysql_create_db() function, 90
mysql_db_name() function, 90
mysql_db_query() function, 90
mysql.default_host configuration
        directive, 51
mysql_drop_db() function, 90
mysql_errno() function, 89
mysql_error() function, 89
mysql_escape_string() function, 57, 89,
        90
mysql_fetch_field() function, 89
mysql_fetch_row() function, 77, 91
mysql_field_flags() function, 90
mysql_field_len() function, 90
mysql_field_name() function, 90
mysql_field_table() function, 89, 90
mysql_field_type() function, 90
mysql_fix_privilege_tables script, 87
mysql_free_result() function, 79
mysql_get_host_info() function, 89
mysql_get_proto_info() function, 90
mysql_get_server_info() function, 90
mysql_list_dbs() function, 90
mysql_list_fields() function, 91
mysql_list_processes() function, 91
mysql_list_tables() function, 91
mysql_pconnect() function, 53, 89, 91
mysql_ping() function, 90
mysql_query() function, 77, 89
mysql_real_escape_string()
        function, 89
mysql_result() function, 91
mysql_select_database() function, 52
mysql_select_db() function, 89
mysql_stat() function, 90

mysql_stmt_init() function, 64
mysql_tablename() function, 91
mysql_thread_id() function, 90
mysql_unbuffered_query() function, 91
mysqli() constructor, 54
mysqli extension, 4, 47–49
    configuring, 49, 302
    connecting to database, 52–54
    enabling in addition to mysql
        extension, 50
    exceptions not thrown by, 189
    features of, 47
    fetch methods, alternative, 50
    migrating to, 48, 82–91
    multiple queries, 78–80
    MySQL versions supported by, 4, 47
    object-oriented interface, 54, 64
    procedural interface for, 50
    SSL-enabled, 80–82
    (see also MySQL)
mysqli object, 64
mysqli_affected_rows() function, 89
mysqli_change_user() function, 89
mysqli_close() function, 89, 96
mysqli_connect() function, 52–54, 89,
        91, 96
mysqli_data_seek() function, 90, 91
mysqli_errno() function, 55, 74, 89
mysqli_error() function, 55, 89
mysqli_fetch_array() function, 50
mysqli_fetch_assoc() function, 96
mysqli_fetch_field() function, 89, 90
mysqli_fetch_object() function, 50
mysqli_fetch_row() function, 50, 79,
        90, 96
mysqli_free_result() function, 78
mysqli_get_host_info() function, 89
mysqli_get_proto_info() function, 90
mysqli_get_server_info() function, 90
mysqli_info() function, 90
mysqli_init() function, 53, 54, 55
mysqli_insert_id() function, 55, 90, 96
mysqli_more_results() function, 79
mysqli_multi_query() function, 78, 79
mysqli_next_result() function, 78, 79
mysqli_info() function, 90
mysqli_insert_id() function, 90
mysqli_num_rows() function, 96
mysqli_options() function, 54
mysqli_ping() function, 90

Oracle extension, functions renamed
    for, 296–298
output, filtering, 216
output from PHP, wrappers
    for, 213–216
output from web servers, wrappers
    for, 215
output parameters, binding, 62–63
output, standard (stdout), 213–215
Overload extension, 303

P

parameters
    input, binding, 57–61, 63
    optional, passing by reference, 293
    output, binding, 62–63
parent class, 29
parent prefix, 34
ParentIterator class, 183
parent_node( ) method, 122
parentNode property, 122
parse_url( ) function, 108
pass-by-reference, 16
pass-by-value, 15, 17, 45–46
passing an object handle, 16
password
    database class constructor, 15
    FTP, 207, 212
    HTTP Basic Authentication
      credentials, 209
    MySQL database, 52, 84, 86, 87
PATH_TRANSLATED setting for
    Apache, 299
PEAR (PHP Extension and Application
    Repository)
    Console_Getopt package, 279
    PEAR DB, 82
    SOAP classes, 245
    web site, xiv
    XML_DTD package, 153
PEAR-style naming convention, 13
PECL (PHP Extension Community
    Library) web site, xiv
performance
    CGI version of PHP, 300
    conversion between SimpleXML and
      DOM objects, 129
    MySQL, xv, 49
    PHP, 3, 8
    SQLite, 100, 104

permission to use code examples, xvi
Person class, address book
    application, 261–265
<?php ... ?> markers, enclosing PHP
    program, xv
PHP 3, 2
PHP 4
    DOM extension, 119, 130, 133
      creating XML, 144
      XPath and, 136, 140
    error handling, 185
    history of, 3
    iteration, 158
    limitations of, 1
    query method used by, 56
    recursive iteration, 170
    running with PHP 5
      simultaneously, 7, 300–308
    SOAP support, 238
    XSLT extension, 147
PHP 5, xi
    books about, xii, xiv
    CGI version of, 300, 303–307
    configuring, 300–303
      (see also configuration directives)
    downloading, 7, 301
    enabling on another port, 303, 306
    enabling on directory-by-directory
      basis, 303, 304
    example application (see address
      book application example)
    features of, 1, 3–7
    history of, 2
    installing, 7, 301
    migrating to, 84, 85, 88, 293–299
    namespaces for functions and objects
      not supported, 288
    OO features for, 8
    running with PHP 4
      simultaneously, 7, 300–308
    version used for this book, xv
    XML extensions, list of, 114–117
PHP command line, 213
PHP Cookbook (Sklar;
    Trachtenberg), xv
PHP DevCenter web site, xiv
PHP Extension and Application
    Repository (see PEAR)
PHP Extension Community Library
    (PECL), xiv

PHP mailing lists web site, xiv
PHP Manual, 283
PHP Presentation archive web site, xiv
php wrapper, 207, 213–216
PHPCommunity.org web site, xiv
PHPDocumentor, 227
PHP/FI, 2
php://filter wrapper, 216, 231
php:function() function, 151
php://input wrapper, 215
phpMyAdmin, 87
php://output wrapper, 215
php://stderr wrapper, 214
php://stdin wrapper, 213
php://stdout wrapper, 213
php_user_filter class, 233
PIs (see processing instructions)
ports, enabling PHP 5 on specific
        port, 303, 306
$_POST variable, 213
POST, wrapper for, 215
--prefix=/usr/local/php5 flag, 304
prepare() method, 59, 65
prepared statements, MySQL, 55–65
preserveWhiteSpace attribute, 121, 125
previous_sibling() method, 123
previousSibling property, 123
primary keys, SQLite, 101
private keyword, 20
private methods, 14, 20, 33
private properties, 14, 20
procedures (see functions)
processing instructions (PIs), 285
    creating, 146
    node type for, 123
    SimpleXML not supporting, 127
programming errors, 192
Programming PHP (Lerdorf; Tatroe), xii
Programming Web Services with SOAP
        (Snell; Tidwell;
        Kulchenko), 238
properties, 13
    defining, 19
    encapsulating access to, 262
    final, 35
    inheritance and, 40
    iterating, 176–177, 179
    predeclaring, 19
    private, 14, 20
    public, 14, 19
    static, 28

protected keyword, 30
protected methods, 30
proxy option, http and https
        wrappers, 210
public keyword, 19, 20
public methods, 14, 20
public properties, 14, 19

Q

qualified name, XML, 289
queries
    iterator for, 163–166
    MySQL, 50, 54
        binding parameters for, 57–65
        multiple, 61, 75–80
        number of rows returned by,
            configuring, 53
        prepared statements for, 55–65
        subselects, 65–71
        transactions for, 71–75
    SQLite, 94, 96, 98, 99
    (see also data retrieval)
query() method, 98, 137, 138
question mark (?), substituting for query
        variables, 58
quotes
    around attributes in XML, 284
    automatically escaped by prepared
        statements, 56
    automatically inserted for string
        parameters, 58
    escaped with mysqli_real_escape_
        string() function, 56
    escaping with sqlite_escape_string()
        function, 94

R

-R flag, PHP command line, 295
RAM
    garbage collection and, 18
    in-memory tables, 103
    multiple MySQL queries and, 79
    wrapper for shared memory
        functions, 218–225
readdir() function, 158
recursive iterators, 157, 170–176
RecursiveDirectoryIterator class, 157,
        171–173, 183
RecursiveIterator interface, 174–176,
        183

RecursiveIteratorIterator class, 172, 183
reference-counting method of garbage
        collection, 18
Reflection classes, 6, 237, 250
    exporting overview information
            about classes, 250–252
    inspecting classes, 253
    inspecting methods, 253
    inspecting properties, 253
    methods for, list of, 254–258
ReflectionClass class, 253, 255
ReflectionExtension class, 258
ReflectionFunction class, 256
ReflectionMethod class, 253, 256
ReflectionParameter class, 253, 258
ReflectionProperty class, 253, 257
register_argc_argv configuration
        setting, 296
register_long_arrays configuration
        directive, 298
registerNamespace() method, 141
registerPHPFunctions() method, 150
register_shutdown_function()
        method, 23
regular expressions
    book about, xv
    iterator using, 167
RelaxNG, 287
RelaxNG schema, validating XML
        against, 153
relaxNGValidate() method, 154
relaxNGValidateSource() method, 154
request_fulluri option, http and https
        wrappers, 210
resource failures, 192
resources (see books; web sites)
REST, 282
REVOKE keyword, SQLite not
        supporting, 93
rewind() method, Iterator interface, 161
rmdir() method, for wrappers, 218
ROLLBACK keyword
    MySQL, 74
    SQLite, 106
root element, XML, 286
root node, DOM, 122

S

save() method, 125
saveXML() method, 125

SAX extension, 88, 115, 142, 302
schemas, 286
    database, 260
    formats for, 286
    validating XML against, 153
schemaValidate() method, 154
schemaValidateSource() method, 154
scheme handlers, 150
Schlossnagle, George (Advanced PHP
        Programming), xv
security
    book about, xv
    (see also password; SSL)
SeekableIterator interface, 183
SELECT statement (see data retrieval;
        queries)
self prefix, 29, 35
self-joins, 67
sendmail program, passing extra
        parameters to, 298
$_SERVER superglobal variable, 296
session.hash_bits_per_character
        configuration directive, 298
session.hash_function configuration
        directive, 298
__set() method, 37, 37–40
setClass() method, 244
set_error_handler() function, 197
set_exception_handler() function, 197
setParameter() method, 149
shallow clone/copy, 45
shared memory functions, wrapper
        for, 218–225
Shiflett, Chris (HTTP Developer's
        Handbook), xv
shmop extension, 219
SimpleXML extension, 5, 115, 126
    configuration for, 302
    converting DOM objects to
            SimpleXML objects, 129
    converting SimpleXML objects to
            DOM, 129
    converting to XML, 128
    reading namespaced elements, 134,
            141
    reading XML and searching with
            XPath, 138, 141
    reading XML documents, 127
    reading XML into SimpleXML
            objects, 132
    streams used by, 203

About the Author

Adam Trachtenberg is Manager of Technical Evangelism at eBay, where he preaches the gospel of the eBay platform to developers and businessmen around the globe. Before eBay, Adam cofounded and served as Vice President for Development at two companies, Student.Com and TVGrid.Com. At both firms, he led the front- and middle-end web site design and development, and worked on corporate planning and strategy.

Adam began using PHP in 1997, and is the coauthor of O'Reilly's popular *PHP Cookbook*. He is a frequent presenter at conferences on PHP, XML, and web services, and has written articles on PHP for c|net, *PHP Magazine*, and the O'Reilly Network.

A recent transplant from New York City, Adam lives in San Francisco with his girlfriend, and has a B.A. and M.B.A. from Columbia University.

Colophon

Our look is the result of reader comments, our own experimentation, and feedback from distribution channels. Distinctive covers complement our distinctive approach to technical topics, breathing personality and life into potentially dry subjects.

The animals on the cover of *Upgrading to PHP 5* are Galapagos tortoises (*Geochelone elephantopus*). These giant tortoises, native to the Galapagos Islands, are the largest in the world. They can weigh up to 500 pounds and measure up to 6 feet from head to tail. As their bulk suggests, they are slow-moving animals, with a top speed of 0.16 mph. Their plodding pace applies to more than just their gait—they can live for 200 years and take 20 to 25 years to reach full maturity. Baby tortoises spend a full month digging out of their sandy nests after they hatch.

Galapagos tortoises are herbivores, and their strong, curved mouths allow them to eat the spiny vegetation found on the more arid islands in the Galapagos chain. Their slow metabolism allows them to survive for long periods of time without food or water, which is necessary during the dry season. Their scaly feet help them navigate the islands' rough lava terrain.

Fifteen subspecies of *Geochelone elephantopus* have been found in the Galapagos Islands, an archipelago located about 600 miles off the coast of Ecuador. The different subspecies are identified primarily by their shell morphology: saddle-back and domed shells are the two general types, but there are intermediate variations. The subspecies descend from a common ancestor, but developed their unique characteristics in response to the varied terrain, available food, humidity, and other environmental factors found on the islands. Charles Darwin's observations of Galapagos tortoises and how they adapted to their environments helped him formulate his theory of natural selection.

Galapagos tortoises are endangered, and several subspecies are already extinct. Before whalers, seal fur hunters, and colonists arrived in the 18th century, about 250,000 tortoises lived on the islands. Today, only 15,000 remain.

Genevieve d'Entremont was the production editor and copyeditor for *Upgrading to PHP 5*. Sada Preisch proofread the book. Sarah Sherman and Claire Cloutier provided quality control. Angela Howard wrote the index.

Ellie Volckhausen designed the cover of this book, based on a series design by Edie Freedman. The cover image is a 19th-century engraving from the Dover Pictorial Archive. Emma Colby produced the cover layout with QuarkXPress 4.1 using Adobe's ITC Garamond font.

Melanie Wang designed the interior layout, based on a series design by David Futato. This book was converted by Joe Wizda to FrameMaker 5.5.6 with a format conversion tool created by Erik Ray, Jason McIntosh, Neil Walls, and Mike Sierra that uses Perl and XML technologies. The text font is Linotype Birka; the heading font is Adobe Myriad Condensed; and the code font is LucasFont's TheSans Mono Condensed. The illustrations that appear in the book were produced by Robert Romano and Jessamyn Read using Macromedia FreeHand 9 and Adobe Photoshop 6. The tip and warning icons were drawn by Christopher Bing. This colophon was written by Genevieve d'Entremont.

Need in-depth answers fast?

Related Titles Available from O'Reilly

Web Programming

ActionScript Cookbook
ActionScript for Flash MX Pocket Reference
ActionScript for Flash MX: The Definitive Guide, *2nd Edition*
Creating Applications with Mozilla
Dynamic HTML: The Definitive Reference, *2nd Edition*
Flash Remoting: The Definitive Guide
Google Hacks
Google Pocket Guide
HTTP: The Definitive Guide
JavaScript & DHTML Cookbook
JavaScript Pocket Reference, *2nd Edition*
JavaScript: The Definitive Guide, *4th Edition*
PHP Cookbook
PHP Pocket Reference, *2nd Edition*
Programming ColdFusion MX, *2nd Edition*
Programming PHP
Web Database Applications with PHP and MySQL, *2nd Edition*
Webmaster in a Nutshell, *3rd Edition*

Web Authoring and Design

Cascading Style Sheets: The Definitive Guide, *2nd Edition*
CSS Pocket Reference
Dreamweaver MX 2004: The Missing Manual
HTML & XHTML: The Definitive Guide, *5th Edition*
HTML Pocket Reference, *2nd Edition*
Information Architecture for the World Wide Web, *2nd Edition*
Learning Web Design, *2nd Edition*
Web Design in a Nutshell, *2nd Edition*

Web Administration

Apache Cookbook
Apache Pocket Reference
Apache: The Definitive Guide, *3rd Edition*
Essential Blogging
Perl for Web Site Management
Squid: The Definitive Guide
Web Performance Tuning, *2nd Edition*

O'REILLY®

Our books are available at most retail and online bookstores.
To order direct: 1-800-998-9938 • *order@oreilly.com* • *www.oreilly.com*
Online editions of most O'Reilly titles are available by subscription at *safari.oreilly.com*

Keep in touch with O'Reilly

1. Download examples from our books

To find example files for a book, go to:
www.oreilly.com/catalog
select the book, and follow the "Examples" link.

2. Register your O'Reilly books

Register your book at *register.oreilly.com*

Why register your books?
Once you've registered your O'Reilly books you can:

- Win O'Reilly books, T-shirts or discount coupons in our monthly drawing.
- Get special offers available only to registered O'Reilly customers.
- Get catalogs announcing new books (US and UK only).
- Get email notification of new editions of the O'Reilly books you own.

3. Join our email lists

Sign up to get topic-specific email announcements of new books and conferences, special offers, and O'Reilly Network technology newsletters at:

elists.oreilly.com

It's easy to customize your free elists subscription so you'll get exactly the O'Reilly news you want.

4. Get the latest news, tips, and tools

www.oreilly.com

- "Top 100 Sites on the Web"—PC Magazine
- CIO Magazine's Web Business 50 Awards

Our web site contains a library of comprehensive product information (including book excerpts and tables of contents), downloadable software, background articles, interviews with technology leaders, links to relevant sites, book cover art, and more.

5. Work for O'Reilly

Check out our web site for current employment opportunities:

jobs.oreilly.com

6. Contact us

O'Reilly & Associates
1005 Gravenstein Hwy North
Sebastopol, CA 95472 USA

TEL: 707-827-7000 or 800-998-9938
(6am to 5pm PST)

FAX: 707-829-0104

order@oreilly.com
For answers to problems regarding your order or our products. To place a book order online, visit:
www.oreilly.com/order_new

catalog@oreilly.com
To request a copy of our latest catalog.

booktech@oreilly.com
For book content technical questions or corrections.

corporate@oreilly.com
For educational, library, government, and corporate sales.

proposals@oreilly.com
To submit new book proposals to our editors and product managers.

international@oreilly.com
For information about our international distributors or translation queries. For a list of our distributors outside of North America check out:
international.oreilly.com/distributors.html

adoption@oreilly.com
For information about academic use of O'Reilly books, visit:
academic.oreilly.com

O'REILLY®

Our books are available at most retail and online bookstores.
To order direct: 1-800-998-9938 • *order@oreilly.com* • *www.oreilly.com*
Online editions of most O'Reilly titles are available by subscription at *safari.oreilly.com*